Contents

contents

Acknowledgements

The authors would like to acknowledge the help and support of the following organisations in the preparation and illustration of this book:

Alice In Wonderland Visitor Centre, The Rabbit Hole
Automobile Association
Barclaycard
British Airports Authority
British Association of Conference Towns
Cunard
English Heritage
Granada Studios
Hostelling International
Jorvik Viking Centre

London Dungeon
Madame Tussaud's
Museums and Galleries Commission
National Playing Fields Association
National Rivers Authority
Pleasure Island Theme Park
Royal Botanic Gardens, Kew
South Hams
Victoria and Albert Museum
Youth Hostel Association

A key to the symbols used in this book

This indicates a comprehensive series of tasks that are designed to cover all of the performance criteria of a particular element.

This indicates the suggested time needed to complete the activity.

This indicates that the activity or assignment has been designed so that evidence can be gathered for stated application of number elements.

This indicates that the activity or assignment has been designed so that evidence can be gathered for stated communication elements.

This indicates that the activity or assignment has been designed so that evidence can be gathered for stated information technology elements.

UNIT 4 CONTRIBUTING TO A TEAM ACTIVITY

element 4.1

PLAN AN ACTIVITY WITH A TEAM

Performance criteria

A student must:

1 Check that he or she and other team members have an accurate understanding of the given objectives of the activity.

2 Agree actions which will meet the overall objectives.

3 Contribute to identifying the **resources** which are necessary.

4 Contribute to identifying which team members are going to carry out different parts of the activity.

5 Contribute to identifying actions to deal with **anticipated problems** and maintain **health and safety**.

6 Contribute to producing a realistic team plan for the overall activity.

7 Agree and produce a realistic individual plan which provides details of own role in the activity.

RANGE

Resources: finance, people, materials, equipment, information

Anticipated problems: given, identified by the team

Health and safety associated with: self, other people, materials, equipment

INTRODUCTION

This element, as for the other elements that make up this unit, is a practical one. During this unit you will carry out the three main stages in dealing with a problem or an activity. In this element we will focus on the planning of the activity. This means that we will be looking at all the things you should do and consider, and the ways in which you can split up the work within the team to make the best use of the skills you have and the time available to do the job. The next element covers the actual carrying out of the activity and the final one looks at the way in which the activity was handled and gives you a chance to review what you did.

We have detailed the activity in the element assignment on pages 9–10. You will therefore have to refer to the activity to make sure that you follow all the planning procedures needed to cover this element. We will be giving you advice as to how to plan the activity properly throughout. You can continue to follow this activity through the other elements of this unit.

Although we have provided you with a framework for a complete activity for this unit, your tutors may choose to use an activity taken from one of the other units of the Foundation course. If this is the case, they will have to make sure that you follow all the procedures and stages detailed in this unit as well as the performance criteria of the other unit.

4.1.1 *Check that he or she and other team members have an accurate understanding of the given objectives of the activity*

As we have already said, you will either be using the activity detailed in the element assignment or an activity related to one of the other units of the Foundation programme. Regardless of the nature of the activity, the first thing you must make sure of is that you all understand exactly what you have to do. There are two parts to this:

1 What has to be done before we can start this activity and what do we need to know?
2 What will be expected of us by the time that the activity is over?

The individual tasks and questions that are detailed in the element assignment will help you with this; read them and make sure that you understand what they require of you. If you do not understand them now, you will not be able to plan the activity. Are you clear about what needs to be done and the evidence you will have to produce to prove that you have carried out all the tasks? If you are unsure, ask your tutor now – later will be too late!

4.1.2 Agree actions which will meet the overall objectives

One of the best ways to agree the actions that you will have to undertake is to discuss the activity's objectives as a group. As explained in the last section, you should all understand what is required of you. There will probably be some dis-agreement about how you will carry out the vari-ous activities, but this is a natural part of any discussion.

Talk about the activity together, and make sure that all the members of the group give sugges-tions and ideas to the discussion. Remember that if you have a good idea about how you should do things and do not say anything, you will only have yourself to blame later if things go wrong.

Your main aim is to produce an overall action plan that will cope with all the demands of the activity. After the discussion, you should fill in the group action plan that is used by your centre. In the next two performance criteria, you will have to identify the resources you will need and agree how you will split the work between you. You may want to start thinking about this as you draw up a list of all the things you have to do.

4.1.3 Contribute to identifying the resources which are necessary

There are very few activities that do not need resources. Exactly what you need will depend on the activity itself. In this performance criterion, we have concentrated on the resources you will

Fig. 4.1.1 The British Association of Conference Towns (BACT) offers a wide range of conference facilities, including training workshops for teams.

need to carry out the activity detailed in the ele-ment assignment. Obviously, if you are doing something different, the resources will be differ-ent too.

RESOURCES

There are several different types of resource; basically they fall into the following categories:

▼ **finance**
▼ **people**
▼ **materials**
▼ **equipment**
▼ **information**

For the purposes of this assignment, you will need to consider all of these. Before we have a look at them in any great detail, however, let us draw up a list of needs. The basic things that you will need for this activity are the following:

▼ **paper and pens**
▼ **graph paper**
▼ **flip-charts and overhead-projector sheets**
▼ **access to a photocopier**
▼ **use of a computer**
▼ **a map of your centre**

This is only part of the list. You will be able to come up with other ideas and needs, as these will depend on how you are intending to carry out the activity. Do not be influenced by what we have suggested – you might not need some of these items in the end. It is a good idea to try and decide what you will definitely need, then make another list of things that would be useful but not essential. Most of the basic resources will be provided by your tutor or will be available somewhere within the centre.

Finance

Although your centre will be providing the majority of the resources that you will need for this assignment, you should draw up a form which details the cost of each item you use. You will have to ask your tutor for the cost of photocopying, overhead transparencies and flip-charts, for example. You should keep a detailed list of what you use – not just the physical items, but also the cost of telephone calls and other services. At the end of the activity, you should be able to provide your tutor with a full list and total of all the expenses.

People

When we think about people involved in an activity, we tend to consider only the main team members. Make a list of *all* the people who you think you will have to talk to, or use the skills of, to

Fig. 4.1.2 The Kew School of Garden Design offers a five-week course with lectures on historical and contemporary landscapes. This picture shows a group of students from one of the courses working together as a team.

carry out the whole of the activity. Librarians, technicians, friends and family may all be useful sources of help and advice throughout the activity and you should not forget them.

Materials and equipment

Throughout the course, you will have been using various sorts of material and equipment. Make a list of the things you will need to carry out this assignment. It is always a good idea to think about what you will need before starting a particular piece of work – remember that things may not be available exactly when you need them. Materials and equipment you may need include:

▼ **photocopiers**
▼ **staplers**
▼ **envelopes**
▼ **paper**

Fig. 4.1.3 Large organisations have video-conferencing facilities to assist team activities. Different individuals or groups, who are thousands of miles apart, can engage in team activities via cameras, satellite links and monitor screens.

▼ overhead projectors and
    transparencies
▼ flip-charts and marker pens
▼ computers and printers
▼ folders
▼ paper clips
▼ rulers and pens

Your centre should be able to provide you with the majority of the materials and equipment you need, but some you will own anyway. Some lucky people have computers at home and will be able to do parts of the work away from the centre.

Information

In addition to the information provided in this book and the companion volume *Foundation Leisure and Tourism,* you will be able to use the library as a main source of books, articles and other materials.

If your centre has computers with CD-ROM drives, then they may have encyclopedias and other useful sources of information available. You will be able to look things up and get print-outs of relevant articles and features.

As we said earlier, people are also a very useful source of information and will be able to give you up-to-date material. If they do not know about a topic themselves, they will be able to point you in the right direction.

4.1.4 Contribute to identifying which team members are going to carry out different parts of the activity

Trying to decide who will be responsible for the various parts of the plan is one of the hardest things to do. All of you will want to do the interesting parts of the plan and no one will want to do the boring bits. Try to think of all the parts of the plan as being equally important.

If you feel strongly that you should carry out a particular part of the plan, explain to the other members of the team why you think you are best suited to the job. If you cannot decide who should do the various tasks, the fairest way is to draw lots, as follows. Write all your names onto small slips of paper and fold them up so the names are hidden. Get someone who is not involved with the activity to choose a slip of paper. The person who has their name chosen first should then pick a task. Continue like this until all the tasks have been allocated to a team member.

Some of the tasks will need more than one person to carry them out. In such cases, try to work with a team member that has skills you do not have. Some people are good with words, others with numbers; some can draw, others are good on the computer – we are all different. Most of us have a skill that we are proud of, so this is a chance to use that skill for the benefit of the whole team.

If you are still unsure about how to divide up the various tasks, each member of the team should make a list of the things they think they are good at. Compare your lists as a group. With a bit of thought and discussion, the ideal person for each task should be fairly obvious.

If you really want to get the most out of the activity, you could choose a task that you are not very good at. Remember, the only way to learn something is to try it. Consider this as a way of splitting up the tasks if all else fails.

4.1.5 Contribute to identifying actions to deal with anticipated problems and maintain health and safety

ANTICIPATED PROBLEMS

Even the best plans do not always go right. No matter how well you have planned an activity, you may have forgotten one little thing that could upset the whole plan. This is very common – even expert planners forget things once in a while.

Alongside your list of tasks, you should therefore begin to try to identify problems that might come up. Think about your plan: what are you relying on? Do certain things have to be done before you can get on with the main parts of the activity? What will you do if you cannot get the resources you think you need?

Once you have identified what might go wrong, you then have to decide what you will do if things go as badly as you feared. You should always have a back-up plan to cope with situations like this. Hopefully you will not need to use it, but you never know!

Against each of the potential problems, you should write possible solutions. Your tutor might be able to offer you a form or sheet that is ideal for this. If you want to create one for yourself, use the following column headings:

▼ **anticipated problem**
▼ **first solution**
▼ **second solution**

By the time that you have completed this list of potential problems, you should be ready for almost anything!

Given problems

The whole of the assignment, including the related activities and tasks, can be viewed as a set of problems to be solved. If you are not following the activity through in the right way, your tutor will let you know and you will have to identify a way to get back on track as quickly and painlessly as possible. In order to test your planning and ability to cope with problems as they arise, your tutor may decide to put other problems in your path as you get on with the work at hand. There is no way of predicting what these may be; only time will tell whether your plan was good enough to cope with them.

Problems identified by the team

By now, you will have identified problems that may crop up in the course of the activity. You should also have planned how you will deal with potential problems. If not, you should review your plan and spend time devising a back-up strategy in case things go wrong. Your tutor will be keen for you to have a good reserve plan and will probably not let you start the activity until you have done this.

HEALTH AND SAFETY

You do not need to know all the details of health and safety law, but you should be aware that your actions must not put you or other people at risk. For a full description of the possible dangers, hazards and problems, refer to Unit 5. This unit looks at health and safety in much greater detail.

Health and safety associated with self

Remember that potential hazards surround us all the time. Nearly every object can pose a threat if treated in the wrong way, and the most innocent action can be dangerous if you are not careful. In a work environment you will be expected to take care of yourself and not take risks. You should adopt the same approach during your course.

Health and safety associated with other people

Just as you can be a danger to yourself, so can others. If they are not careful with materials and equipment, you can be put into unnecessary danger by their actions.

It is always wise to make sure you know the rules about handling items of equipment in the centre. Not only must you be aware of what you should and should not do, but you also need to make sure that other people are not doing things that could cause you harm.

If you intend to collect information from outside your centre (perhaps from local leisure and tourism facilities or members of the public), do not go there alone. It is safer for a small group of two or three students to work together in such circumstances.

Health and safety associated with equipment and materials

Although most pieces of equipment and different materials are not a danger in themselves, there is always the outside chance that something could go wrong and you could find yourself in difficulties. Remember that electricity is dangerous and lethal in certain circumstances. Also, equipment like guillotines and staples are designed for office use and not for minor surgery to yourself or others! No doubt you will have been warned about

7

the dangers that surround you in the workplace – be aware that many of these dangers are with you now.

4.1.6 Contribute to producing a realistic team plan for the overall activity

To fulfil the requirements of this element, you should produce the following:

▼ **an action plan for the whole of the activity, along with a back-up plan to deal with the possible problems that you might encounter along the way**
▼ **an agenda for the initial meeting and other meetings that you will have in planning the activity**
▼ **an activity schedule, including a list of the activities and how long you expect them to take (approximate times are fine for this)**
▼ **individual lists of tasks and duties that are to be performed by each member of the team**
▼ **individual and group targets, which should include what has to be done by the end of each session, day or week by both the team as a whole and each of the individual team members**

This may sound like quite a lot of work to do before you have even started the activity itself. Remember, however, that everything you plan and organise now will help you later. Not having

thought the activity through will mean that, if you get into problems later, you will not have the time or means to deal with them.

The individual schedules and targets will help you to assess whether your actions are going according to plan. You should always slightly overestimate the time that you think will be needed. If you underestimate, the activity is bound to get behind schedule and you will be putting unnecessary pressure on yourselves. You will be given a date for the completion of the whole of the assignment; work back from that and you will be able to allocate the time for each part of the activity accordingly.

4.1.7 Agree and produce a realistic plan which provides details of own role in the activity

If you have completed all the aspects of planning we have described, you will have a good idea as to your own part in the activity. To double-check that you have listed all the things you will have to do as your part of the work, it is a good idea to create a separate action plan of your own. In this plan, which should run alongside the main team plan, you should write down (in order) all the activities for which you are personally responsible. Your centre will have a particular form for this, either designed by the centre itself or recommended by the awarding body. You will be expected to complete this before moving on to the activity proper.

assignment

ELEMENT 4.1

PC 4.1.1–7
COM 1.1, 1.2, 1.3, 1.4
AON 1.1, 1.2, 1.3

In order to cover all the aspects of this unit, we have suggested an assignment and related tasks that can be based on the college or school you are attending. There are lots of things to think about and do. Remember that you will often have to work as a member of a team; few tasks (apart from very basic and simple ones) are carried out on your own. Ideally, the team should be at least three strong – perhaps more if the scope of a task is broad.

Before we look at the activity, let us recap on the requirements of this element alongside the performance criteria that make up the element itself. This will give you a format to refer to when you construct your overall team plan.

PC 4.1.1 *Describe the main aims of the activity.*

PC 4.1.2 *Describe the actions and tasks that will have to be undertaken in completing the activity.*

PC 4.1.3 *List and describe the resources that will be needed and identify where these can be obtained.*

PC 4.1.4 *Identify who will be responsible for each of the actions and tasks that make up the activity as a whole.*

PC 4.1.5 *Identify the actions that will be undertaken in the face of potential problems.*

PC 4.1.6 *As a final check that you have covered all the planning tasks, consider the following points:*

- *Have all the options been considered within the timescale that you have been given?*
- *Have all the resources been identified and are they available in the quantity, quality and time available?*
- *Does everyone in the team understand exactly what their jobs are?*
- *Does each individual member of the team have a clearly defined role?*

PC 4.1.7 *Create an individual action plan which describes your own actions throughout the whole of the activity.*

You will need to keep a log outlining your contribution to the team planning exercise. You should also keep a log of all the actions you have to undertake personally. Remember that this log should be accurate, as the assessor will need to verify the account as a true record of what you have done.

Team activity

As we mentioned, this activity is designed so that you can follow it through the three elements of this unit. You will not see any performance criteria against the tasks in this assignment; they relate to the planning stage that we have already looked at.

Scenario

Your school or college is keen to make the best use of the leisure facilities at the centre. It believes that the sports facilities are not being used as much as they could be, particularly by groups and individuals in the community. To this end, it has asked you to carry out a survey which investigates the leisure pursuits of the students and staff at the centre, as well as the views of the local community. You are also expected to arrange publicity for the leisure facilities at your centre and work out the costs of inviting the local press and local prominent members of the community to an event.

task 1

Design a questionnaire that asks the students, staff and members of the public about their leisure activities and whether they would like to use the facilities at your centre. You may wish to ask your tutors about the probable costs of hiring the facilities so that you can mention this on the questionnaire. You should try to get at least 50 questionnaires filled in by the various groups of people.

task 2

After you have collected the information, you should collate the results and put your findings into a format that can be easily understood. Give an oral presentation of your findings to your tutors, supported by visual aids and summaries of the information that you have collected. As part of this presentation, you should suggest which forms of leisure activity you consider to be the most popular.

task 3

You should also suggest suitable charges for hiring the facilities and propose a way in which this money could be collected. Alongside this, you will have to create a way of recording the bookings so that you can keep track of the times when the facilities are available for hire and when they have already been booked.

task 4

The final task is to organise a launch party to publicise the availability of the facilities. In order to do this, you must undertake the following:

- Draw up a list of 50 people to invite. These should include representatives of local sports and leisure groups, journalists and reporters, and other people involved in local leisure and tourism.

- Working from the following costs and assuming that 50 people will attend the event, calculate the total cost of the event:

    Buffet costs: £5.00 per head
    Cost of printing the invitations: £10.00
    Postage costs: 19p per invitation.

element 4.2

UNDERTAKE A ROLE IN A TEAM ACTIVITY

Performance criteria

A student must:

1 Carry out the activities in the agreed individual plan and the agreed team plan.
2 Make best use of available **resources**.
3 Maintain **health and safety**.
4 Co-operate effectively with others as required by the plans.
5 **Respond** to **problems** promptly and in the correct way.

RANGE

Resources: finance, people, materials, equipment, information

Health and safety associated with: self, other people, materials, equipment

Respond: taking action to resolve the problem, reporting the problem to person(s) responsible

Problems: anticipated, unexpected

4.2.1 Carry out the activities in the agreed individual plan and the agreed team plan

Having planned the activity, the main point of this performance criterion is to make sure that you carry out the tasks which you have agreed and written down in your individual and team plans.

It may become obvious to you during the activity that some people have not done everything they were supposed to do; others may have taken on additional tasks they were not asked to do. Bear in mind that you will have been observed and monitored whilst preparing your individual and team action plans. Your tutor should be aware of what you proposed to do and will compare this with the tasks you are now undertaking.

Your tutor will consider the following:

▼ **Have you fulfilled the promises you made in your plans?**
▼ **Have you made the best use of available resources?**
▼ **Have you considered health and safety throughout?**
▼ **Have you co-operated fully with one another throughout the activity?**
▼ **Have you responded correctly and promptly to problems as they have arisen?**

As we said in Element 4.1, the exact nature of the tasks you are undertaking will depend on the type of activity you have been given to perform. Remember that your tutor will be looking at you both individually and as a group; although you may be performing well yourself, this does not necessarily mean that the group is performing as well as it should. Since this unit focuses specifically on developing your skills as a team member,

you should bear this in mind throughout all your actions from now on.

It is a good idea to begin monitoring and comparing actual behaviour with the agreed plans you made earlier. You can do this by writing down the initials of the person(s) undertaking various tasks against each of the tasks, and then comparing them to the individuals who were supposed to carry out those tasks. Some of the roles in the group may have changed without any of you noticing. Provided that there is a good reason for this and the work is shared out fairly, it may be acceptable to your tutor. You should note and explain the reasons for any changes in your review of the activity. It is, however, a good idea to avoid swapping roles as this can lead to confusion and, at worst, some of the tasks may be overlooked or carried out twice.

You may wish to use the following column headings to keep a track of what has been done, by whom and how long it took them:

▼ **task**
▼ **planned person**
▼ **actual person**
▼ **time taken**

Be aware that filling in a form like this may cause friction within the group, particularly if someone is not pulling their weight. If you all agree to fill in a form like this, such problems can be avoided – everyone will know that the other team members are keeping an eye on what they are doing.

4.2.2 Make the best use of available resources

RESOURCES

In Element 4.1, we gave a description of the types of resources that you might need to carry out the team activity. Within your individual and team plans you will have identified the resources which you thought were necessary and are available to you. Your tutor will be looking at how you use these resources and whether you make the best use of what is available. You should make sure that you do not ask for items or information that you had not planned for. If you do this, it will show that your original plans were not thought through sufficiently.

In this performance criterion, we will be suggesting ways of monitoring your use of resources throughout the team activity. It will be your responsibility to list and account for any item, materials, equipment, information or assistance you make use of, in order to support your approach to the activity. Bearing in mind that you will have to review your activity in Element 4.3, it is a good idea to keep track of what you have and have not used – you will find it very difficult to remember everything once the activity is completed.

Finance

As we mentioned in Element 4.1, the use of almost anything has a financial implication. Photocopies are not free; neither are the running costs of machines and equipment. Every time you use paper or envelopes these will have to be replaced at a cost to your centre. In this unit, you do not need to cost people's time when you ask them for assistance or information. However, you should, at the very least, list all the **consumable materials** (items which are used during the activity, such as paper, flip-charts and overhead-projector transparencies). Your tutor will advise you as to the cost of these items.

You may find the following column headings helpful in keeping track of the consumable items you have used:

▼ **item**
▼ **used in (task number)**
▼ **cost per item**
▼ **total cost**

At the bottom of the page, you will have a final total which shows all expenses related to the activity.

People

As we said earlier, you will not need to cost the time of any individual who you have consulted. It would be a good idea, however, to list the individuals consulted and note down the questions asked of them and a brief summary of their responses. The following column headings may help you to do this:

▼ **name of person**
▼ **information requested**
▼ **answer details**

It is worth remembering that other group members may be a valuable source of information or, at the very least, will know someone who can help you with a particular problem. Since we all have different backgrounds and experiences, it is worth asking the group members first before attempting to gain information elsewhere. As we will see later in this performance criterion, you will be credited for your ability to obtain information from any source – particularly if you can identify where or to whom you should go for that information.

Materials and equipment

Although you will have listed the consumable items used in the activity when you completed your summary of expenses, you also need to list the types of materials used and any equipment you required during the activity.

Again, it is probably a good idea to list the materials and equipment against the particular tasks, mentioning which member of the group used these and why. The following column headings may help you to do this:

▼ **equipment/materials used**
▼ **used by**
▼ **used in (task number)**
▼ **problems found**

We have added the last column to enable you to note down any difficulties you encountered in using particular equipment or materials. For example, you may have wanted to print out something from a computer, but found that the computers were unavailable.

Information

If you are using the activity detailed in Element 4.1, the majority of the information you need will have been collected by you and your team in the form of questionnaires. If you were overambitious and collected too much information, you are probably now wondering what to do with it all. On the other hand, if you have not collected enough, you are now faced with the prospect of collecting more (or even considering the option of making up facts in order to cover your lack of information).

The first problem is more easily solved than the second. If you find yourself with a mountain of information and cannot see how you will be able to process it all in the time you have been given for the activity, you should consider analysing only 50 of the questionnaires, as recommended in Element 4.1. You may wonder, 'how do we know whether the 50 questionnaires are a true reflection of the opinions of all the people who filled in questionnaires?' The basic answer is that you do not, but there is no sure way of picking these without going through all the questionnaires you have collected. A better solution is to keep your questionnaires in two batches which relate either to individuals within your centre or individuals from the community, and then take some from each set. A quick and relatively fair way of choosing the questionnaires is to simply count out the top 25 from each pile.

Addressing the second problem of not having collected enough data raises an altogether different set of concerns. Your tutor may not be happy with you trying to draw conclusions from a very small sample of questionnaires. However, you cannot trade information with other teams, as they may have taken a different approach to the one you used. The only alternative is to go out and collect more data. You will have to explain why you did not collect sufficient data in the first place, particularly if you had more questionnaires printed than you used. After all, in your team plan you agreed to get a certain number of questionnaires filled in and you have not fulfilled this.

Faced with a pile of completed questionnaires, you will have to think of a way to process the data and obtain totals for each of the questions. As long as you have used questions which have only a limited set of answers, you will only need to add up the number of times each answer was given to fully process your data. The easiest way to do this is for one person to have a blank questionnaire and the other members of the team to have a pile of filled in questionnaires each. Those with the completed questionnaires call out, in turn, the response to each question on the sheet in front of them. The person with the blank questionnaire can then use a simple 'bar and gate' (tally) method of counting the responses to each question.

For those of you that used more open questions, which allowed individuals to express their opinions in words, the processing of the information can be rather more lengthy. The best approach is to look through all the questionnaires and highlight some of the more interesting responses and, at the same time, try to get a feel of the overall opinions of the people who filled in the questionnaires. You cannot hope to include all the opinions and should try to cover the most popular ones.

The ideal questionnaire has features of both of the above approaches. The majority of the questions should be **closed** (which means that the person filling in the questionnaire can only make a limited set of responses, such as yes, no, sometimes or maybe). Some of the other questions can be more **open** (which means you leave space on the questionnaire for people to write their own opinion or statement).

Apart from the information collected from your questionnaires, there may be other things you need to know to help you with the activity. If you are undertaking our series of tasks outlined in Element 4.1, you will have to discover the names and addresses of local people to invite to the event. Some of these names and addresses will be easy to obtain, but you may have to ask for assistance in finding others. Perhaps your librarian, tutor, friends or family will be able to help you in this. You should always note down the source of any information you receive. The following column headings may assist you in doing this:

▼ information sought
▼ from whom
▼ information obtained
▼ alternative source

Again, it is a good idea to use these headings as early in the activity as possible, as you will find it very difficult later to remember the type of information you needed at a particular time and who you went to for it. When you review the activity you will have to mention any problems that you encountered in collecting information and whether this had a bearing on your ability to complete the tasks and meet deadlines.

4.2.3 Maintain health and safety

HEALTH AND SAFETY

You will find a full description of health and safety considerations in Unit 5. The main point of this performance criterion is to make sure that you have maintained health and safety throughout the activity and that your actions have not put yourself or other members of the team at risk. Rather than repeat what we have already said in Element 4.1, you will find under each section of this performance criterion a suggested set of headings which could help you log and monitor any potential health and safety concerns that you and your team may have had during the activity.

Health and safety associated with self

As a result of the part you played in the team activity, you may have experienced health and safety concerns which you should note for future reference and for review purposes in Element 4.3. If you did not note any health and safety considerations associated with your own actions, you should say so. The following column headings

may help you to log your health and safety concerns:

▼ problem encountered
▼ date
▼ action taken

Health and safety associated with other people

There is no way of predicting what you may or may not have encountered as a result of other people's actions during the activity. Whilst we suggested possible health and safety concerns, you may well have experienced unexpected problems. Again, you should note down any health and safety concerns that were associated with other people. You may find it useful to log these using the following column headings:

▼ problem encountered
▼ date
▼ action taken

Health and safety associated with materials and equipment

This is the area in which you are most likely to encounter health and safety concerns. You will find a full description of the things to look out for in Unit 5.

If you have encountered any serious problem relating to materials or equipment, you should report it to your tutor. Your centre will want to know immediately if anything is faulty or dangerous. The following column headings may help you to log any health and safety concerns associated with materials and equipment:

▼ equipment/materials used
▼ problem encountered
▼ date
▼ reported to

You will be expected to review the maintenance of health and safety throughout the activity in Element 4.3. Bear in mind that you will have to

15

suggest ways in which health and safety can be improved within your centre in relation to all the aspects covered in this performance criterion.

4.2.4 Co-operate effectively with others as required by the plan

Carrying out all the tasks which you agreed in your individual action plan is not sufficient to claim that the team activity was a success. You must try to ensure that the whole team activity, including everyone's individual part in it, has been undertaken to the best of all your abilities.

Some members of the team will have worked far harder than others. Some may believe that they have undertaken more of the tasks and worked harder than anyone else. This may be the case, as you cannot predict accurately how much work will be involved in any individual task at the beginning. The main point about dealing with team activities is that you have to co-operate as much as possible and try to sort out problems as and when they arise. Try to agree on the best ways in which to approach problems and avoid bullying individuals within the team. Remember that your behaviour towards one another and your approach to the activity in general will be observed by your tutor throughout. Your tutor will be looking for clues and evidence which will support your claims that you have worked well as a team. Try to give your tutor every opportunity to recognise your skills as a team – not weaknesses and inability to co-operate.

Remember that co-operation also involves taking some of the load off other members of the team who are struggling. Perhaps they were given too much work or responsibility, or maybe they have been waiting for others to complete an earlier task before they can get on with theirs. Co-operation is all about getting involved in the activity as a team, without wasting time arguing

about who has responsibility for things. If you have finished your part of the activity, do not sit back and watch other members of the team struggle to complete their parts. This does not show good co-operation.

4.2.5 Respond to problems promptly and in the correct way

RESPOND

There is a right and wrong way of handling any given situation. This performance criterion aims to help you correctly identify the right action that should be taken and the person to whom you should report the problem.

Taking action to resolve the problem

Many of the problems you encounter in the completion of this or any other activity will have to be handled by you and your team in the first instance. You cannot necessarily rely on someone else to sort out a problem for you. As problems arise, rather than attempting to solve them individually, you should discuss your difficulties as a team and arrive at the best solution for all of you. One of the other team members may have, in fact, encountered a similar problem in the past and might be able to suggest the perfect solution to the problem.

As long as the action you are proposing to take is acceptable to the whole team and will not cause additional problems, you may not have to refer to anybody else before doing it. Remember, however, that simple problems may not always have simple solutions and you should think your actions through before you do anything that will make the situation worse. If you are unsure what course of action to take, you should ask the opinion of your tutor. You do not want to lose more time by having to work around another set of problems that have arisen as a result of your poor choice of solution.

Someone within the group will have to take responsibility for seeing through the team's solution to a particular problem. You do not want to make that person deal with additional trouble because of the decision you have taken. If you cannot agree on a particular course of action, you should go with the decision of the majority of the team or refer the matter to your tutor.

Reporting the problem to the person(s) responsible

In most cases the person you should refer your problems to is your tutor. He or she will be able to deal with most disagreements or problems that arise and suggest a range of options available to you (which will be expected to choose from). Do not expect your tutor to give you the answer every time. Remember that your tutor will be looking at your ability to cope with problems and carry out different courses of action.

Some problems will be of a technical nature, which may involve faulty equipment or the lack of materials or resources. Your tutor may not be on hand to suggest solutions and you may have to refer to a technician, librarian or other member of staff to help you. Unless the problem involves a health and safety matter, it will again be up to you to decide exactly which solution to follow.

In most cases, you will be expected to record the problem and your solution on a monitoring sheet (provided by the centre or awarding body). It will be useful to refer to these in Element 4.3, when you have to review the activity and your actions.

PROBLEMS

As we will see, there are problems that are obvious and you know will happen. They are unavoidable. Other problems are unforeseen and you can never predict whether they will happen or when they will occur. In this part of the element we will be trying to help you cope with anticipated and expected problems.

Anticipated problems

Problems that you can anticipate are likely to relate to the availability of information, materials or equipment. If you have created a flexible individual and team action plan, as suggested in Element 4.1, you will have thought of alternative ways of completing the activity if these problems arise. This is a good opportunity to show how good your action plan was in the first place – demonstrating that you anticipated certain situations and worked out ways of getting around them. Again, you should record the fact that these anticipated problems arose and state whether your suggested solutions worked. If your suggested solutions did not work, you can count these as unexpected problems.

Unexpected problems

Having spent a considerable amount of time working out the team plan and allocating specific tasks to individuals within the team, you may be faced with the prospect of having to carry out the activity without one of the members of the team. Sickness, for example, can never be anticipated. Your tutor will be looking at the way in which the remainder of the team deals with this problem and accepts responsibility for the tasks that have been allocated to the absent team member. Once again, you should always make a note of any unexpected problem and identify the way in which the team dealt with it.

assignment

ELEMENT 4.2

PC 4.2.1–5
COM 1.4
AON 1.1, 1.2, 1.3

As you will be performing the tasks related to each of the performance criteria during the team activity, there is no specific element assignment. In order to help you think about the kinds of things your tutor will be looking at, we have created a number of personalised questionnaires for you to complete. These will help you to assess your own abilities and strengths and weaknesses. Where possible, we have linked these questionnaires with the performance criteria of this element, although some of the questionnaires cover more than one performance criterion, as well as core skills.

task	**1**	PC 4.2.1

Answer this set of questions, using the following responses: always, sometimes, occasionally, never.

 1 *Are you able to work long hours?*
 2 *Do you find problems a challenge?*
 3 *Can you come up with good ideas to get out of problems?*
 4 *If you started an activity and were struggling, would you be prepared to continue with it?*
 5 *Are you able to keep working at something until it is completed?*
 6 *Are you able to stick with a problem through to its solution?*
 7 *Would you always put your own duties before anything else, including your leisure activities and family?*
 8 *Do you consider success to be measured in terms of how much praise you get?*

 9 *Can you cope with being unsure about what you have to do in a particular task?*
10 *Do you consider yourself to be self-confident?*
11 *Are you able to take criticism?*
12 *Do you ask others to give you feedback on your performance in the hope that you can do something better next time?*
13 *Do you feel that your success or failure relies on others too much?*
14 *Do you tend to be a leader in group situations?*
15 *Are you good at finding the right person or source of information to help you achieve what you want?*
16 *Do you have the ability to realise that you may need help in certain circumstances?*
17 *Do you set high standards for yourself?*
18 *Do you take risks rather than being cautious?*
19 *Are you healthy?*
20 *Do you have the ability to pass jobs onto others?*
21 *Are you able to identify important decisions and unimportant ones?*
22 *Do others think of you as a survivor?*
23 *Do you find coping with problems a real difficulty?*
24 *Do you respect other people's views and opinions?*
25 *When other people express an opinion or offer advice and information, are you able to accept what they say?*

If you have answered these questions with mainly 'always' or 'sometimes' responses, you are probably a good leader.

task 2 PC 4.2.4

Consider the statements below and give one of the following responses to each: I agree, I neither agree nor disagree, I disagree.

1 I want to control the tasks I am set.
2 I want to be involved in everything.
3 I find it impossible to pass on a job to someone else.
4 I hate being uncertain about things.
5 I do not trust other people's ability to do a job.
6 I hate asking other people for favours.
7 I like to be alone when I have things to do.
8 I always check and change other people's work.
9 I would rather stop doing what I am doing to carry out a task than let someone else undertake that task.
10 I lose interest in a task if someone else interferes in what I am doing.

If you have agreed with the above statements, this shows you are more an individual than a team worker. If you have neither agreed nor disagreed with the statements, you may be either unsure of how you behave in certain situations or unconcerned whether you work alone or as part of a team. Those that have disagreed with the majority of the statements should be reasonable group workers.

task 3 PC 4.2.1/5

Time management concerns not only other people, but also physical items such as paperwork. It involves the constant monitoring of what needs to be done. Consider the following statements and give a 'true' or 'false' response to each.

1 I have identified my strengths in relation to time management.
2 I have identified my weaknesses in relation to time management.
3 I know where and how I waste my time.

4 I know why I allow my time to be managed badly.
5 I am able to decide which tasks should be done first.
6 I can quickly process and decide on the importance of information.
7 I understand the reasons behind my time-wasting behaviour.
8 I can use a variety of different methods to manage my time.
9 I can cope with other individuals who try to stop me getting on with my tasks.
10 I am able to control my time.

If you have responded 'true' to the majority of these statements, you have already begun to manage your time effectively. If you have made a number of 'false' responses, you may have to consider making stricter rules for yourself and others.

task 4 PC 4.2.5

Decision making is an important skill that must be looked at by any individual within a leisure and tourism facility. We all make lots of decisions on a day-to-day basis, but we may not recognise them as such. In order to help you understand the process of decision making, it is useful to spend some time thinking about how you make decisions. This way, when the time comes to make one, you will be prepared to consider the options and make the right choice.

Many problems arise without prior notice. There are many ways of handling such situations – one of the most common and least productive responses is to panic.

Consider the following statements and give a 'yes' or 'no' response to each.

1 I can identify the nature and sources of problems before they happen.
2 I have already examined the possible solutions before I make a decision.
3 I have clear ideas that help me arrive at a solution.

4 I am able to compare possible solutions and choose the right one.

5 I can put decisions into action and monitor the results.

6 I am able to guess that a problem might come up before it does.

7 I never make a snap decision.

8 I would rather think about the problem at length than risk making a wrong decision.

9 I do not find decision making stressful, but it is challenging.

10 If I manage information correctly then decision making is relatively easy.

If you have responded 'yes' to the majority of the statements, this shows you have some grasp of the decision-making process and are able to solve problems. If you said 'no' to the majority or some of these statements, you are perhaps being a little more honest with yourself. There are only a handful of highly experienced managers who could claim that they always make the right decision and are invariably able to solve problems effectively.

task	5	PC 4.2.2

Following on from decision making and problem solving, the collection and handling of information is another key skill. The information that you are able to obtain, handle and process, will be vital in establishing your ability to communicate within a group.

Again, consider these statements and give a 'yes' or 'no' response to each.

1 I know what information I need.

2 I know from whom or where I can obtain the information.

3 I know why I want the information.

4 I have a good idea of the deadline involved.

5 I know how I want the information to look.

6 Once I have the information, I know what I have to do with it.

7 I can look at the information and know what is valuable and what is useless.

8 I can process the information and present it in a clear and logical way.

9 Once I have tackled the information, I can draw clear conclusions from it.

10 I know the use of the information and to whom it should be given.

If you have given a 'yes' response to these statements, this shows you have a fairly clear understanding of handling information. However, if you have a mixture of responses, or mainly 'no' responses, you should not consider yourself a failure in this respect. A cautious user of information may see things that the more confident handler misses.

task	6	PC 4.2.4/5

The use and development of communication skills is an important consideration when attempting to establish relationships with others. Consider the following statements and give a 'true' or 'false' response to each.

1 I can use a variety of communication methods.

2 I can listen effectively.

3 I am able to make myself understood by others.

4 I have better communication skills than other members of the team.

5 I do not have any trouble in communicating with different people in different circumstances.

6 I know the right questions to ask to get the information I need.

7 I am able to understand what people are really saying to me.

8 I appreciate that I need to listen as well as talk.

9 I am able to communicate well in written form.

10 I am able to present information in a variety of different ways.

If you have responded 'false' to a number of the above statements, you should consider how you can improve these communication aspects.

---

task | **7** | PC 4.2.3

Health and safety concerns are important in everything that we do. Consider the following statements and give a 'true' or 'false' response to each.

1 *I would never put myself in a position where I felt unsafe.*

2 *I would never use equipment that I have not been instructed how to use.*

3 *I find it hard to understand why people get hurt at work.*

4 *I do not believe that electrical equipment is necessarily dangerous.*

5 *People who get hurt at work deserve it because they are probably being careless.*

6 *Simple pieces of equipment do not really have health and safety problems at all.*

7 *If I saw something dangerous, I would definitely avoid it.*

8 *I have noticed dangerous things and have reported them.*

9 *If I saw something dangerous at my centre, I would know who to report it to.*

10 *I know all there is to know about health and safety laws.*

If you have responded 'true' to the majority of these statements, you are probably a little overconfident; you are possibly overlooking things that may be more dangerous than you think. Several 'false' replies will show that you, along with the majority of people, think about health and safety but are not always sure whether you are at risk or not.

element 4.3

REVIEW THE ACTIVITY

Performance criteria

A student must:

1 **Review** the extent to which the overall objectives of the activity were met.
2 **Review** use of **resources**.
3 **Review** whether responses to **problems** were effective.
4 **Review** maintenance of **health and safety**.
5 Provide clear and constructive **feedback** to others on their performance.
6 Respond constructively to **feedback** from others.
7 Make and record suggestions for **improvements** in the way similar activities are tackled in the future.

RANGE

Review: of the team's overall performance, of individual team members' performance; through team discussions, through discussions between individual team members and teachers/tutors

Resources: finance, people, materials, equipment, information

Problems: anticipated, unexpected

Health and safety associated with: self, other people, materials, equipment

Feedback: on success in undertaking the activity, on aspects of performance which may be improved

Improvements to: the team's performance, the student's performance, the use of resources, the responses to problems, the maintenance of health and safety

4.3.1 **R**eview the extent to which the overall objectives of the activity were met

REVIEW

This element aims to see whether you have met all the performance criteria of not only this element, but the other two elements of this unit as well. Your tutor will have reviewed your progress regularly and given you feedback on your performance so far. This element gives you, your team and your tutor the opportunity to look at the activity in detail and review your performance throughout.

In the element assignment you will be asked to produce a log which outlines your performance in the team review of the activity. In order to help you do this, we thought it would be useful to look at some key skills in writing a log.

1   A good way to get started is to divide your experiences and ideas into 'good' and 'bad'. It might be useful to list them under headings, such as:
   • I was good at . . .
   • I was bad at . . .
   • I felt this went well . . .
   • I felt this went badly . . .
2   Keep to the point and do not waffle; you only need to write a summary.
3   Some things may occur to you as a result of your tutor's comments. Did you agree with what was said at the time?
4   Be yourself and do not feel that you have to hide things. You will learn more by being honest.
5   Write exactly what you want to say and do not be frightened of the comments you might get back as a result.
6   Try to be positive, productive and useful. After all, how else will you be able to progress and improve?

7   Imagine you are writing the log for yourself and not for your tutor; this may help you to show your real thoughts and feelings.

Review of the team's overall performance

The activity that forms the basis of this unit requires teams of students to plan and complete a series of tasks. One of the difficulties that your tutor will face in assessing the team's overall performance is identifying the parts played by individual members of the team. If you have followed our advice throughout this unit, you will have made it clear at each stage exactly what your contribution was and whether you undertook tasks beyond those which you had been allocated. As long as you have logged your contribution, it will not necessarily matter if your tutor did not actually see you do it. You are providing evidence that you have completed the task.

When working as a group, there is often a tendency for some members of the team to concentrate on certain tasks at the expense of other aspects of the assignment. This is why many assignments ask you to repeat tasks or follow a series of stages to completion.

Review of individual team members' performance

Your tutor will give you feedback about your performance during the activity but, at the end of the day, it is your own opinions which really matter. Provided you have logged as evidence the various situations and occasions you felt were important during the activity, you can draw your own valid conclusions about your performance. In other words, you are saying 'next time I will . . .'

You will have opportunities to give your own opinion in the discussion sessions that make up part of this performance criterion and in the feedback sessions of performance criteria 4.3.5 and 4.3.6. The more you remember now, the more valuable your contribution to these sessions will be.

Review through team discussions and discussions between individual team members and teachers/tutors

It can be extremely useful to get feedback from someone like your tutor who has watched you undertake an activity. As we will see in performance criterion 4.3.5 when we look at feedback, some people find it difficult to tell you how you actually performed, but even more people find it difficult to accept what is being said about them. The main point of this performance criterion is to try to decide whether the team as a whole performed well and met the objectives of the activity.

It is a good idea to begin by thinking about what we actually mean by the word discussion. It is not an opportunity for you to make accusations against other team members for not having worked hard enough during the activity (although if you feel that the team's overall performance was hindered by one of the team members not pulling their weight, you should say so). Here are some questions you may wish to think about when reviewing the team's performance during any discussions you have:

▼ **Why did you decide to approach the activity in the way you did?**

▼ **What could you have done to have made the activity easier?**

▼ **Did you take everyone's opinion into account when you planned the activity?**

▼ **What should have been done that was not done?**

▼ **Were all the team members happy with the workload allocated to them?**

▼ **Were all the team members happy with the end result of the activity?**

▼ **How could the team's performance be improved if you were asked to complete this activity in the future?**

4.3.2 **Review use of resources**

RESOURCES

No doubt some of the resources you had hoped to use (and had noted in your individual and team plans) were not available when, where and in the quantity you needed them. Although it may not be of help to you now, if you highlight the resource problems you encountered during the activity, your tutor will be able to ensure that the resources you identified are available next time the activity is run.

As we will see in this performance criterion, your tutor will discuss with you the resources available, how they were used and whether you should have used them in a different way. We will begin by looking at finance.

Finance

If you followed our suggestions in Element 4.2, you will have recorded the costs of all consumable items used in the activity. Your tutor can get a better idea of the costs of the activity for each team by seeing your cost totals. If you were asked to stay within a particular budget at the beginning of the activity, you now have the opportunity to compare your actual spending with the recommended amount.

You should also consider whether you actually needed to use these resources and whether the money was well spent. Individual members of the team and your tutor may have very different views on this. If you have spent money on items that were not really needed, this shows you did not consider the financial side of the activity enough.

People

Again, you should have noted down occasions when you had to approach someone for information or guidance. Hopefully you did not take up too much of any individual's time in trying to get the activity completed. You probably used your tutor as the main source of advice and information and he or she will let you know if you relied on him or her too much. Other individuals, who may not be able to give direct feedback on how much you used them during the activity, may also have views that are valuable. It may be a little harder to obtain these opinions. Perhaps your tutor has already spoken to some of them.

Bear in mind that the more you actually do on your own, the more you can claim that the end result of the activity was due to your own actions. You should begin to learn that it is not advisable to seek other people's help all the time.

When reviewing people as a resource, you should also consider whether the advice and information they gave you was actually useful. Did you explain to them what you really needed and did you get from them what you expected? Your experiences in this activity may well have an impact on who you ask and how often you ask for help in the future.

Materials and equipment

When reviewing your use of materials and equipment, there are many aspects to consider. For example, you may have discovered that the items you detailed in your action plan in Element 4.1 did not actually prove to be all that useful. Equally, as we mentioned earlier, the materials and equipment may not have been available at the time you needed them or in sufficient quantity or quality. You may have felt that your performance in this assignment was hindered by shortcomings in the materials and equipment, but as you will discover, work is often like that and individuals often have to undertake tasks without the support they were expecting. You may wish to consider some of the following questions in assessing and reviewing your use of materials and equipment:

▼ **Did you make sure that the materials were on hand and of the right quality and quantity before you actually needed them?**
▼ **When you had to use equipment, did**

you know exactly how to operate it?
▼ **Were there times when lack of materials meant that tasks were not completed on time?**
▼ **Were there times when confusion over the operation and availability of equipment meant that tasks were not completed on time?**
▼ **Were there materials and equipment that you had requested which were not available in the event?**
▼ **Were there materials and equipment that you had not requested which you found you needed and consequently wasted time obtaining?**

Again, your tutor will have noted your use of materials and equipment throughout the activity. No doubt some materials and equipment were suggested to you as being useful in completing the activity. You may wish to think about whether this advice was, in fact, relevant or useful in the event. Finally, you could compare your use of materials and equipment with other teams. To this end, you may want to consider the following questions:

▼ **Did other teams identify materials and equipment that you did not?**
▼ **If so, did this make their job easier or harder?**
▼ **What influenced your choice of materials and equipment?**
▼ **Do you think that you would have been able to carry out the activity more efficiently if you had requested a different set of materials and equipment?**

Information

Knowing where to get information is only one part of handling information itself. Once you have obtained information, the most important thing is how to use it. You may have collected a large amount of information and, at the end of the day, either decided not to use it or found that you did not have time to use it. This may have been as a result of not obtaining the information as early as you should have done. Bear in mind that informa-

25

tion is never in the format you need it to be in; all information has to be processed in some way to make it useable.

If you were using our assignment detailed in Element 4.1, you should ideally have constructed a questionnaire which focused on the information you needed to collect and had a format that made it easy for you to process. The information should then have been easy for you to use. If you found that you were not able to use the information, you should consider whether this was due to the design of your questionnaire.

Obtaining information from individuals or from books, articles and magazines is never an easy job. Often the information is not written in a way which makes it easy to understand or use; neither is it necessarily up to date. Faced with information in this state there is often a temptation to ignore it, but this may be a mistake. In terms of reviewing your use of information, you should think about the following questions:

▼ **Were you able to collect all the information you wanted?**
▼ **How much time did you use in collecting this information and was it worth the time spent?**
▼ **How much time did you use in trying to make use of information that you had collected?**
▼ **Were there times that you needed information and had to pause whilst it was being collected?**
▼ **Should you have used other forms of information collection to have made this aspect of the assignment easier?**
▼ **Did you find yourself with information that you did not use at all?**

It is also worth remembering that information seeking and information handling are grading criteria for your award. These criteria look at how you identify and use information sources. There are two aspects to this:

1 Identifying information needs. You are expected to independently identify the information that you need for the various tasks.
2 Identifying and using sources to obtain

information. You are expected to independently collect a variety of information and identify where this can be found.

4.3.3 *Review whether responses to problems were effective*

PROBLEMS

No matter how skilled or experienced you are in tackling various tasks and assignments, you will always reach a point when a particular problem will stand in your way. In this performance criterion we will try to help jog your memory about the various problems that caused you difficulty in completing the assignment.

Anticipated problems

A good action plan will have considered various problems that could arise in the completion of an assignment, as explained in Element 4.1. Your tutor will have encouraged you to have thought about different ways of tackling tasks during the activity. It is always wise to think of at least two ways of doing anything. Sometimes this is not possible, as we need to have carried out certain tasks before others may be attempted. If, for example, you encountered problems in collecting information, it would be impossible to process or analyse it. You may wish to think about some of the following questions when reviewing the way you dealt with anticipated problems:

▼ **Did you anticipate all the problems? (If not, were these unexpected problems?)**
▼ **What were your main anticipated problems? Did they relate to people, materials, equipment or information?**
▼ **Could you have avoided an anticipated problem by attempting a different way of handling the assignment?**

▼ **If you had to carry out this activity again in the future, would you be more aware of any of your anticipated problems than you were this time?**

▼ **How many of the anticipated problems arose as a result of the team's actions?**

Your tutor will have been assessing your ability to switch from one set of actions to another during the course of the activity. He or she will have looked at how smoothly you managed to work around an anticipated problem and dealt with any unexpected problems.

Unexpected problems

In this part of the performance criterion you should consider problems that were beyond your control. You may wish to think about the following questions:

▼ **Although unexpected when you wrote your action plan, how many of the unexpected problems became anticipated problems when you got further into the assignment?**

▼ **How many of the unexpected problems should have really been anticipated problems and you just failed to recognise them as such?**

▼ **Were the unexpected problems harder to handle as a result of the fact that you had not considered ways of getting round them in your action plan?**

▼ **How many of the unexpected problems arose as a result of your own actions and how many arose as a result of other people's actions or the non-availability of materials and equipment?**

▼ **Were there any unexpected problems that you could not cope with?**

▼ **How many unexpected problems in this activity would be anticipated problems in a future activity?**

Your tutor will not expect you to be a mind-reader or have the ability to look into the future. Although you will have identified some antici-pated problems in your action plan, you will be assessed on your ability to handle the unexpected and act swiftly to cope with any problems.

4.3.4 *Review maintenance of health and safety*

We have already outlined the possible health and safety considerations associated with self, other people and materials and equipment in Elements 4.1 and 4.2. Rather than repeating ourselves here, you should now think about any health and safety concerns which came up during the activity. You should consider the following questions in your review:

▼ **Were you responsible for any act that put you or your health in danger during the activity? If so, why did you do this and how will you avoid this situation next time?**

▼ **Were you responsible for any act that put other people in danger during the activity? If so, why did you do this and how will you avoid this situation next time?**

▼ **Was another person responsible for any act that put a member of your team in danger during the activity? If so, why did they do this and how should this situation be avoided next time?**

▼ **Do you consider that the whole of your team was aware of health and safety implications during the activity? If not, how could you ensure they were next time?**

▼ **Are there any materials or equipment which you would avoid in the future due to their health and safety dangers? If so, have you reported them?**

4.3.5 **P**rovide clear and constructive feedback to others on their performance

4.3.6 Respond constructively to feedback from others

We have put these two performance criteria together, as they are linked aspects of the review process.

FEEDBACK

Obviously the content of feedback will vary according to the work carried out. Bear in mind that constructive feedback is not necessarily positive, as the review process is intended to contribute towards your learning and help you improve your performance. Constructive feedback will take the form of comments, opinions and suggestions about both the team's successes in undertaking the activity and aspects of performance which could have been improved. Non-constructive feedback, which typically takes the form of personal comments not related to the work, should be avoided.

As we said earlier, it is often easier to accept feedback and criticism from tutors than from other members of the team. Although at the time it may not seem like it, even criticism can be valuable. In order to make sure that feedback is useful, it is worth considering the following points:

▼ **How do you know that something happened if you do not have evidence of it? In other words, if something was**

important enough to log at the time, you will have evidence that it actually happened, even if the individuals involved cannot remember the incident. You will then have this to refer to if the incident is mentioned in feedback.
▼ **Did you take the feelings of other team members into account when you did something? This refers to situations when you were bossy or lazy, for example. You should consider how the other team members felt when you were behaving like this.**
▼ **Can you step back and criticise yourself? Although you may not have noticed things during the activity, it is worth thinking very hard about what you did. Even the most obvious things can be useful for feedback.**
▼ **Were there more positive things about the activity than negative ones? Did you hate the activity and find it impossible to work with the other team members? Did you keep too quiet at the beginning of the activity, particularly when it was planned, and as a result feel that the way in which the activity was tackled was wrong?**

4.3.7 **M**ake and record suggestions for improvements in the way similar activities are tackled in the future

IMPROVEMENTS

One of the main reasons for reviewing anything that you have done is to try to recognise ways in which you could improve your performance or use of resources next time. In this performance criterion, we will be looking at ways in which you can make these vital improvements that will be a great advantage to you in the future.

Improvements to the team's performance and the student's performance

Your tutor may have his or her own ideas about how to approach this part of the performance criterion. If this is not the case, or you want to try to identify improvements you would wish to come out of the activity, you might want to consider the following steps:

▼ **Individually, think about and write down at least two occasions where you found difficulty in the activity. One occasion should be when you handled the situation well and one should be when you handled the situation badly. What was the outcome of these two occasions?**

▼ **Pairing up, describe the situations you have written down to one another. Listen to your partner's description of how he or she handled each situation and try to suggest ways in which the problems could have been solved.**

▼ **In your teams, describe the situations you have been talking about, as well as your proposed solutions. See if the rest of the team agrees with what you have suggested.**

Improvements to the use of resources

Having reviewed your use of resources, you are now in a position to make valuable comments in response to the tutor's observations. Provided that you can justify your use of resources throughout the activity, you will be able to answer any queries or criticisms which may be levelled at you. Remember that any suggestions about improving your use of resources are meant

to be constructive. Listening to these suggestions will put you in a much better position when you use resources for your next activity. Make sure that this feedback session is a two-way process where you can explain to your tutor the shortcomings of any resources; he or she will then be able to address these problems and make sure the resources are available next time.

Improvements to the responses to problems

When you reviewed your list of responses to anticipated and unexpected problems, you may already have identified a way in which you, as a team, could have improved a particular response. On the other hand, you may not have been able to work out a better way to have approached the situation. Your tutor may have noticed or be able to suggest a better way of handling the situation, and you should listen to his or her advice and guidance in this. Bear in mind, however, that the tutor will not be able to put him or herself in your position and think about the things you, as a team, were considering at the time.

Improvements to the maintenance of health and safety

As we will see in Unit 5, there are various ways of reducing the common risks to individuals in the workplace. The following questions should help you in considering potential improvements to the maintenance of health and safety:

▼ **Were there situations when health and safety problems arose that could have been prevented?**

▼ **Were there situations when health and safety equipment should have been available?**

▼ **Were there situations when health and safety problems arose as a result of someone not following the correct procedure?**

▼ **Were there situations when health and safety problems arose which could** have been avoided had you been suitably trained?

▼ Were there situations when a health and safety problem arose as a result of problems with equipment or materials?

If you have answered 'yes' to any of these, this shows there is room for improvement in health and safety. You should inform your tutor immediately if there is a hazard. Your tutor may have noticed certain behaviours or use of equipment and materials that could have resulted in health and safety problems during the activity. Listen to this advice and consider the ways you, as a team, could improve your performance.

---

assignment

ELEMENT 4.3

PC 4.3.1–7
COM 1.1, 1.2, 1.3

Assuming that you followed our advice from the beginning of this unit, you will have a fairly detailed log which outlines your performance throughout the activity. In this part of the unit you are expected to undertake a review of your performance and evaluate your contribution. Your tutor will be responsible for some of the aspects of this element, particularly those relating to feedback. Your review should match the performance criteria of this element and we have broken down the content of your review in task form below.

Your review should take the form of a log sheet, provided by your tutor, which is an accurate record of your performance. Remember that this will have to be verified by your tutor or assessor. Your log will be compared to the notes and observations made by your tutor throughout the activity, so it is essential that your log is accurate.

| task | 1 | PC 4.3.1 |

Comment on your performance against the roles and tasks which were allocated to you as part of the overall activity. Also mention whether your actions allowed the overall objectives of the activity to be met.

| task | 2 | PC 4.3.2 |

Comment on whether you think that the resources needed were used effectively.

| task | 3 | PC 4.3.3 |

Comment on whether you believe that your responses to problems were effective.

| task | 4 | PC 4.3.4 |

Comment on whether you felt that health and safety was maintained throughout the activity.

| task | 5 | PC 4.3.5–6 |

Comment on whether you have received constructive feedback from others and whether you have given constructive feedback to the other members of your group.

| task | 6 | PC 4.3.7 |

Write a list of suggestions for improvements in your performance.

PRESENTATION AND DISPLAY

element 5.1

INVESTIGATE WAYS OF DISPLAYING AND PRESENTING INFORMATION

Performance criteria

A student must:

1   Describe, with examples, **common types of presentation** and **display**.
2   Match different **materials** used for presentation and display with different types of presentation and display.
3   Identify local examples of displays and **describe** selected ones.
4   **Evaluate** the effectiveness of selected displays **in terms of** their **key features**, and summarise the findings.

RANGE

Common types of presentation: sales promotions, sales seminars, product launches, sales conversations

Common types of display: window, point of sale, public places, advertising sites

Materials: videos, slides, overhead transparencies, brochures, leaflets, posters, props, notices, goods; printed, handmade; adhesives

Describe: what is displayed, why it is displayed, how it is displayed, where it is displayed

Evaluate in terms of key features: timing, location, target audience, style (format, use of colour, images, lettering)

5.1.1 *Describe, with examples, common types of presentation and display*

COMMON TYPES OF PRESENTATION

As the aim of this unit is to allow you to appreciate the importance of presentation and display skills, we will be looking at the most common types of display and presentation in this element. It is also important that you recognise that some forms of display and presentation are more effective than others in certain situations. Later in this element you will need to look at some local displays and evaluate them.

For now, however, we will turn our attention to the main types of presentation, which include:

▼ **sales promotions**
▼ **sales seminars**
▼ **product launches**
▼ **sales conversations**

Sales promotions

Sales promotions are used to achieve a number of different goals. These include encouraging customers to make repeat purchases; building up long-term customer loyalty; and encouraging customers to visit a particular facility. In order to do this, sales promotion ideas include:

▼ **price reductions**
▼ **vouchers**
▼ **coupons**
▼ **gifts**
▼ **competitions**
▼ **lotteries**
▼ **cash bonuses**

These sales promotion ideas are very common in the high street, but are being used increasingly in facilities offering leisure and tourism products and services.

Sales seminars

It is vital for sales staff to know about products and services and the process of selling them to customers. Unfortunately, however, the quality of training differs greatly between facilities. The staff will need to have the following:

▼ **knowledge of the product or service being offered by the facility**
▼ **an ability to demonstrate and use the product or service**
▼ **an ability to handle complaints and faults related to the product or service**
▼ **awareness of other products and services in competition with those on sale at the facility**
▼ **understanding of the customers' needs**

Proper training is expensive but, as customers' needs become more complicated, it is vital that sales staff know about the products available. Often the staff will have to work in an advisory role, working closely with customers.

Sales seminars are held to explain the product and its uses to the staff. Without such training schemes, the staff cannot hope to be able to sell the product to the customer. Ideally, these seminars should be held before the product is offered to the customer.

Product launches

New product or service launches aim to broaden the appeal of the facility. Typically, this will involve some of the following:

▼ **exhibitions**
▼ **displays**
▼ **demonstrations**
▼ **use of the product by the customer for a trial period**

In promoting a new product, the facility aims to bring it to the attention of customers; stimulate an interest in the product; and encourage customers to try the new product. It is vital that the four Ps, or **marketing mix**, are considered when launching a new product. These are:

1   *Product.* The nature of the product must be clear and obvious to staff and customers.
2   *Place.* Customers should know where they can obtain the product.
3   *Price.* Customers should be aware of the price structure and feel it is reasonable.
4   *Promotion.* The facility must choose an appropriate form of promotion that offers the best chance of letting customers know about the product.

Sales conversations

Sales staff play an important part in convincing customers to part with money for a product or service. They can do this by having sales conversations. These take place when sales staff speak (either face to face or via a telephone) with customers. In the leisure and tourism industry, typical sales conversations would occur in travel agencies, leisure centres and via the telephone with staff of a tour operator.

Some organisations have stopped using the titles 'salesman' and 'saleswoman' or 'salesperson'. Nowadays, they prefer to use the following terms:

▼ **advisors**
▼ **counsellors**
▼ **consultants**
▼ **representatives**

Whatever the job title, selling is a skilled and professional occupation. Any facility needs customers and an active salesforce will make sure that customers are both attracted and kept. Salespeople can help to make sure that customers are retained by:

▼ **establishing a good relationship with customers**
▼ **checking that customers' are actually sold what they ask for**
▼ **checking that customers receive the right information and advice before, during and after the sale has been made**

COMMON TYPES OF DISPLAY

Depending on the layout of the facility, there may be areas that are set aside specifically for displays. Other facilities may be desperately short of display space and have to consider smaller displays or posters. In terms of different display types, we shall consider the following:

▼ **windows**
▼ **point of sale**
▼ **public places (perhaps other than the facility itself)**
▼ **advertising sites (both outside the facility and in other places)**

These include window displays in shops and other places, exhibitions at local facilities or museums, and displays promoting forthcoming productions at local theatres or cinemas.

As we have said, display area is often limited. A good display will be carefully considered in terms of the budget, make full use of the available space and avoid waste.

Window

Window areas can be used for a variety of different displays. Typically, these would include the following:

▼ *posters* **– stuck onto the glass or on boards in the window area**
▼ *pelmets* **– pasted along the edges of the window**
▼ *dummy packs* **– useful for filling window areas**
▼ *trade figures* **– large life-sized cut-outs of product characters or personalities**
▼ *illuminated displays* **– with flashing lights or permanent lights as a particular part of the display**

Obviously, windows may feature a mixture of the above. The most important thing is that a window display needs to be striking and eye-catching to encourage the passer-by (potential customer) to take note and be influenced by it.

Point of sale

Point of sale areas are also known as point of purchase. The most common point of sale area is beside the cash register, but it can include the whole of a shop, reception area or beside food or drink dispensers in a leisure centre or tourist attraction. Their main purpose, as we already know, is to encourage sales. Here are some examples of point of sale features:

▼ *mobiles* – cut-out displays which move with the air currents and are suspended from the ceiling
▼ *posters* – colourful, bright and used to announce special offers or facilities/services
▼ *pelmets* – usually posted along the top of the window or along a shelf in a shop
▼ *dummy packs* – empty boxes used to display the product
▼ *dumpers and dump bins* – ideal to encourage impulse buying
▼ *wire stands* – small enough to be hung near the cash register
▼ *show cards* – portable displays that can be moved around
▼ *dispenser boxes* – sturdy, ideal for leaflets

Public places

Rather than have a display in a window or beside a cash register, the facility may use areas that are thoroughfares for the public (such as entrance halls or corridors) or they may have a refreshment area. Given the fact that the display should not cause an obstruction or be in a place that could cause a health and safety problem, a refreshment area offers greater opportunities since the display may be larger. You should also consider the fact that the public place used may not be in the facility at all, but may be at another site that allows displays of local facilities. Such sites would usually be libraries, museums or other public areas.

Many of the types of display mentioned for windows could be used, but other possibilities include:

▼ *illuminated displays* – possibly spot lights or limited flashing light displays
▼ *display stands* – either standard or carton-made to promote a particular product or service
▼ *dispensers* – ideal if the public place is limited in space
▼ *video screens or TVs* – useful for showing activities being carried out or giving demonstrations

Advertising sites

Outdoor advertising is probably the oldest form of advertising. Advertisements can stay in a particular place for weeks or months, but it is common for the poster to be changed every 13 weeks or so. When we are considering advertising sites, we should include the following:

▼ bus and railway stations
▼ airports
▼ advertisements on buses or trains
▼ inside buildings

Whatever the site, the following points should always be considered:

▼ the size of the poster
▼ the colours used
▼ the number of words (should be brief)
▼ the placement of the poster (using the minimum number of posters to get the maximum effect)

5.1.2 *Match different materials used for presentations and display with different types of presentation and display*

MATERIALS

You will probably be limited in the choice of materials that you can use for your display. Perhaps you will be lucky enough for the facility to be able to provide you with most of the necessary materials. In most cases, however, you will need to make your own display out of materials available to you.

Videos

This is becoming a popular and versatile medium. It is used in many stores and facilities to display advertisements for products and services. No doubt you will have seen the Post Office Videoservice, where there is a continuous presentation of video advertisements. The video advertisement is ideally supported by references to leaflets and brochures that are available near the screen.

Making video advertisements can be complicated and should only be attempted at centres which have adequate editing and sound facilities. Poorly constructed videos can look very unprofessional and will give a bad impression of the services or products that you are trying to promote.

Slides

Slides are an ideal way of showing still photographs of the facility to the public. The use of a projector, with a cassette or carousel of slides on a continuous loop, can be a very effective method of display. The slides should be visible for a minute or so, continually changing so that the viewer does not get bored with the same picture. The facility should have some photographs available that could be turned into slides. Again, it is a good idea to back up the slides with leaflets or brochures and perhaps some of the slides should be worded to direct the customer to the dispenser holding the sales literature.

Overhead transparencies

The problem with using an overhead transparency is that you are limited to a single image. This means that it is only valuable as a backdrop for other display materials or if someone is on hand to change the transparency at regular intervals.

It is a good idea to have an overhead projector available if the display is to be manned. One advantage of using overhead transparencies is that they can hold a great deal of information. You should remember, however, that the viewer can only take in so much, and the letters or images need to be big enough to read with ease.

Brochures and leaflets

The processes that are available to you will differ from centre to centre, as will the quality of the finished product. At this stage it is worth thinking about the nature of the message you want to get across in the brochure or leaflet. The following points will help you:

▼ **remember that the brochure or leaflet is designed to sell a product/service or remind customers of its existence**
▼ **use repetition when necessary as it helps customers to remember what you are saying**
▼ **avoid boring customers with unnecessary words – you do not want to lose their attention**
▼ **make your language clear – if customers are unsure what you are saying, they will lose interest**
▼ **use short sentences**

▼ use short words
▼ use short paragraphs
▼ make the message easy and quick to read

Posters

If the poster is in an area that will allow the reader to pause and consider the words and message, then you can get away with using lots of words and making the poster complicated. If the poster site is likely to attract the passer-by for only a brief moment, however, the poster design needs to be as simple as possible. With this in mind, it is a good idea to minimise the number of words you intend to use on the poster. If possible, always use pictures and images rather than words to get the message across; only use basic words and keep the message simple.

If you refer back to what we have already said about advertising sites, this will give you a greater understanding of how to design the right kind of poster for the job.

Props

If you are displaying a particular sport or recreational activity, it is a good idea to use props such as sports equipment for your display. Bear in mind that this equipment should be kept secure so that it cannot be stolen or taken away. For displays that are set up behind glass cabinets or in windows, this may not be a particular problem. Props also include any boxes, 3-D displays or similar items that can enhance the overall look of the display.

Props are not always necessary and you may not be able to think of any that would be relevant for your display. Remember that any form of physical item could be useful. For example, if you were displaying winter holidays in a travel agency window, then skis or even an item of ski clothing would be ideal props.

Notices

Notices are extremely common display materials, used in nearly all facilities. They provide valuable and easy ways of putting across simple instructions or messages to customers. Notices should be every bit as appealing and attractive to the eye as posters. The major difference is that notices tend to have more words on them and do not rely so heavily on visual aids to help get the message across. Notices can be used at the point of sale; they can also be placed in areas that are not good for more elaborate displays. Notices are particularly suitable for public places where there is only a limited display area available.

Goods

Simple displays of goods are very common, not only in tourist and recreational facilities but also in shops and supermarkets. The packaging of

Fig. 5.1.1 This basic leaflet, produced by a swimming pool, shows the nature of the activity, times and price.

Fig. 5.1.2 A multi-purpose poster which can be overprinted with specific event details (courtesy of Granada Studios).

most products is designed to promote an attractive image to the customer. Careful use of the product's packaging can therefore form the basis of an attractive display. Again, it is important to consider when and where products are used for displays. They should be in clear view of the staff at all times to avoid theft and tampering with the display. A simple pile of products can be sufficient, but it is better to think about how the products should be placed in the available display area.

Using goods for display would be ideal for a shop or merchandising area within a facility, but not for other public places where the display cannot be watched or easily locked away afterwards.

Printed and handmade materials

Many facilities will already have a variety of printed materials that can be used for displays, such as posters, leaflets or brochures. It is important to make sure that the display reflects the image that the facility wants to put across. This can be easily achieved by making use of the facility's own materials. Posters, for example, can be used as the background for a display, whilst other materials, such as props or 3-D items, can be used in the foreground and central part of the display.

Smaller facilities may not have a wide range of printed materials for you to use. You may therefore have to create your own materials for your display. In this respect, you have a little more freedom, but are limited by your ability to create professional-looking materials.

Most centres and facilities will have computer software that can help you create quite professional-looking materials. You should try to use these graphics and word-processing packages rather than rely on handdrawn display posters, leaflets and brochures.

Adhesives

Naturally, you should take great care in dealing with adhesives and other potentially toxic or dangerous materials in constructing your display. You will probably have to use adhesives to make your display strong enough to withstand handling, moving and general wear and tear. Always ensure that you read the labels and instructions on adhesives. Take precautions to avoid getting them on your skin and never use them in confined areas where the noxious fumes could affect you – remember that inhaling the fumes from these adhesives can cause brain damage. Consider carefully which type of adhesive you should use – some are more suitable for gluing specific materials; some are better for covering large areas.

5.1.3 *Identify local examples of displays and describe selected ones*

DESCRIBE

This part of the element is practical. You need to have a good look around your local area and identify all the examples of leisure and tourism displays you can find. These will include:

▼ **window displays**
▼ **point of sale displays**
▼ **displays in public places**
▼ **displays at advertising sites**

You then have to choose three different displays and describe them in detail. Your descriptions should include the following:

▼ **what is displayed**
▼ **why it is displayed**
▼ **how it is displayed**
▼ **where it is displayed**

Please use the information in this performance criterion as guidance in attempting the element assignment on page 41.

What is displayed

If the display is a good one, it will be obvious what it is meant to achieve. Perhaps it is displaying a product or a service, or perhaps it is announcing an event or a forthcoming attraction. A good display will tell the whole story to the customer. It should be straightforward and designed to get a message across.

Sometimes, you will find a display that is just designed to fill a space, such as a window. In such cases, the display may involve an attractive arrangement of leaflets, brochures or items that will be interesting and informative for the customer.

If you are unsure about the display and what it is meant to show, then this is probably not a suitable example to use for your descriptions. You could mention the fact that the display is not very good and comment on why you think it has failed.

Why it is displayed

As we have already mentioned, the reason behind the display should be obvious. The facility will have constructed the display to get across a particular message. The following are typical reasons for a display:

▼ **to promote a new product**
▼ **to promote a popular product**
▼ **to promote a service**
▼ **to promote an event**
▼ **to announce a forthcoming event**

FIGURE IT OUT

PC 5.1.3
COM 1.1

00:10

*C*an you think of other reasons for a display? Discuss this as a group.

How it is displayed

How things are displayed may be restricted by the space or materials available. In some cases, the display may be based on materials supplied by the manufacturer of a product. In other situations, the display may have to be handmade and will include materials that have been constructed by the staff at the centre. If you refer back to Section 5.1.2, we have looked in detail at the most common materials used in displays.

Where it is displayed

The site of the display, as we have seen, can determine the nature of the display itself. In areas that are limited in space, the display needs to be simple and straightforward. In other cases, such as window displays, the materials may need to cover a large area.

In many cases, there will be a variety of different displays set up in the same facility. The facility may have chosen to show the wide range of products or services that it offers. You could consider these displays separately or as a whole.

5.1.4 *Evaluate the effectiveness of selected displays in terms of their key features and summarise the findings*

Evaluate in terms of key features

Once you have decided on the three displays you are going to describe in detail, you must consider their effectiveness.

▼ **Are the displays appropriate in terms of their timing?**
▼ **Have the displays been located in the right place?**
▼ **Do the displays cater for the target audience?**
▼ **How good is the style of each display (in terms of the use of colour, images and choice of lettering)**

We will look at these key features in some detail to help you make decisions for the element assignment.

Timing

Timing of displays is crucial. Clearly, the display should be constructed prior to an event it is promoting or the date of a special activity at the centre. However, there is little point in putting up a display just before (or after) something is going to happen. The customers will not have time to take in the display or respond to it. It is also inappropriate to have a display which announces or promotes something in the distant future. By the time the event actually takes place, the customers will have forgotten all about it.

Displays should be designed to encourage an immediate response from customers, so the facility needs to be geared up to cope with this. If the display is informing customers of a forthcoming event, for example, the tickets should be available as soon as the display goes up.

Location

The display should be located where the target audience will see it. Consider how appropriate the location is. Will plenty of people see the display? Is the display prominent enough for casual passers-by to notice it? Remember that some locations, although they are busy and attract a number of customers, are not places where customers have time to read or look at displays.

The display also needs to be located in a place that can be monitored. Perhaps the display includes leaflets or brochures. Staff need to be able to respond to the demand for these materials and top them up as necessary. A remote location could mean that a number of staff have to visit the site specifically for this purpose.

Target audience

Target audience means that the facility has a particular sort of person in mind for the display. The display not only has to be located in a place that will be visible to the target audience, but also has to appeal to these customers. For example, if the facility is a theme park, the display should be designed to appeal to children and families.

Identifying the target audience can be difficult, particularly if the facility is offering a new product or service. It is not always obvious what type of customer will be interested. In most cases the facility should have a good idea about the type of customer that currently uses the facility and its services. It should consider this when designing the display. Obviously, complicated and wordy displays are not a good idea for small children; they need to look attractive and exciting.

Style

As we have said earlier in this element, the style of the display (format, use of colour, images, lettering) should be determined by the target audience and the available expertise. There are a number of points you should consider in terms of style:

▼ **use buzz words like 'now', 'new', 'today'**
▼ **use action words like 'buy', 'enjoy', 'hear', 'try', 'see', 'do' or 'come'**

▼ **use exciting words like 'magnificent', 'splendid', 'wonderful', 'amazing', 'inexpensive'**
▼ **use repetitive sounds like 'amazingly attractive', 'super service', 'excitingly educational'**
▼ **use informal, chatty English like 'what's', 'you'd' and 'don't'**
▼ **use short headlines or slogans**
▼ **use different typefaces for the subheadings**

---

assignment

ELEMENT 5.1

PC 5.1.1–4
COM 1.2, 1.3, 1.4

You will have already looked at the basics of display to help you with this assignment. In order to fulfil all the performance criteria of this element, you should tackle the following tasks:

task **1** PC 5.1.1

Describe in general terms the common types of display and presentation. Give two examples of presentations and two examples of displays.

task **2** PC 5.1.2

List and give examples of the following types of materials used for presentations and displays:

▼ *videos*
▼ *slides and overhead transparencies*
▼ *brochures and leaflets*
▼ *posters*
▼ *props*
▼ *notices*
▼ *goods*

You should match each material with the types of presentation and display for which it can be used.

task **3** PC 5.1.3

Identify all the examples of leisure and tourism displays found locally. Describe three in terms of what they display and why, how and where they display it.

task **4** PC 5.1.4

Evaluate the effectiveness of the three displays you have identified and summarise your findings.

Notes
Your tutors should encourage you and arrange visits to leisure and tourism displays in the locality.

element 5.2

PROPOSE A DISPLAY IDEA

Performance criteria

A student must:

1 Generate **ideas** for a **display** in accordance with a given **brief**, and present those ideas.

2 Select an **idea** which meets given **requirements**.

3 Modify the selected **idea** if necessary to ensure that it makes effective use of available **resources**.

4 Present the **idea** in a suitable **format**.

5 Suggest **ideas** for **information materials** to support the **display**.

RANGE

Ideas: what to display, why to display it, how to display it, where to display it

Display: window, point of sale, public places, advertising sites

Brief: display objectives, audience profile

Requirements: timing, location, content, style (necessity to conform to house style, format, use of colour, images, lettering)

Resources: materials, time, skills, finance

Format: verbal, written, graphic; appropriate to the student's presentational preferences

Information materials: videos, slides, overhead transparencies, brochures, leaflets, posters, props, notices

5.2.1 *Generate ideas for a display in accordance with a given brief, and present those ideas*

IDEAS

The whole of this element is concerned with the proposal of a display idea. It operates as the planning stage for Element 5.3.

You could work in groups for the assignment covering the two elements. Your tutor will organise the assignment around a local facility that needs a display constructed, or may give you the option to come up with your own idea. You can present your ideas in any form that suits your own preferences, provided that you have addressed all the performance criteria of the element.

What to display

Having looked at all the local leisure and tourism facilities, you should now have some ideas on what your display will be about. You will need to have this clear in your mind before continuing with the rest of the assignment.

Why to display it

There needs to be a reason for displaying whatever you have chosen; perhaps the product or service is new or has been improved. If you are considering a theatre or theme park, for example, there may be new rides or programmes that need to be publicised. For this aspect of the assignment, you will need to say why you are creating a display for the product, service or event.

How to display it

Depending on the site and available space, you will now have to decide how you are going to display the products, services or attractions. This is often one of the hardest things to do since you will have to make sure that the materials you want to use are available. Make sure the size and nature of your display is appropriate. Do not make things difficult for yourself by trying to create a display that is overambitious.

Where to display it

It is essential to take into account the location of the display. If you are using a shop window, for example, it will be important to consider the fact that the display will be seen at all times of the day. The rear of the display should also be tidy as this may be in view at times by customers in the shop.

The location of the display will depend on the arrangements made by your tutor. Your group may be asked to design a display on an aspect of leisure and tourism of your own choice, or to contribute a particular display as part of a whole exhibition. In the latter case, all of the groups will design a display for that exhibition. Each group will have equal space and materials in order to produce an attractive and effective display.

DISPLAY

Different types of location (window, point of sale, public places and advertising sites) require slightly different approaches. For example, a window or public place will offer far greater scope than a point of sale display. As we have said in the previous element, the exact location of the display may determine the nature, style and size of the materials you will be able to use.

If your display is produced on behalf of a facility, you will have to conform to certain rules about what you use and how the display is constructed. We will look at this in more detail later.

Brief

Your tutor will expect certain things of the display, particularly in terms of meeting the display objectives and catering for the audience profile.

Display objectives

The display needs to be of a high enough standard. It must be clear and informative to the customer. The display has to be constructed in such a way as to get across the intended message.

Audience profile

Whether the display is at a facility or not, the level of information and approach should be aimed at a particular target audience. Your tutor will help you form an idea of the audience, but this may be obvious to you. Remember that the audience may be made up of people who do not know as much about the subject of the display as you. You should design your display so that everyone can understand. There should be something in the display for everyone, from the ones who know a lot about the subject to those who have never heard of it before.

5.2.2 Select an idea which meets given requirements

REQUIREMENTS

The basic requirements of the display will have to be considered when you are planning its design. Not only do you have to think about the appearance of the display, but also the timing and location and any problems that may arise as a result of these.

Timing

The timing requirements are very important. You should make sure that you understand how long you have to create the display. Again, you should not be overambitious in your design. Remember that displays take time to get ready; it may be difficult to construct a complicated design by the date you have been set. Also think about when the display needs to be set up, particularly if the purpose of the display is to promote a particular event on a particular day. For long-term displays that just show a series of activities, products or services, timing may not be so crucial.

Location

Turning to the location, you need to think again about the availability of space and the size and nature of the display. In other words, what is to be displayed and what is the purpose of the display? If your display is part of a large-scale open event organised by your centre, it will have to be located where the visitors to the event will be able to see it easily.

Content and style

The content and style of the display should conform to given requirements. These will include:

▼ **house style – there may be a general approach that should be used by all the displays at your centre, or you may have to use the style and approach of a particular facility**
▼ **format – you may be required to use a certain approach and basic materials; for example, all displays may be on display boards, tables or in poster format**
▼ **use of colour – you may be required to use a particular colour scheme associated with your centre or the chosen facility**
▼ **images – the availability of photographs, logos and other images will influence the way in which you design your display**
▼ **lettering – again, the centre or facility may use a particular style of lettering; you will be expected to follow this through in your display**

The London Dungeon, 28/34 Tooley Street, London, SE1 2SZ
Tel: 071 403 7221 Fax: 071 378 1529

Fig. 5.2.1 All materials produced for The London Dungeon must conform to the house style, which incorporates this logo.

The content and style should reflect your own ideas of what is meant by the brief or requirements of the display. You will be given guidance on this by your tutor. It is also worth remembering that the content and style may be influenced by the availability (or non-availability) of resources.

RESOURCES

Once you have considered all the requirements of your display, you may need to modify or slightly change your approach. Your tutor will be keen to see that you have not only stuck to the brief of the display and thought about the requirements of the display, but also realised that there are a number of resource problems that could be encountered.

Materials and time

We have already talked about materials and timing in detail, but both of these should be looked at again. You must be sure that you have access to the materials you think you will need and enough time to do the whole job.

Skills

In terms of skills, try not to be overambitious about what you intend to produce. It takes years of practice and experience to produce a really effective and professional display. Your tutor will be able to suggest ways in which you can get your ideas across using the skills that you have, and this will not make your display any less impressive.

Finance

Finance, or the purchase of materials for your display, is the final consideration here. Remember that all displays, no matter how grand, are constructed on a limited budget. Your tutor will tell you what your budget is for the display and you will have to stick to it.

5.2.3 *Present the idea in a suitable format*

FORMAT

It will be up to you (or perhaps this will be decided by your tutor) how you present your display idea. You need to make sure, however, that your tutor and any other interested parties understand exactly what you are proposing to do. You can present the idea in the following formats:

▼ **verbal**
▼ **written**
▼ **graphic**

Remember that your choice should reflect your own abilities. You could, of course, use more than one of the above formats in your presentation.

Verbal

It may be difficult for you to simply describe the display (particularly if you have something complicated in mind). If you choose this method, you should have some back-up notes to help you make sure that you have covered everything. Remember that your ideas should cover the following:

▼ **what will be displayed**
▼ **why it needs displaying**

VICTORIA AND ALBERT MUSEUM

The Victoria and Albert Museum is the world's finest museum of the decorative arts. Its collections, housed in magnificent Victorian buildings, span 2000 years and include sculpture, furniture, fashion and textiles, paintings, silver, glass, ceramics, jewellery, books and prints from Britain and all over the world.

The V&A, a magnificent Grade I listed building, also contains the National collections of watercolours, portrait miniatures and the art of photography, as well as the National Art Library. The Collections constitute a unique international resource; some four million objects exist at the V&A, ranging from Constable paintings to Oriental lacquerware, massive plaster casts to exquisite jewellery.

The Museum was founded in 1852 as a Museum of Manufactures. In 1857 it moved from Marlborough House in the centre of town to the fields of Brompton, where it was known as the 'South Kensington Museum'. In 1899 it was renamed 'The Victoria and Albert Museum' in honour of Queen Victoria, who laid the foundation stone of the building in that year, and of her husband Prince Albert.

Highlights include the world's greatest collection of paintings by Constable and the national collection of watercolours; the famous fifteenth-century Devonshire Hunting Tapestries; the Dress Collection showing the history of fashion from the seventeenth-century to the present day; a superb Asian collection of Renaissance and Victorian sculpture; the Jewellery Gallery; fine collections of British and European furniture and the 20th century Gallery, devoted to contemporary art and design. There are magnificent new galleries devoted to European art and design, glass and ironwork, Chinese, European and Indian art, and the architect Frank Lloyd-Wright. The Raphael Gallery is due to reopen in October 1996, and Phase I of the Silver Gallery is due to open in December 1996.

There is a changing programme of exciting **temporary exhibitions:** Exhibitions for 1995/1996 include: **The Peaceful Liberators: Jain Art from India**, 23 November '95 -18 February '96, **William Morris**, 9 May '96 - 1 September '96; **American Photography 1890 - 1960**, 14 November '96 - 26 January '97.

Free guided tours daily. Restaurant, shops, access for visitors with disabilities. Groups are welcome.

Museum opening hours:
Tuesday to Sunday 10.00 - 17.50
Monday 12.00 - 17.50

Visitors are asked to make a voluntary donation at the entrance. (Suggested amount £4.50 adult, £1 concessions, children under 12, V&A Patrons and Friends of the V&A are asked not to make a donation.) There are separate charges for temporary exhibitions.

Telephone: 0171-938 8500
24 Hour recorded information:
General V&A information: 0171-938 8441
Current V&A exhibitions: 0171-938 8349

Nearest underground South Kensington. Buses C1, 14 and 74 stop outside the Museum.

PLEASE RING THE V&A MARKETING DEPARTMENT ON 0171-938 8627 FOR FURTHER DETAILS ON GALLERIES AND OBJECTS AND FOR SUPPLY OF IMAGES.

Victoria and Albert Museum South Kensington London SW7 2RL Telephone 071-938 8500 Facsimile 071-938 8379 A charity exempt from registration

Fig. 5.2.2 This information sheet, produced by the Victoria and Albert Museum, contains a short history of the museum and details of forthcoming exhibitions for 1995–7. The opening hours, entrance fees and methods of getting to the museum have also been included.

▼ **how you will display it**
▼ **where you will display it**

You must explain how you intend to cater for your target audience and what the display objectives are. You should also describe the materials you will need to get the display ready.

Written

The written format is perhaps the easiest way of presenting your proposals. You will be able to state clearly the exact nature of the display and how you intend to tackle the construction and collection of materials. A written proposal does not need to be long or complicated, but should cover all the basic requirements of the display. It must include what is to be displayed and why,

how and where you will display it – as for the verbal presentation.

Graphics

Sometimes there is a need for the display to be presented in graphic format. This is especially useful if you need to get across a lot of ideas and complicated designs in a relatively easy way. For example, a basic diagram of the display will help your tutor or other interested party to understand what you are proposing to do. The drawings do not need to be complex or to scale, as long as you get across the basic look of the display and show how the parts of the display make up the overall design.

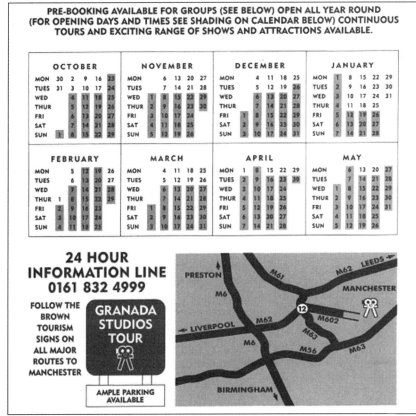

Fig. 5.2.3 A section from a Granada Studios Tour leaflet, which uses a calendar and map to get across important information to potential visitors.

Appropriate to the student's presentational preferences

As we said earlier, you should choose the format which best suits your personal abilities and preferences. If you do not feel that any of the main forms of presentation we have described suit you, choose one that does or use a mixture of different presentation types.

5.2.4 **Suggest ideas for information materials to support the display**

INFORMATION MATERIALS

Finally, you must identify the information materials that are needed to support the display, such as videos, slides, overhead transparencies, brochures, leaflets, posters, props and notices. You need to consider not only materials that form a part of the display, but also materials that customers or visitors will be able to take away with them to help them remember your display and the reasons for the display.

Preparing materials like leaflets or brochures can be as time-consuming as (if not more so than) organising the display itself. You need to think about the size of such supporting materials and the detail you are proposing to include.

Notices are useful for providing specific information about key aspects of your display. This may include:

▼ **costs of the activities**
▼ **times of transport**
▼ **a map showing the location**

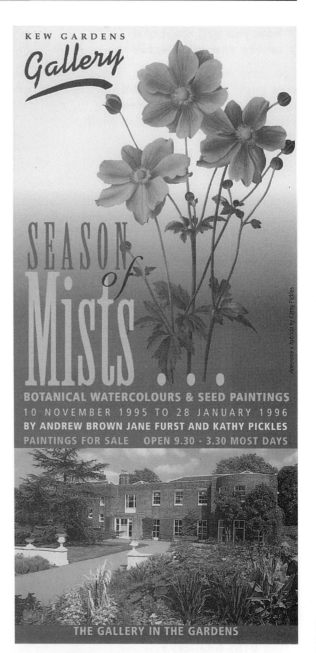

Fig. 5.2.4 This is just one of many different leaflets produced by Kew Gardens. It details the 1996 exhibition season in the Kew Gardens Gallery.

element 5.3

SET UP A DISPLAY

Performance criteria

A student must:

1 Describe **health and safety requirements** relevant to the display.

2 Identify and prepare available **resources** needed for the display.

3 Prepare the display area with due regard to health and safety.

4 Set up the display in accordance with a given **specification**, and following **health and safety requirements**.

5 Leave the display area clean, tidy and safe.

6 Return, or correctly dispose of, all unused **resources**.

RANGE

Health and safety requirements (including hygiene where appropriate) relating to: people, display environment, materials, equipment

Resources: media/materials, tools and equipment, other (time, skills, finance)

Specification: plans, recorded proposals (for schedules, costs, location, design, resources)

5.3.1 Describe health and safety requirements relevant to the display

HEALTH AND SAFETY REQUIREMENTS

The display environment should be safe to work in and should be left safe after the display has been set up. You should consider not only your own health and safety, but also the health and safety of those working on the display. Do not forget that the safety of the visitors or customers looking at the display should also be a major concern.

When dealing with food, particularly as an integral part of the display, remember that hygiene requirements will have to be taken into account.

Health and safety requirements relating to people

There are many things that could happen to people at the display site (or indeed in any place of work). We have looked at the main health and safety concerns above. The injuries that most commonly occur in the workplace fall into the following categories:

▼ *eye injuries* – eyes are very delicate things; they could be injured by flying particles, dust, chemicals, molten metal, gases and radiation
▼ *ear injuries* – loud noises can affect your ears, even if you are exposed to them for only a short period of time
▼ *head and neck injuries* – hair can get tangled in machinery, your face can be splashed by chemicals or you could get hurt in extreme temperatures
▼ *hand and arm injuries* – your hands and arms (often the part of the body that is in direct contact with machinery) can be damaged by crushing, burns or cuts, be splashed by chemicals, receive electric shocks, be hit by falling objects, or lose skin from rubbing
▼ *feet and leg injuries* – slipping is the most obvious cause, but feet and leg injuries may also be due to cuts, stepping on sharp objects, falling objects, heavy weights and chemical splashing
▼ *body injuries* – intense heat and cold in certain situations may damage the body, but injuries may also be caused by chemicals, pressure and being hit by things

Fire is also a constant concern in most workplaces. After all, we all use electrical equipment and this is a major source of fire hazards. Here are some general points to think about in relation to fire – maybe you can identify reasons why they are good things to remember:

▼ make sure that you know what the fire drills are and practise the evacuation at least once a year
▼ make sure that you read all the fire notices displayed around the workplace
▼ make sure that you know where the fire equipment is and how to use it in an emergency
▼ make sure that the fire exits are always clear and not blocked at any time
▼ make sure that anything that could catch fire (this is known as inflammable) is stored away
▼ make sure that any inflammable materials or objects are stored out of direct sunlight, as this may make them catch fire
▼ make sure that you do not smoke in areas that have been designated non-smoking areas. There may be very good reasons for this

Health and safety requirements relating to the display and its environment

Much of what we have said about potential health and safety concerns regarding people should also be applied to the display and its environment.

You should make sure that the display itself does not present any particular hazards to the people working on it or the general public. You must also ensure that the display environment is safe from any potential health and safety problems. Check that the exits are clear and that none of the displays are causing an obstruction. Always make sure that the display is secure and that all electrical equipment is turned off before leaving.

Health and safety requirements relating to materials

There are a number of things to think about when you are handling materials in the display area. Obviously, the types of health and safety problems that may crop up will depend on the particular materials used in the display. Here are some points you should consider:

▼ **materials should be stored in places where they are easily accessible, particularly if they are heavy or bulky**
▼ **materials should be stored in places where they are kept dry and safe**
▼ **materials that are not being used should be put away again as soon as possible**
▼ **materials should never be left in a place that would cause an obstruction to others**
▼ **materials should always be kept in the containers which are designed for them**
▼ **materials need to be disposed of if they become useless; they could become a hazard if left lying around**

Health and safety requirements relating to equipment

Probably the most important thing to consider when you are using machinery, tools or other equipment, is whether they are powered by electricity. There are specific health and safety requirements related to the use of electrical equipment:

▼ **make sure that you always use the closest power point when plugging in a machine, tool or piece of equipment**
▼ **remember that trailing wires and flexes can cause accidents if they are left across areas that other people have to cross**
▼ **never overload an electrical socket when you could use another one. It is very unwise to plug several pieces of equipment into the same socket using a multi-adaptor**
▼ **if there is anything wrong with the machine, tool or piece of equipment, never be tempted to try to mend it yourself. Always report the fault to your supervisor or a technician**
▼ **the same point should be remembered when you spot a broken socket, plug or loose wire. Never try to mend these yourself**
▼ **always switch off the machine if you see that there is something wrong with it. Never mess around with machines, tools or equipment if they are still plugged in**
▼ **when you have finished using a machine, tool or piece of equipment, always turn it off and unplug it. Make sure that you unplug all equipment at the end of the day, without fail**

The following are some general points to remember when using machines, tools or equipment:

▼ **always follow the manufacturer's instructions**
▼ **never try to use a machine, tool or**

piece of equipment for a purpose for which it is not designed

▼ if the machine is bulky and not meant to be moved, never try to move it. It has been placed there for a reason

▼ always read the instructions related to the piece of equipment before you start to use it

▼ make sure that you can see what you are doing, never try to use machinery in poor light

▼ always use the protective equipment provided for the job; do not even switch on the machinery before you have put on this protective equipment

▼ make sure that you know the safety rules regarding the machinery before you attempt to use it

▼ never try to use a piece of equipment that you have been told not to touch or if you have not received relevant instructions or training.

Fig. 5.3.1 Madame Tussaud's gift shop contains many impressive displays of gifts and souvenirs, encouraging customers to take a memento home of their visit.

5.3.2 *Identify and prepare available resources needed for the display*

RESOURCES

In the previous element you identified the resource requirements of the display. You will now, hopefully, have access to these and will be able to use them to put the display together.

Remember to be logical about the way in which you construct the display. Take care not to waste any of the resources you have been given to prepare the display area.

We will now look at the resources you will be using and the best ways to handle them in the preparation phase of this assignment.

Media/materials

This refers to all the leaflets, posters, brochures and other printed materials that may have been provided to you by your centre or a leisure and tourism facility.

Remember that these materials are expensive to produce and you should make the best use of them. None of the materials are inexhaustible, so you will need to use only the amount that you have ordered or been supplied with. The suppliers of the materials expect you to use them, but will be unhappy if you waste some by not thinking about what you are doing.

If you have made your own materials, you will realise how much work has gone into their preparation and will be keen to make the best use of them.

Tools and equipment

If you have been supplied with tools and equipment, you need to ensure that these will be secure at all times. Never leave equipment unat-

Fig. 5.3.2 A display of working machinery and equipment at Queen Street Mill, Burnley.

tended as this could result in theft. Always monitor and control access to the tools and equipment.

You will need to position any equipment so that you make the best use of its features. Television screens, for example, are not easy to see if they are in direct sunlight or illuminated by spot lights.

Other resources

We looked at other resources, such as time, skills and finance, in the previous element. You should always have an idea about how long things will take you to construct. A simple timetable, counting down to the opening of the display, will help you to make sure that you are ready on time.

You may need to employ the skills of others, particularly in advising you about the way in which the display is organised. Listen to the advice and take heed of any suggestions.

You will be expected to remain within the budget that has been allocated to you. You will not be able to add to the cost by producing additional material later. It is therefore important that you make sure the materials you intend to produce cover all the necessary aspects of your display.

You may also need other props and fittings for your display. Make sure that you have informed your tutor of your requirements before this stage.

5.3.3 Prepare the display area with due regard to health and safety

5.3.4 Set up the display in accordance with a given specification, and following health and safety requirements

You should now be in a position to prepare the display area. Make sure that you have thought about all the health and safety considerations we looked at earlier in this element. Remember that you will be expected to amend or change the display if your tutor feels it is a health and safety hazard. Rather than cause this extra work and worry, think about what you are doing before you make a final decision about the display area.

SPECIFICATION

Your original plans, taken from Element 5.1, will form the specification for your display. You will have agreed a certain format for the display and now you will be expected to put the display together so that it is as close to your original plan as possible. Again, make sure that you are not creating any health and safety problems.

You will be expected to keep a record of the display and the stages you have covered in constructing and setting it up. You must make sure that the display meets the original specification, and that you have considered the needs of the display in the context of the location and the practicalities of the situation.

Plans

It is important that the display matches the original plan you put forward for Element 5.2. You should try to draw a diagram or take a photograph of the display, so that you have a permanent record of what it looked like after all your hard work preparing and setting it up.

Recorded proposals

A single list of all the parts of the proposal (schedules, costs, location, design and resources) and how they worked in reality is important. This is particularly true if you are intending to set up another display in the future. It will give you a good idea of how the display proposals worked on this occasion.

You will need to make sure that you have stuck to your original proposals in respect of the following:

▼ **Have you stayed on schedule and got everything done on time?**
▼ **Have you stuck to your original costs? Have you been able to save money or have you needed more?**
▼ **Is the location as good or as useful as you expected it to be? What are the problems related to the location?**
▼ **Is your design a good one and does it work in practice?**

Although you don't need a map to get around Madame Tussaud's (the route is very well signposted), you might find this plan an interesting guide to which floor each environment is on.

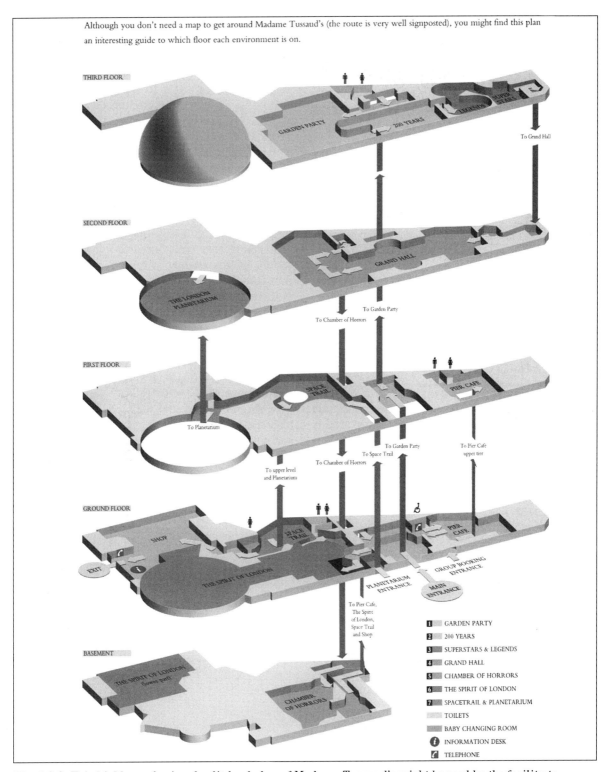

Fig. 5.3.3 This highly professional split-level plan of Madame Tussaud's might be used by the facility to identify areas where appropriate displays could be included or extended.

▼ Have you been able to get all the resources you needed? Were they really necessary?

5.3.5 Leave the display area clean, tidy and safe

5.3.6 Return, or correctly dispose of, all unused resources

At the end of each of the manned sessions, you will be expected to make sure the display area is every bit as clean, tidy and safe as when you set it up for the first time.

You should always ensure that the display area does both you and the centre credit. A poorly maintained and untidy display area can look awful and give a bad impression. The whole purpose of the display is to attract customers and visitors and it would be pointless if an untidy display area caused them to be less than impressed.

Once the duration of your display comes to an end, it is possible that, in a matter of only a few hours, someone else will be using the area to display something else. For this reason, as well as pure politeness, it is important that you completely clear the area of your materials and resources once you have finished there.

Anything that was borrowed from the centre should be returned to the person from whom it was taken. It should also, of course, be returned in the state in which it was lent. This means that you should not return anything which is damaged or dirty, but must try to make sure it is in good working order and clean.

If you are left with any rubbish which is of no further use to you or anybody else, make sure you dispose of it correctly. Any paper that is left over should be put in a paper bank and any rubbish that cannot be recycled should be collected and put into a bin bag or bins that may be provided at the site of the display.

element 6.1

PRODUCE A SCHEDULE FOR A VISIT

Performance criteria

A student must:

1 Identify the **main features and activities** of the visit to be included in the **schedule**.
2 Plan the **timings** for the visit and allocate them on the **schedule**.
3 Identify **resources** available for the visit.
4 Identify **constraints** which need to be taken into account when planning a **schedule**.
5 Produce a **schedule** for the visit taking account of any **constraints** and the **resources** available.

RANGE

Main features and activities: talks, seminars, physical activities, meetings; refreshments

Schedule: brief introduction to the facility/attraction/event (name, location, nature of activities), arrival time, meeting point, person(s) to meet, activities (timings, locations), timings of refreshments, departure time, relevant travel information

Timings: length of the visit, length of individual activities, times (of arrival, departure, breaks)

Resources: money, equipment, premises, refreshments, people, transport

Constraints: health and safety, security, confidentiality, other people visiting

6.1.1 *Identify the main features and activities of the visit to be included in the schedule*

MAIN FEATURES AND ACTIVITIES

In producing a schedule for a visit, the best starting point is to identify the main features and activities which will be included. We can break down the features and activities into three distinct groups:

1 activities which involve no participation by the visitors, such as talks
2 activities which involve participation by the visitors, such as seminars, physical activities and meetings
3 support services required by the visitors, such as refreshments

In this first performance criterion of the element, we will be looking briefly at these different features and activities.

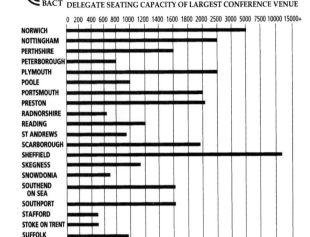

Fig. 6.1.1 This graph, taken from the British Association of Conference Towns (BACT) 'Destinations' directory, shows the size or capacity of various venues around the UK which are used regularly for conferences, talks and seminars.

Talks and seminars

Broadly speaking, a talk is a presentation to a group of visitors regarding the facility itself or perhaps a particular subject. In the first case, a representative from the facility will provide an interesting and informative speech about the facility and the services offered by it. In the second case, the facility will probably be used only as a venue for the talk and the subject of the speech may not relate to the facility at all.

Seminars are rather more informal and intimate as they usually involve fewer people and smaller rooms. Seminars are basically discussion groups which could be organised after a talk, pre-sentation or speech. They provide a valuable opportunity to discuss various matters in detail.

Physical activities

The most popular events, as far as the general public are concerned, are physical activities. The general public are not 'business users', although they may be members of a group, club or association. Club secretaries or organisers have to arrange adequate facilities as well as bookings for their groups. Normally the facilities will be booked for sole use by the visiting group and many facilities offer these opportunities during the day time or slack periods when fewer members of the public use the facility. Obviously, the range of physical activities available will be dependent on whether the facility is indoor or outdoor. These activities could form the basis of training, coaching, competitions or simply enjoyment and team-building exercises.

Businesses also use physical activities to build team spirit and co-operation within their workforce. Typical activities would include:

▼ **orienteering**
▼ **paintballing**
▼ **assault courses**
▼ **canoeing and rafting**

Meetings

Organisers of meetings have to work very closely with the staff of the facility being used in order to ensure that all the requirements of the delegates are met. The facility has to be of a sufficient size and offer various conference and meeting facilities, such as video walls, public address systems and administrative support. Many hotels, as well as conference centres, offer comprehensive services at an all-in price based on the number of delegates attending the meeting or conference.

Refreshments

Refreshments can be either an integral part of the overall schedule or an additional service or benefit for the members of the group. For day-long visits, refreshments would feature in the schedule and would normally be provided as part of the whole package by the venue being used. The organiser should ensure, before the visit is underway, that he or she has asked the members of the group whether they have any particular dietary requirements. During a visit to a facility, the following refreshments would need to be organised:

▼ **'welcome' coffee, tea and biscuits**
▼ **lunch, which could be a buffet or waiter/waitress served**
▼ **afternoon tea, coffee and biscuits**
▼ **end-of-conference refreshments**

6.1.2 *P*lan the timings for the visit and allocate them on the schedule

SCHEDULE

When planning a schedule, it is important that the people taking part in the visit have all the information they will need. Being thorough in the planning and preparation stages will help to ensure that the visit is successful. If you are responsible for arranging a schedule for a visit, you should start by making yourself a list of things to do.

The first thing to do when arranging a schedule is to determine the day and date of the visit. Diaries should be checked at this stage to make sure that no other meetings or visits have been arranged for that date. The person or facility being visited should be contacted to find out whether the day and date is convenient for them. Once the date has been provisionally booked, this entry should be made in the diary so that nothing else can be booked for then.

When thinking about the day and date of the visit, other considerations should be taken into account. For example, the amount of traffic likely to be encountered on the journey can differ from day to day and at different times of the year. The ease with which visitors will be able to park their car if they are driving to the meeting place can also vary depending on the day of the week or time of the year in some towns and cities. Both of these considerations would have to be taken into account when arranging the schedule; extra time may have to be allowed for travelling to the meeting point to ensure the visitors do not arrive late and flustered.

DERBY

Derby could easily become the destination for your next successful conference. A beautiful historic city surrounded by magnificent countryside. Derby's central location makes it easy to reach from near or far. It lies at the crossroads of a communications network of railways and motorways, and is within 15 minutes of East Midlands International Airport.

Derby's history is impressive. It is home to the world famous Royal Crown Derby china, renowned as the birthplace of Midland Railways and respected as the producer of Rolls Royce aero-engines. Today it is a thriving city which offers its visitors everything from industrial heritage and splendid architecture to active sports and lively nightlife.

As a conference city Derby has much to offer. The major venue is the Assembly Rooms - an impressive complex capable of handling between 5 and 1500 people. The venue's greatest asset is its high degree of flexibility, specially designed to meet the varying needs of the business community. This is coupled with a superb catering operation and a team of professional staff always ready to assist.

The Assembly Rooms is supplemented by an extensive range of well equipped meeting facilities, both modern and traditional, provided by the hotels and other specialist venues. There is also an excellent choice of accommodation with prices to suit most budgets.

Delegates with a few hours to spare can join regular visitors to the city in discovering the numerous nearby attractions - magnificent stately homes, exciting theme parks, nostalgic transport trips, factory shop bargains, and the beautiful Derbyshire Dales and Peak National Park.

Whatever your requirements, Derby has something special to offer. Our NEW conference brochure will give you some ideas, and we can support you with a range of services.

Why not give us a call and see what you might have missed?

CONTACT
Marion Nixon
Tourism Officer
Derby City Council
Council House
Corporation Street
Derby DE1 2XJ
Tel: 01332 253766
Fax: 01332 255549

Access
AIR: East Midlands - 15 mins
RAIL: Derby Station
ROAD: M1, J25 - 10 mins;
A/M42, J13 - 20 mins; M6 J4/4A
- 40 mins

Conference Venue Capacity
Max. seating of major
conference venue 1500

Accommodation
1512 hotel/venue bedrooms with
ensuite facilities
715 hotel/venue bedrooms
within 1 mile radius of main
venue
1097 hotel/venue bedrooms
within 5 mile radius of main
venue

Exhibition Capacity
Max. exhibition space
1820 sq m in one venue

Services
* Venue advice/selection
* Delegate information
* Preparation of bid documents
  & presentation
* Advice on access and local
  transport
* Advice on tours/social
  programmes
* Familiarisation visits
* Advice on local support
  services

Assembly Rooms

Fig. 6.1.2 Derby is one of many conference venues. As this information shows, it offers a comprehensive range of services and support facilities (courtesy of the British Association of Conference Towns).

REFRESHMENTS

We can arrange the following special catering options in **The New Restaurant**:

Coffee/tea and shortbread £2.00 per head

Cream tea £4.00 per head
A traditional English cream tea includes tea, 2 scones, jam and cream.

Sunday Jazz Brunch £7.75
Make the most of a Sunday morning: enjoy live music or read the Sunday papers.
Full English breakfast from 11.00 to 13.00 or roast lunch from 13.00 to 15.00.
Group rate £7.75 (13 plus people).

We offer a free tea/cream tea or Jazz Brunch voucher for tour leader or coach driver (one per group). An area of the restaurant can be set aside if booked in advance. All catering options are charged per person, include VAT, and are additional to the guided tour price.

SHOPS/GUIDE BOOKS

The V&A shops are well known for their excellent range of quality gifts, stationery, books, ceramics and textiles, with designs inspired by the V&A collections.

Guide books are available from both shops.

Introducing the V&A looks at the Museum's highlights, costs £2 and is printed in English, French, German and Japanese.

The Victoria and Albert Museum full-colour souvenir guide costs £8.95 in English, French and German and £9.95 in Japanese.

Fig. 6.1.3 A section from the 'Tours and Talks for Groups' leaflet produced by the Victoria and Albert Museum, showing the refreshment facilities available to organised parties and groups.

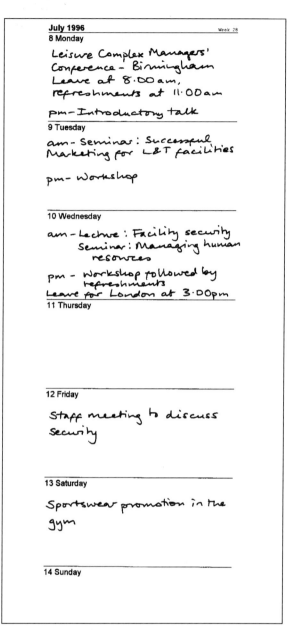

July 1996 Week 28
8 Monday
Leisure Complex Managers' Conference - Birmingham
Leave at 8.00 am, refreshments at 11.00 am
pm - Introductory talk

9 Tuesday
am - Seminar: Successful Marketing for L&T facilities

pm - Workshop

10 Wednesday
am - Lecture: Facility security
Seminar: Managing human resources
pm - Workshop followed by refreshments
Leave for London at 3.00pm

11 Thursday

12 Friday
Staff meeting to discuss security

13 Saturday
Sportswear promotion in the gym

14 Sunday

Fig. 6.1.4 A page from a diary.

Brief introduction to the facility, attraction or event

If the group is visiting the facility, rather than just using it as a venue for a meeting or conference, it is common practice for the facility to organise a brief introduction which would outline the main features and activities available. This may well be provided by a member of the reception staff or a manager who has responsibility for welcoming visitors to the facility. In this initial talk, the visitors will be told about the structure or schedule which has been arranged for them and will probably be given a printed version of the schedule so that they know when particular activities will take place. Obviously, all this needs to be organised ahead of the visit so that the facility's staff are aware of the size, nature and interests of the group and can modify their introductory speech to suit the audience.

*T*hinking about the town or city in which you live, what considerations would you have to take into account when arranging a schedule, particularly with regard to the day of the week and the time of the year? Do you think that you would have to consider extra traffic problems, maybe on a market day? Discuss this first in pairs and then as a group.

Arrival time and meeting point

Much embarrassment can be caused if someone arrives late for a meeting or is delayed because it was unclear where they should be reporting for the meeting. The schedule should show clearly where and at what time the meeting is being held.

Person(s) to meet

The schedule should also give the names of the people the visitors are expected to ask for when they arrive at the facility. These may not be the people they will be visiting, but could be a receptionist or gatehouse person who regularly greets visitors and then directs them to the people concerned.

Activities

In co-operation with the visit organiser, the facility will attempt to create a detailed schedule which identifies when and where the various activities will take place. Again, these timings and locations will be announced to the visitors in the introductory talk or perhaps provided in written form in a pack given to the visitors upon arrival.

Timings of refreshments

When scheduling the information on how the day is to be spent, make sure that you allow some time for 'comfort breaks'. Show when refreshments will be served so that visitors know, for example, that coffee will be served at 11.00 and lunch at 13.00 hours. This will make the visitor feel more relaxed and not under so much pressure. If you are planning the visit to your own organisation or centre, be sure that visitors are aware of the location of the toilets so that they can visit them during the refreshment breaks if necessary.

Departure time

You should indicate on the schedule the proposed departure time for the visitors. If you are entertaining visitors to your own facility, try to keep to this time whenever you can. The visitors may have long journeys ahead of them and will not want to be kept much longer than the expected finish time.

Relevant travel information

If your visit involves a lot of travel for several people, be sure to give them as much useful information as possible when sending them the schedule. This could include:

▼ a road map which shows clearly the location of the venue
▼ a street map which gives more detail of how to get to the meeting point
▼ directions on how to get to the venue from the railway station (if necessary)
▼ information which makes it clear to the visitor where the facility or centre is situated and to whom they should report on arrival

TIMINGS

When planning a schedule, either for your own visit or for that of someone else, the timings involved are very important. You need to consider whether enough time has been allocated for both the journey to the visit and the visit itself, and whether the times arranged are conve-nient for all concerned. It is always wise to confirm timings with the person or centre being visited, as well as those who are visiting. This confirmation can be made verbally (by telephone or in person, although by confirming in this way you will have no written confirmation) or in writing (by letter, fax or electronic mail message).

Length of the visit

When booking the appointment for the person or group of people concerned, it is important that it is clear to everybody involved exactly how much time is to be put aside for the visit. If this is not clear at the outset, confusion could occur on the day. It would be unfortunate for a visitor to travel for some length of time to what he or she considers to be an all-morning visit, only to find out that the activities will only last for one hour.

In addition, it should be confirmed that the

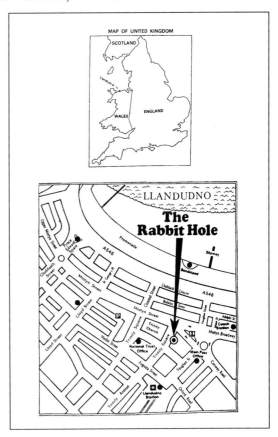

Fig. 6.1.5 The Rabbit Hole, which houses the Lewis Carroll collection, provides visitors with a map of its position in the centre of Llandudno and identifies the town's location in the UK.

length of the visit will allow for all the activities or meetings to take place. It would be unsuitable, for example, to book the visit to last one hour if there is at least two-hours worth of exhibition to see or activities to carry out.

Once again, when planning the schedule for the visit it is important to take the length of time available and the length of time needed into consideration and to try to make the two as flexible as possible. The probable length of the visit should also be confirmed with the person or group of people concerned.

Length of individual activities

Whether you are planning a schedule for someone who is visiting you or for someone visiting an exhibition or seminar, that person will need to know what the proposed activities are likely to be. Find out as much information as you can in the planning stage and list this information on the schedule. If workshops are being held during the day, list their start and finish times. If different activities are being undertaken at different times during the day, list the expected start and finish times of each one. By knowing how the day is expected to take shape, people will see that the visit has been well planned and be satisfied that they are getting the most out of the day.

Times of arrival, departure and breaks

It is of prime importance that people involved in the visit know what time to arrive. Whether the visit is one that you are arranging for yourself or for another person, it would look inefficient and be embarrassing for all concerned if you or the visitor were to arrive late. When arranging the start time, make sure that enough time is allowed for travelling and parking or, if the journey is being made by train, that the visitor has time to travel from the railway station to the venue itself. If the venue is some distance from the home town or workplace and the start time is early in the morning, you may need to arrange facilities for an overnight stay.

The departure time is equally important; firstly so that everyone involved knows when they are likely to finish, and secondly so that travel arrangements can be made for the homeward journey. Again, the start and finish times should be confirmed with the person or group of people concerned at the time of booking.

The timing of breaks for refreshments and rest should be included in any organised activity. It is also worth mentioning the availability of refreshments and facilities in case the participants need to bring their own refreshments.

FIGURE IT OUT

PC 6.1.2
COM 1.2
IT 1.1, 1.2, 1.3

`00:60`

*I*magine that you have arranged a visit to a leisure centre of your choice. You now need to confirm this in writing by means of a letter. Word process a letter to the organisation concerned – we will leave the details of the visit and the timings up to you.

6.1.3 *Identify resources available for the visit*

RESOURCES

If you are arranging a schedule for a visit to your own organisation by other people then, in addition to the arrangements we have already covered, you will need to consider what resources they will require whilst attending. Visitors may be coming along to your organisation in order to give a talk to a large group of people; on the other hand, they may be showing some slides or a video to just one or two people.

When planning the schedule for the visit, you need to consider what resources visitors will require once they arrive and the best location within the facility for them to use. The following list of headings will help you consider these resource requirements.

Money

Nearly all visits have to be organised under fairly strict budgets. Depending on the circumstances, the following arrangements may be made regarding payment for the visits:

▼ **the total cost will be borne by the organisers of the visit**
▼ **the total cost will be shared between the visitors and the organisers of the visit**
▼ **the total cost will be borne by the venue (this may be because the venue wishes to use the visit as an information-gathering exercise or for publicity purposes)**
▼ **the total cost or part of the cost will be borne by sponsorship, charitable donations or local councils**

Equipment

In some cases, particular pieces of equipment will be needed as a result of visitors' attendance – to illustrate a talk, for example. Naturally the facility will be expected to provide this. The equipment could include any of the following:

▼ **an overhead projector and screen**
▼ **a video and slide projector**
▼ **a computer software package**

Premises

If equipment is being used, a suitable room will have to be arranged. It would be useless, for example, to provide a video in a room with no blinds to shut out the light or no electric sockets. In addition, the size of the room is important if many members of staff or the public are to be involved in the presentation or if a large audience is expected. Suitable premises (rooms or buildings) should be timetabled for the day so that the visitor(s) have the use of its resources or equipment and the audience are comfortable and not too cramped. Heating of the premises should also be considered here. If the room is too small it may not only be too cramped, but also get too hot. If this is the only room available, the heating could be turned off for the duration of the activity to make it more suitable.

Refreshments

To make the visit run as smoothly as possible, refreshments should also be regarded as a resource requirement. During the coffee and lunch breaks, visitors and members of staff usually continue to talk about business and often strong and lasting working relationships are formed at these times. When arranging the refreshments for your visit, you should consider the following points:

▼ **What time will refreshments be served?**
▼ **Where will the refreshments be served?**
▼ **What refreshments will be served?**
▼ **Who will serve the refreshments?**

It is often preferable to serve coffee and lunch in a different room to the one in which the meeting is taking place. This gives the people concerned the chance to relax and talk informally.

People

People are also resources and are known as **human resources**. When planning the visit, it may be necessary to list the people the visitor(s) may need to see and to make sure they are available at given times during the day.

Transport

As we mentioned earlier, visitors will have to know how to get to your organisation. If they are driving, you should send a clear map which gives directions. Alternatively, a car may be sent to the railway station to collect visitors and bring them to the facility or centre. Whatever transport arrangements are made, be sure to notify visitors of the arrangements in advance and give the timings of all the transport details.

FIGURE IT OUT

PC 6.1.3
COM 1.1, 1.2,
IT 1.1, 1.2, 1.3

00:60

*W*orking in pairs, imagine that you are expecting a visitor to the place in which you are studying this course. Your visitor is going to give a talk to a group of 45 students about career opportunities in your nearest large city and is travelling from there to see you all. This careers advisor will be showing a video and will need an overhead projector and screen. The visit is to last for the whole morning and your timetables have been cancelled for that time.

Using the headings in this performance criterion, plan and word process a schedule for the visit, making sure that all the necessary resources will be appropriately arranged.

6.1.4 **Identify constraints which need to be taken into account when planning a schedule**

CONSTRAINTS

Constraints are things which make planning more difficult (or sometimes impossible). For the purposes of this performance criterion, constraints should be regarded as additional considerations. The following headings are the additional considerations which should be taken into account when arranging a schedule for a visitor to your facility or centre.

Health and safety

Health and safety is an important consideration in all aspects of the working world. When people visit a facility or centre, their health and safety has to be virtually guaranteed. This is the case even if someone is only visiting for one morning or day rather than on a regular basis. When arranging your schedule, you must consider the health and safety requirements of the visitors, particularly if they are using any equipment within your organisation.

FIGURE IT OUT

PC 6.1.4
COM 1.1

00:20

*T*hinking about the previous activity when you arranged a visit for a careers advisor, you should now discuss in pairs what health and safety requirements that visitor would have. What would your centre need to ensure? What can you do to help keep the visitor safe at all times?

Security and confidentiality

Another constraint which must be considered by any organisation that receives visitors is security and confidentiality of information.

Naturally, any facility would not want a visitor to be allowed to wander around its premises without supervision, or be allowed to gain access to information which might be of a confidential nature and useful to its competitors. In order to avoid potential problems, organisations tend to have a strict set of rules which visitors to their premises must follow. These may include the following:

▼ **Visitors will have to report to reception or the gatehouse keeper before they are allowed any further into the building. The receptionist will keep a log which details the name and business address of each visitor, the time they arrive and the time they leave.**
▼ **Visitors will be accompanied on their journey to the meeting point.**

▼ Visitors will be issued with a badge which lets everyone see they are visiting the organisation and not working there.

▼ Members of staff will know what the policy is regarding visitors and security and confidentiality of information, and will be updated at regular intervals.

▼ Passwords and codes will be in use within the organisation for access to safes, files and computers.

Other people visiting

In large facilities, it is often the case that several visitors will be meeting at the centre in order to go to different rooms with different groups of people or carry out a variety of activities. This could be a constraint on the resources the organisation has for use by the visitors. In such cases, the planning of the schedules is even more important to ensure that equipment is available for those who need it and not lying in a room where it is not required.

Other people visiting could also cause problems if more than one visitor needs to see the same person or use the same facilities for activities. The diaries of the different activity co-ordinators will have to be arranged carefully so that they can allow each visitor some of their time.

Another resource which has to be considered when this constraint is in force is refreshments. If the visitors are competitors, for example, they would not want to be taking their refreshments at the same time. In this case the refreshment breaks for each of the activities could be staggered so that they do not coincide, or the refreshments could be taken in different rooms.

6.1.5 *Produce a schedule for the visit, taking account of any constraints and the resources available*

Now that we have discussed all the various aspects of a schedule for a visit, you must produce one for yourself. Following the performance criteria, you must ensure that you have covered all the aspects given below:

▼ a brief introduction to the facility, attraction or event
▼ times of arrival and departure
▼ details of the meeting point and person(s) to be met
▼ timings of the individual activities and refreshments
▼ any relevant travel information

Your schedule should be supported with notes identifying any constraints which need to be taken into account and the resources available for the visit.

Your tutor may require you to create a schedule for a simulated visit, or you will be expected to prepare a schedule for a visit to a leisure/recreational facility or a tourism attraction/event as part of the course. In this instance you will have the opportunity to talk to professional schedule organisers at the particular venue.

element 6.2

MAKE A BOOKING

Performance criteria

A student must:

1 Identify the **booking requirements** of a specified person.

2 Suggest alternatives if some requirements cannot be met.

3 Make a booking that meets the **booking requirements** by completing all necessary **documentation and records** clearly and accurately.

4 **Confirm** the booking accurately with the person for whom it is being made

---

RANGE

Booking requirements: date, time, place, equipment, people, services, transport

Documentation and records: booking logs, reservation slips, diary, letter of confirmation

Confirmation: oral, handwritten, electronic

6.2.1 *Identify the booking requirements of a specified person*

BOOKING REQUIREMENTS

This element is a practical one. Using the information that we outlined in Element 6.1, you must now make a booking following all the headings given below.

Date

It is extremely important to find out the correct date for the booking, as nearly all the other information and booking details will depend on the availability of accommodation, equipment, people, services and transport on that day. Remember that when you make a booking you not only need to know the departure date (if applicable), but also the dates of particular events or activities that will occur during or as part of the main booking.

FIGURE IT OUT

PC 6.2.1

00:05

*A*n individual needs to visit London on the last Monday of June this year. What is the date of the visit?

Time

It is essential that you ensure that each of the days involved in the booking is accurately timetabled and scheduled. Individuals making the booking may have to be in particular places at particular times, so you will have to make sure that they have sufficient travelling time between each event. Equally, individuals will not wish to arrive after a long journey and be expected to give a presentation to a group of people or to participate in activities without having had the chance to freshen up.

FIGURE IT OUT

PC 6.2.1

00:05

*A*n individual needs to arrive in Birmingham at ten o'clock in the morning for a meeting at twenty to eleven, but must leave Birmingham by three o'clock in the afternoon. What are these times using the 24-hour clock?

Place

The place of the event could be a room or another venue; it may be located in a different part of the country or abroad. It is also possible that the event is part of a larger activity or event such as a holiday.

Taking into account the fact that a group will need more space than a single individual, you must make sure that you have booked adequate room for their activities and events, and for any overnight accommodation which they may require.

FIGURE IT OUT

PC 6.2.1

00:10

An individual needs to meet someone in a city that neither knows. List at least five places that are common to most cities as potential meeting places.

Equipment

If there is any particular need for business equipment, such as overhead projectors, video screens, presentation boards or slide projectors, this must be included in the booking. Equally, the individuals may need more sophisticated equipment that is not generally available in a facility, centre or hotel venue. Local organisations may have to be contacted in order to provide telecommunications equipment, computers and other materials.

FIGURE IT OUT

PC 6.2.1

00:05

A representative of an organisation has to attend a trade fair and must be able to carry with her all the equipment she will need. There will be display boards provided, so what must the representative take with her?

People

When making a booking, you should find out if any of the people involved have specific needs which must be taken into account. There are two aspects to consider:

1   The individuals within the group who have made the booking may have specific needs. For example, some may be vegetarian, others may need rooms on ground floors due to mobility problems.

2   The individuals who are providing services to the group may have specific needs themselves.

FIGURE IT OUT

PC 6.2.1

00:05

*I*f a group of sales representatives are due to have a meeting at a local hotel and there are no support staff available from the organisation, where would you obtain individuals who could take minutes of the meeting and run errands for the group?

Services

Individuals may require services whilst on route to the location or once they get there.

Refreshment and meals, private facilities, access to toilet facilities, entertainment and more specialised services may all be required, depending on the nature of the booking.

FIGURE IT OUT

PC 6.2.1

00:05

*H*ow would you find out which services are available at a particular hotel before confirming a booking with them?

Transport

Not only will the group or individual need transport to and from the location, but they may also require transport once they get to their destination. This may be necessary as they could have to visit a number of places close to the hotel or main venue. The form of transport should be appropriate to the needs of the individual or group; it is not worth booking a coach for a handful of people, for example. You should choose transport which is big enough, comfortable enough, flexible enough and available on demand.

PC 6.2.1

00:15

*W*hich would be the most appropriate form of transport in the following situations:

- *an individual who needs to attend a meeting in a town 200 miles away*
- *an individual who needs to take a range of samples from his organisation to show a group of potential customers*
- *a group of ten people who need to attend a conference in a city 300 miles away*

6.2.2 *Suggest alternatives if some requirements cannot be met*

There are bound to be certain occasions when the requirements cannot be met. The reasons behind these problems may be:

▼ **the venue is inadequate for the intended purpose**
▼ **the timings are not right for the venue and are already booked**
▼ **something happens at the last minute that means the arrangements have to be changed**
▼ **additional needs are identified at a later date that cannot be accommodated by the venue**

In most cases, the venue will be only too happy to try to rearrange or accommodate your requirements. The best plan is to get in contact with them as soon as you know things need to be changed.

As long as you have not been overambitious in your plans and schedules, things should not go wrong. There are a number of things that could happen that would be out of your control, but these will (usually) either be covered by insurance or dealt with using alternative suggestions by the travel operator or venue organiser.

6.2.3 *Make a booking that meets the booking requirements by completing all necessary documentation and records clearly and accurately*

DOCUMENTATION AND RECORDS

As with all tasks which are carried out by individuals within an organisation, it is necessary to record the fact that something has been done when making a booking. It is vital that this information is recorded accurately and clearly. When confirming a booking for an individual, you should always keep a copy for yourself or for the file so that the information can be retrieved at a later date if required.

If bookings are made on a regular basis, it may be useful to keep a log of these. Certainly, when providing evidence that you have made bookings for this unit, it would be useful to include a log of that information in your portfolio of evidence.

Booking logs

A booking log is a list of the requirements that have been met. As you will see in Figure 6.2.2, this can be a very simple form which is completed each time a booking is made. It will provide evidence that the booking has been made and by whom.

Reservation slips

A reservation slip may be required by the organiser of the meeting or visit to confirm that the person attending actually requires the place. A copy of the reservation slip should be kept so that you have written confirmation of making the booking.

Diary

Any booking you make should be entered in your own diary, as well as that of the person who requested you to carry out the task. As soon as the booking is made and confirmed, even if this is only over the telephone, you should enter the details in the diaries. This will avoid any double-booking and will act as a reminder, to both you and the person concerned, that this event is taking place on that particular date.

Letter of confirmation

It is always advisable to write a letter of confirmation for any booking you make. This letter may be to a hotel or to confirm attendance at a meeting. You should always retain a copy of the letter in case any problems are encountered later on.

6.2.4 *Confirm the booking accurately with the person for whom it is being made*

CONFIRMATION

For this performance criterion, you need to confirm the booking you have made. Confirmation can be made in the following ways:

▼ **verbally**
▼ **in writing**
▼ **electronically**

TO: MEETING PLANNERS & CONFERENCE ORGANISERS

If you would like to receive a complimentary copy of the 1996 edition of the 'British Conference Destinations Directory', as well as news on the latest developments within the conference industry, please complete the following form by ticking all the appropriate boxes.

YOUR DETAILS

Mr/Mrs/Miss/Ms First Name . . . .

Surname. . . . .

Position. . . . .

Organisation . . . .

Address . . . .

. . . .

Postcode . . . .

Tel Number. . . . .

Fax Number . . . .

YOUR ORGANISATION *(please ✓ appropriate boxes)*

What is your main area of responsibility?

Conference/Events organiser ☐

Personnel/Training ☐

Secretarial/Administration ☐

Sales/Marketing ☐

Other *(please specify)* . . . .

WHAT TYPE OF ORGANISATION DO YOU WORK FOR?

Professional assoc./institution ☐ Trade union ☐

Voluntary assoc./charity ☐ Government agency ☐

Educational body ☐ Venue finding agency ☐

Conference/event production co. ☐

Other *(please specify)* . . . .

What is your organisation's main business activity? . . . .

FAMILIARISATION VISITS

I am interested in BACT familiarisation visits ☐

I would like to visit *(BACT Members)* . . . .

. . . .

. . . .

YOUR EVENTS *(please all ✓ appropriate boxes)*

How many events do you arrange each year?. . . . .

What types of events do you arrange?

Conferences/meetings ☐ Product launches ☐

Exhibitions ☐ Corporate hospitality ☐

Training ☐ Incentive Travel ☐

What sizes of events do you arrange?

Up to 50 delegates ☐ 51-100 delegates ☐

101-200 delegates ☐ 201-500 delegates ☐

501-1000 delegates ☐ over 1000 delegates ☐

What facilities/venues would you consider using?

Purpose built conference centre ☐

Civic Hall ☐ University/College ☐

Hotel ☐ Unusual Venue ☐

Which of the following regions would you consider?

Scotland ☐ West Midlands ☐

Wales ☐ East Anglia ☐

Northern Ireland ☐ North West England ☐

South West England ☐ North East England ☐

South East England ☐ Isle of Man ☐

East Midlands ☐ Channel Islands ☐

Please ✓ if you hold events overseas ☐

YOUR LARGEST EVENT

How many attend your largest annual event? . . . . .

What kind of event is it? . . . .

What time of year do you normally hold this event?

Winter ☐ Spring ☐

Summer ☐ Autumn ☐

In which town did you hold this event in

1992 . . . .

1993 . . . .

1994 . . . .

Please post or fax the completed form to:
BACT, 1st Floor, Elizabeth House, 22 Suffolk Street, Queensway, Birmingham B1 1LS.
Fax Number: 0121 616 1364

Fig. 6.2.1 The British Association of Conference Towns (BACT) uses this questionnaire to gather relevant information from potential conference organisers.

LOG OF BOOKINGS MADE

DATE	BOOKING FOR (PERSON)	DEPARTURE DATE/TIME	ARRIVAL DATE/TIME	TRAVEL BY (MODE)	DESTINATION	MADE BY

Fig. 6.2.2 A booking log.

BOOKING FORM

Please complete this form to pre-book educational groups into the ARC, Jorvik Viking Centre and/or Barley Hall, or to obtain further information about the activities of the Trust. Schools resources can be pre-booked using the list overleaf. If you have any enquiries regarding the Jorvik Viking Centre, the ARC and/or Barley Hall please telephone the Bookings Officer on 01904 613711 during office hours.

Name of School: _____

Address: _____
_____
_____

Postcode: _____

Name of Organiser: _____   Tel. No: _____

No. of children: _____   No. of Staff: _____   Age of Group: _____

Visit to:		JVC	ARC	Barley Hall
Date of visit:	1st choice:	_____	_____	_____
	2nd choice:	_____	_____	_____
	3rd choice:	_____	_____	_____
Time of visit:	1st choice:	_____	_____	_____
	2nd choice:	_____	_____	_____
	3rd choice:	_____	_____	_____

Period/Subject being studied: _____

Special Needs: _____
_____

Signed: _____   Date: _____

We would be obliged if the party organiser presents the entire payment for the whole party on arrival (Cheques should be made payable to 'York Archaeological Trust'). We cannot accept payment from individual members of groups.

Please provide further information on the following:

- ☐ Jorvik Festival
- ☐ Friends of York Archaeological Trust
- ☐ Adult Education Courses
- ☐ Past Forward Ltd
- ☐ Volunteer Placements
- ☐ Lectures and Talks

- ☐ Conservation Department
- ☐ Artefact Research Department
- ☐ Training Digs
- ☐ Archaeological Picture Library
- ☐ Special Exhibitions
- ☐ Other (please specify):

Please return forms to: BOOKINGS OFFICE
JORVIK VIKING CENTRE
COPPERGATE
YORK
YO1 1NT   Fax:01904 627097

_____
_____
_____
_____
_____

Fig. 6.2.3 The pre-visit booking form used by educational groups visiting the Jorvik Viking Centre in York.

We will look briefly at the different methods in this section. Obviously, confirmation can only be made once all the necessary information has been passed to the venue or other organisations involved in the booking. They will not be able to confirm something that has not yet been arranged.

Oral confirmation

It is only advisable to confirm a booking by telephone if the details are not complex or this is being used as a second or back-up confirmation at the last moment. You might wish to use this rather more informal way of confirming a booking if you have used the services of a venue or organisation before and know the person to whom you are speaking.

Handwritten confirmation

The request to receive confirmation about a booking can be made when you return the documentation to the booking organiser. Normally you would use a compliments slip with a brief message requesting the confirmation, which should be attached to the other booking documentation.

Electronic confirmation

The large majority of the more up-to-date venues and event organisers are now making use of E-mail. Provided that you have access to this form of communication, they should be able to respond rapidly to your request and provide confirmation electronically via an E-mail message. Obviously they may choose to respond in a more conventional manner to your message.

Faxes are a more common alternative to E-mail. Since the overwhelming majority of venues and conference organisers have fax machines, this is a simple and efficient method of ensuring that your request or confirmation is received by the correct individual.

assignment
ELEMENT 6.2

PC 6.2.1–4
COM 1.1, 1.2
AON 1.1
IT 1.1, 1.2, 1.3

Although you will have probably carried out the majority of these tasks already during the course of this element, we have provided a comprehensive reminder of the requirements of the performance criteria. Bear in mind that you will be observed making a real or simulated booking for a specific person and that all the documents and records should be completed clearly and accurately.

| task | 1 | PC 6.2.1 |

Identify the booking requirements of a specified person.

| task | 2 | PC 6.2.2 |

Suggest any alternatives if necessary.

| task | 3 | PC 6.2.3 |

Make a booking by completing all the necessary documentation and records clearly and accurately.

| task | 4 | PC 6.2.4 |

Confirm the booking accurately.

Notes

You could carry out any of the following:

- *a theatre booking*
- *a holiday booking*
- *a travel booking*
- *a leisure centre activity booking*
- *a sports centre activity booking*
- *a museum booking*
- *a visitor attraction booking*
- *an accommodation booking*

These could either be real or simulated. Your tutor will be able to advise you as to whether he or she can arrange a real booking to coincide with the completion of this element.

element 6.3

PREPARE TRAVEL ITINERARIES

Performance criteria

A student must:

1 Locate travel **destinations** on a map and identify the countries concerned.

2 Establish what the **travellers' needs** are.

3 Select suitable routes and **means of travel** which meet the **travellers' needs**.

4 Using a **timetable**, identify dates and **times** of travel to meet **travellers' needs**.

5 Calculate travel **times** and estimate costs.

6 Prepare **travel itineraries**, including necessary **stops** and present them in an effective way.

RANGE

Destinations: major cities, within the European Union

Travellers' needs: route, time (of year, of day), speed of travel, scenic route, stops on way, few changes of transport mode, appropriate cost

Means of travel: air, rail, car/taxi, coach, ferry

Timetables: bus, rail, coach, air, ferry

Times: departure, arrival; length of journey, transport changes, journey breaks

Travel itineraries: person(s), number of persons in party, date of travel, destination, means of travel, point of departure, time of departure, details of stops, point of arrival, time of arrival, overall travel time, estimated cost

Stops: refreshment breaks, transport connections, seeing places of interest

6.3.1 *Locate travel destinations on a map and identify the countries concerned*

DESTINATIONS

In this performance criterion we will be asking you to locate various travel destinations. Not only will you have to find the city involved, but also name the country in which it lies.

The remainder of this performance criterion is of a practical nature and we will set you a number of tasks. You can use the maps printed in this book, or larger ones provided by your tutor. Bear in mind that the maps will be blank apart from the borders between each country.

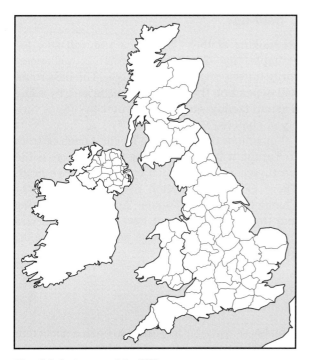

Fig. 6.3.1 A map of the UK.

Major cities

You will have to find a number of cities both in the UK and from within the rest of the European Union. Remember that major cities are not just capital cities. Birmingham, Manchester, Leeds, Glasgow and Norwich are examples of major cities, none of which are capital cities. You may be asked to locate some major cities that you have never heard of before. You will only need to mark the rough location of each of these cities.

Destinations within the European Union

At the time of writing, there are a number of countries which make up the European Union. By the time you read this book others may have joined. To make things simple, we will only list cities in the more well-known parts of Europe.

6.3.2 *Establish what the travellers' needs are*

TRAVELLERS' NEEDS

Before preparing travel itineraries, it is important to find out from the travellers exactly what their requirements and needs are. They may have a preferred route, perhaps one that they have not used before or one that they know and enjoy. They will certainly have a particular day or time of day in mind. Equally, they will have a preferred means of transport and may not wish to travel in a particular way; for example, some people are frightened of air travel or ferries. All these needs must be taken into account.

Route

When considering the possible route to a particular destination, we are often faced with a wide

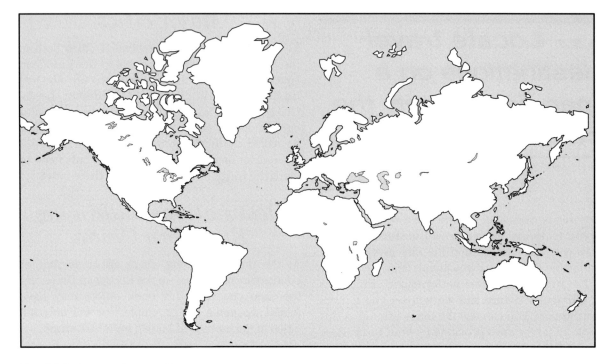

Fig. 6.3.2 A map of the world.

variety of different alternatives. The most direct route is probably by air. Generally speaking, air routes are straight lines linking different airports. Some of the more isolated cities are more difficult to get to and you will have to make several detours, stop-overs or aircraft changes to reach them.

Even rail and coach travel offer a variety of different routes. Travellers do not always want to go directly from the point of departure to the destination. They may wish to stop over and include an extra visit elsewhere on route.

Travelling by car is perhaps the most flexible and personalised form of transport. You can offer the travellers a series of alternative routes and allow them to choose. There are various computer programs which have been created to supply suggestions for different routes, including:

▼ **the quickest route**
▼ **the shortest route**
▼ **the scenic route**
▼ **the motorway route**
▼ **the A and B road route**

▼ **the route least likely to have traffic hold-ups**

By looking at these programs you will see, for example, that the motorway route is not necessarily the shortest or quickest one. The best route will depend on the travellers' needs and, by using a useful facility such as this, you can offer a variety of choices.

Remember that travelling by car, coach or train to Europe will involve having to travel across the North Sea or the Channel by ferry or hovercraft. There is also the option of getting across the Channel using the Tunnel. Any route planning and timing of travel will have to take the extra time to get on and off this additional transport into account.

Time

A business traveller may have to be in a particular place at a particular time. In conjunction with the route information, you will be able to work out

FIGURE IT OUT

PC 6.3.1
COM 1.1, 1.2

`00:15`

*F*ind *the following cities and mark them on a blank map of Europe like the one below. Name the country they belong to.*

- *Copenhagen*
- *Birmingham*
- *Bonn*
- *Dublin*
- *Marseilles*
- *Leeds*
- *Athens*
- *Frankfurt*
- *Milan*
- *Edinburgh*
- *Barcelona*
- *Cardiff*
- *Brussels*
- *Rotterdam*
- *Düsseldorf*
- *Toulouse*

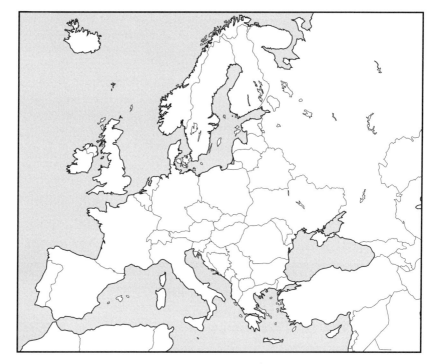

Fig. 6.3.3 A map of Europe.

Compare your suggestions with those of the rest of your group.

whether the traveller will reach his or her destination in time for the appointment.

It is always worth remembering that travelling at particular times of the year can involve additional complications. Travelling during the summer months, for example, will mean that travellers may encounter a greater amount of traffic and probably slow-moving traffic too. If their destination is likely to be busy on a particular day of the week or year, such as a market day, then the travellers should be warned.

The final consideration is to remember that foreign travel also means a change in time. Many countries are either several hours ahead of or several hours behind the UK (the UK time is known as Greenwich Mean Time).

FIGURE IT OUT

PC 6.3.2
COM 1.1, 1.2

00:20

If it is 10 a.m. in London, what time is it in the following cities? Remember to say whether it is a.m. or p.m.

- *Harare*
- *Tokyo*
- *San Francisco*
- *Bogota*
- *Melbourne*
- *Auckland*
- *Cape Town*
- *Tunis*
- *Tel Aviv*
- *Quebec*
- *Buenos Aires*
- *St Petersburg*

Compare your timings with those of the rest of your group.

Speed of travel

This aspect of the travel itinerary will be dependent on the following considerations:

▼ **Are those travelling operating to a tight schedule?**

▼ **Are those travelling restricted in terms of the available transport methods?**

▼ **Are any of those travelling prone to sickness?**

▼ **Do any of those travelling need disabled facilities or have specific requirements?**

▼ **Do the travellers need to be able to talk to each other whilst they are travelling?**

Scenic route

Depending on the purpose of their journey, travellers may wish to take a scenic route to their destination. If they are using scheduled transport, the route will be predetermined. In cases when a coach, mini-bus or car is being used, the choice of route is entirely up to the driver or organiser of the party. You should consider the following aspects:

▼ **if the journey is a short one, the opportunities for a scenic route may be limited**

▼ **if the journey is a long one, the travellers may just wish to get to their destination as soon as possible**

▼ **if the journey is neither too short nor too long, this may be the opportunity to seek an alternative scenic route**

With regard to your itinerary, you will need to weigh up the benefits and disadvantages of each of the different modes of transport in respect of the speed and comfort of the route.

Stops on way

Assuming that the mode of transport is large enough to contain toilet and refreshment facilities, there may not be a particular need to stop on the way. However, coaches in particular, despite the fact that they have toilet and refreshment facilities on board, do tend to stop at regular intervals so that travellers can stretch their legs and the drivers can change over. Obviously you will need to build the time and duration of each stop into your itinerary.

Few changes of transport mode

It is inevitable that certain journeys will involve the switching of transport. If, for example, you were travelling by rail into London, bound for Heathrow Airport, you would have to get off the train, onto the tube and then make your way to the airport. At the other end of your journey you will probably be taken to your final destination by coach or taxi.

Apart from the interruption to the journey, the basic problem with changing to different modes of transport is that the travellers' baggage and belongings have to be transferred each time and may be mislaid in the process. In your travel itinerary, it is best to organise a route which has as few changes of transport mode as possible.

Appropriate cost

As with many things, operating within a particular budget is one of the key elements of preparing a realistic travel itinerary. There are inevitably best ways of getting to and from a destination, but you should always consider what the travellers can afford. Students travelling abroad, for example, often have to use coaches instead of aircraft to get to continental destinations – although coach travel takes longer, the cost is half that of air travel.

6.3.3 Select suitable routes and means of travel which meet the travellers' needs

MEANS OF TRAVEL

When preparing an itinerary and deciding which means of travel to select, it is obviously important that the needs of the travellers are taken into account. The main consideration would be whether the travel is of a local, national or international nature.

Local travel normally means within a particular area near to the travellers' office or home. It is often not necessary for the visit to be more than one day; therefore, hotel accommodation would not always be a requirement.

With national travel, a one-day visit is not always possible. Therefore, hotel accommodation may have to be booked for one or more nights.

Depending on the length of the visit, international travel can be much more complicated and involved than national travel. It is, however, possible to fly to The Netherlands and back in a day from the UK, making overnight accommodation unnecessary. In most cases, though, an international trip will involve more arrangements with regard to travel and accommodation. In addition, other key considerations have to be taken into account; we discuss these a little later in this element.

Air

Air travel is possible within the UK. For example, regular services are provided daily from Norwich to Aberdeen, making it possible for someone to travel to Scotland from the south of England and back in the same day. This method of transport is expensive, but not in terms of time. If a manager needs to be in a conference which will last only 2

Fig. 6.3.4 A Virgin Atlantic aircraft on the aircraft parking area at Gatwick Airport.

or 3 hours, this method will allow him or her to be back in the office the following day.

Flying is probably the most convenient method of travel for international visits. It is certainly the quickest. However, because airports are usually located well outside major cities, additional rail or road travel to the venue of the meeting may be required. Air travel can also be very expensive for long-haul flights in particular and may involve long waits at airports for connecting flights. All these features should be taken into account when arrangements are being made.

Rail

Rail travel may be suitable if the arrangements can be made satisfactorily. Sometimes, particularly in rural areas, connections cannot be made easily or the service does not run very frequently. If the venue of the meeting is convenient for the rail station and the train times allow it, however, rail travel is a possibility – certainly for local and national travel.

Rail travel is often a good option for business journeys. It allows staff to arrive more refreshed than they would be if driving was involved and gives them time during the journey for working on papers, etc. If more than one member of staff are travelling together, they may use the travelling time to have pre-meeting discussions.

For international travel, the rail service can be expensive and involve waits for connections. Rail travel is therefore not as popular as flying because of the length of time it takes to complete the journey. However, the opening of the Channel Tunnel has meant that the journey time from London to Paris has been reduced.

Again, the location of the train station may mean that travellers need to change to another mode of transport to reach their final destination.

Car or taxi

This is probably the most convenient method of transport for local travel. An organisation may pay the expenses for a member of staff to use his or her own car, or it may provide a company car or allow for a car to be hired. If road travel is considered to be the best option, detailed instructions should be given on the most appropriate route to take.

Road travel is often the most economical method of transport, particularly if more than one person is travelling. The petrol costs, or even the car hire costs, could be far less than the cost for four people to travel by train. Road travel can, however, be tiring – particularly for the driver. This may be an important consideration for business travellers.

Although road travel is a popular and less expensive way of travelling if several people are visiting a foreign country on holiday, it is not so popular for international business trips. This is due mainly to the length of time road travel can take when compared to air travel. Additionally, road travel to a country either within or outside the European Union will involve the crossing of the Channel. This can add expense to the visit. The opening of the Channel Tunnel has made this crossing a quicker process, although not necessarily a cheaper one.

Taxis are available at most stations and airports, and throughout most major cities. It is their job to know where potential customers may be, so areas with businesses tend to be well served by this type of transport. Travellers who are working on a tight schedule may have to prebook taxis so that they can ensure they are picked up at a particular place and time. This can be arranged quite a long while in advance, but it

Fig. 6.3.5 This night-time view of Heathrow Airport, the world's busiest international airport, shows that many of its 52 million passengers per year travel to the airport by car or other forms of road transport.

is not too difficult to organise a taxi at fairly short notice. In areas which are not served by taxis, a mini-cab service will be available. Travellers will have to decide whether the comparatively high cost of using a taxi can be justified if there is readily available public transport at hand.

Coach

When you consider coaches as a means of travel, you should recognise that there are two ways of using this type of transport:

1 *Private coach hire.* The driver and coach is dedicated to the travellers' use only and is hired to carry travellers from the point of departure to the destination, making any requested stops or detours along the way.
2 *Scheduled coaches.* There are a wide variety of different coach lines in the UK. These run regular and reliable services, linking various towns and cities around the country. Careful planning can mean that the traveller can 'coach hop' and reach fairly remote destinations with the minimum of fuss. It is normally advisable to book ahead when using scheduled coaches as they are relatively cheap compared to rail or air travel and are often fully booked.

Coaches are generally better than buses for long journeys as they stop at fewer places. In fact, many coaches are non-stop and this is their appeal. Another major advantage of coaches over buses is that they tend to have refreshments and toilet facilities on board, as well as the capacity to carry luggage.

Coaches not only provide a comprehensive national service, but they also serve as an alternative form of transport for international destinations. There are regular services to most of the main European cities, however this may mean overnight travel and journeys of over 24 hours.

Ferry

When compared to air travel, sea travel takes a much longer time. In addition to this added time factor, you must take into account the fact that additional transport will be needed once the port is reached.

Ferries are considerably cheaper than air travel. They offer the foot passenger, car passenger or coach traveller the opportunity to break their journey and stretch their legs. The quality of facilities on board the newer ferries has been much improved over the past few years. Many travellers actually prefer the slower crossing for these reasons.

6.3.4 *Using a timetable, identify dates and times of travel to meet travellers' needs*

TIMETABLE

Timetables are available for most methods of transport which offer services to the general public. There is generally no charge for timetables and they are readily available on request

Fig. 6.3.6 Although it is not strictly speaking a ferry, the Cunard Princess *represents a memorable way of getting around the Mediterranean.*

from stations, airports, ports, coach and bus stations, travel agents and the AA and RAC.

Bus

Bus timetables can be obtained in advance of the departure date. They will state where the starting point is and where the bus will terminate. A time will be given for the beginning of the journey and for all stops between this and the termination point. Remember that the times tend to be estimated and it is advisable to arrive at the stop at least five minutes before the bus is due.

Rail

The rail timetable for your local area and connections to large cities can be obtained by telephone; a recorded message is usually transmitted, giving relevant details. Rail companies issue timetables which are revised twice a year for all the services they offer. They will answer enquiries regarding the best routes, prices and times of trains. In addition, they will take advance bookings for tickets and seats, although the reservation of seats can incur an additional charge.

Coach

In a similar way to a bus timetable, coach operators will state the departure and arrival times of their scheduled coach services. The major difference between coaches and buses is that a coach tends to stop at fewer places.

Air

Since many air operators offer a flexible and regular service to and from a variety of different destinations, travellers can easily become confused with the assortment on offer. Probably the best thing to do is to pre-book the air flight through a local travel agent. If this is not possible, most operators will accept bookings via the telephone using a credit card. Some of the departures are so regular from the major airports that it is possible to literally 'turn up and take off'. The one thing that nearly all operators insist upon is that you pay before you get on the plane. In many respects, air travel has become so easily available that it is really no different from getting on a train.

Ferry

Since the building of the Channel Tunnel, ferry operators have begun to offer a far more flexible and regular service. This is the only way that they can hope to survive. This is a good thing for travellers, as regular sailings mean they do not have to organise their whole day around the departure or arrival of a ferry. On less popular routes, such as those to Ireland, Scandinavia and Holland, the ferry times are not as regular (although extremely reliable) and it is important to book ahead.

TIMES

The vast majority of timetables will be created using the 24-hour clock. You will have to get used to this type of timing and remember that if the number is over 12, it is p.m. So, for example, 18.00 hours is 6 p.m.; 00.00 hours is midnight.

Bear in mind that when you look at timetables involving travel abroad, the country of destination may be several hours in front of or behind the UK time. For example, a ferry leaving Dover at 08.30 will appear to take two and a quarter hours to get to Calais, but a similar ferry leaving Calais at 08.30 (French time) will appear to take only a quarter of an hour to get to Dover.

When you look at timetables, you should consider the most convenient travel times for the travellers. They may not wish to travel overnight; equally, an early travel connection may mean that they will have to start their journey very early. You should find out what their needs are before you go any further with your itinerary.

Departure and arrival times

Remember that the departure and arrival times are only approximate – you will find a brief note stating this fact on many timetables. The times will normally be shown using the 24-hour clock and will always be stated in local time (the time of the country involved). Changes to the departure and arrival times may affect transfer from one mode of transport to another. If possible, a certain amount of additional time should therefore be incorporated into the itinerary to ensure safe changeover.

Length of journey

The length of the journey should be expressed in terms of the actual number of hours which will be spent travelling. This information should be provided in addition to the arrival and departure times. You cannot assume that travellers will understand the fact that there are different time zones and make the correct calculations.

Transport changes

The travellers need to know exactly where they have to go once they get off a particular mode of transport, as well as being assured that their luggage and belongings are being transferred along with them. The last thing that travellers would wish to discover is that they are being transported to Bristol and their baggage is on the way to Glasgow.

Journey breaks

Typically, journey breaks would include the following:

▼ **toilet stops**
▼ **refreshment stops**
▼ **sleep stops**
▼ **stops to pick up other travellers on the way**
▼ **stops to view particular sights**

Again, these should be included in the itinerary, with an estimated time of arrival, duration of the stop, nature of the stop and estimated departure time.

6.3.5 Calculate travel times and estimate costs

This is a practical performance criterion and you may wish to use it as the basis for your whole travel itinerary for this element. You will find that the tasks you are asked to undertake will be useful in focusing your mind on the complexities of travel itineraries.

6.3.6 Prepare travel itineraries, including necessary stops, and present them in an effective way

Travel itineraries

An itinerary is a summary of the details and plans for the visit, including all times, accommodation and methods of travel. If a visit is a particularly long and complicated one, the itinerary will be very detailed and could be pages long. In such a case, a briefer version containing only essential information could be printed onto cards so that the travellers can carry this in a pocket.

You may be required to make travel and/or accommodation arrangements for visitors to your organisation. On the other hand, your manager or other members of staff may have to travel during the course of their duties, in which case you may be asked to arrange the travel and accommodation requirements for them. It could be that this would involve making the arrangements for just one individual, or for several. The travel may be by various methods and may involve arrangements for within the UK, within the European Union or to countries further afield. As always, attention to detail is the key factor to be observed. In this performance criterion, we will discuss the main considerations in dealing with the preparation of itineraries.

Person(s) and number of persons in party

The larger the group, the more difficult it is to arrange complicated and flexible travel itineraries. If there are stop-overs or visits involved, you will have to check ahead that the intended facilities can cope with the number and needs of people in the group. There are many things to consider, including:

▼ **Do the type of transport and intended stops have facilities for disabled people?**
▼ **If it is going to be a long journey, is there entertainment available on the means of transport?**
▼ **Is there any prospect of losing people along the way and what can be done to avoid this?**
▼ **Have the scheduled stops got facilities for refreshments and, if so, do any of the travellers have special dietary requirements?**
▼ **Is the travel organiser going to assume responsibility for any paperwork that needs to be carried by the group?**

FIGURE IT OUT

PC 6.2.2
COM 1.1, 1.2, 1.3
AON 1.1, 1.2, 1.3

*T*he group within your centre is to make an educational visit to Paris. This will be a one-week trip and you are to make the necessary enquiries and arrangements. You will be travelling by coach and ferry and will make the booking through a company that specialises in student travel. You will need to stay in a hotel in the centre of Paris on a bed and breakfast basis. Included in the amount you are prepared to pay will be several excursions to some of the following places:

- *Disneyland Paris (a one-day visit by coach)*
- *Versailles Palace (a half-day visit by coach)*
- *The Eiffel Tower*
- *The Louvre*
- *Montmartre area (and the Sacre Coeur)*
- *A half-day coach tour of the sights of Paris*
- *The Opera House*
- *A boat trip along the Seine*
- *The Notre Dame*
- *An opportunity to spend free time for shopping*

In order to complete this activity you should contact several tour operators and ask them to send you copies of their brochures. From these brochures you should identify the tour operators who provide a coach trip to Paris and compare their costs and the facilities provided. You should then work out how much it would cost each student to participate in the visit and draw up an itinerary for the whole trip, including the excursions which can be fitted in during the time in Paris itself.

Remember that you will require the coach to stay with the group for the whole of the visit so that the excursions can be carried out using it. The hours that the coach driver is allowed to drive will have to be taken into consideration here. You should also remember that ferry crossings will have to be booked, so adequate time will have to be allowed for the coach journey from your centre to the port.

Those students who are involved in the visit will require passports and E111 forms. You should write a list of the necessary documentation which would have to be taken with you.

```
                            ITINERARY

                        FOR SARAH BROWN

                        25 JANUARY 19..


Monday 25 January 19..


Depart:          Norwich                        0930

Arrive:          London Liverpool Street        1105

Hotel:           Regent Palace
                 Piccadilly Circus
                 London
                 Tel:  0171-273-6290

Seminar:         At the hotel


                      Registration             1230
                      Lunch                    1300
                      Interpersonal skills     1400
                      Afternoon tea            1530
                      Plenary session          1545
                      Close                    1630



Theatre:             The Adelphi Theatre
                     'Sunset Boulevard'         2015



Tuesday 26 January 19..


Seminar:         At the hotel


                      Dealing with customers   0930
                      Coffee                   1100
                      Role play exercises      1130
                      Lunch                    1300
                      Aggressive callers       1415
                      Afternoon tea            1530
                      Plenary session          1545
                      Close                    1630

Depart:          London Liverpool Street        1800

Arrive:          Norwich                        2000
```

Fig. 6.3.7 An example of a travel itinerary.

Date of travel and destination

Naturally, the location of the meeting will have an effect on the travel and accommodation requirements. Ideally, the accommodation will be as near to the venue of the meeting as possible, but key considerations are the car-parking facilities, the location of the railway station or airport, and the distance to the establishment in which the meeting is to take place.

For local and national travel, the following steps should be taken when producing an itinerary:

▼ agree the dates for travel and accommodation requirements with all those concerned and enter them in your diary
▼ book any hotel requirements
▼ arrange the meetings and appointments that the travellers will be required to attend during their visit
▼ arrange any rail tickets, seat reservations or car hire
▼ gather together any documents the travellers may have to take

---

finding out

PC 6.3.5
COM 1.1, 1.2
IT 1.1, 1.2, 1.3

Word process a letter to the hotel of your choice enquiring about accommodation for two nights for two travellers. They will require breakfast but no evening meal and they each need a single room with bath. Find out the price for accommodation and ask them to send any literature to assist the travellers in finding the hotel, railway station and the venue of the seminar they will be attending.

For international travel the following would also have to be taken into consideration:

▼ book any air tickets
▼ arrange any insurance requirements
▼ book hotel accommodation and arrangements
▼ arrange any vaccinations or inoculations that may be required
▼ apply for any visas that may be required
▼ check that the passports of all those travelling are up-to-date and will not expire whilst the visit is taking place
▼ collect together any information you can regarding the country being visited, including information about food, drink and places of interest
▼ arrange taxis or hire cars for transfer from the airport to the hotel and vice versa
▼ check with the AA and RAC for regulations regarding Green Card Insurance or an International Driving Permit if the traveller is driving
▼ confirm that a Form E111 is available
▼ order travellers' cheques, foreign currency or a Eurocheque book from the bank or travel agent if required

Means of travel

As we have seen, there are a variety of different means of travel to choose from. Before any firm decision is made as to the preferred mode, it is a good idea to make a final check that none of the travellers have medical reasons why they should not travel this way. Provided this is not the case, you should include the means of travel on your itinerary and state any changes that will be necessary during the trip. For example, on a trip to France you might use a coach down to Dover, then take the ferry across the Channel and get back onto another coach at Calais.

Point and time of departure

You must state clearly on the itinerary exactly where the travellers should congregate in order to begin their journey. Always make it an obvious place that cannot be confused with any other location. Make sure that you ask the travellers to arrive at the point of departure well before they actually need to leave, otherwise you could be putting the rest of the itinerary in danger and may miss vital travel connections as a result of somebody being late. Remember that you should state the time of departure using the 24-hour clock. This will avoid any confusion, such as travellers arriving at 10 a.m. instead of 10. p.m.

Details of stops (refreshment breaks, transport connections)

Travellers will want to be assured that they are not travelling for any great length of time without a chance of stretching their legs. Obviously, if the means of transport is an aircraft then this is impossible. You should state on the itinerary when and where the stops will be made, and indicate the length of each stop so that the travellers can pace themselves and decide whether they should eat at a particular stop or just have a snack and a rest.

It may be necessary for the travellers to make transport connections on route to their destination. If the connection times are for ferries or trains, for example, then the timetables are already set. You will have to ensure that the travellers reach the point of connection in good time so that there is not a panic to switch modes of transport. If you work backwards from the connection time, you can work out what time you will have to set out to get there.

Point and time of arrival

The point of arrival is just as important as the point of departure, particularly if there will be someone waiting for the travellers at the other end of their journey. In such situations, you should always try to find out from the person whom the travellers are meeting where the best termination point may be. He or she will know the local area and be able to suggest a suitable meeting point that will not cause confusion or unnecessary delay. Remember that the time of arrival should be stated using the 24-hour clock and, if the point of arrival is in another country, you should always give the local time and not UK time.

Overall travel time

This is one of the most important factors governing the method of transport to be used. If the visit is within the UK, it is often much quicker to travel by air than by train. However, the cost consideration may not allow this. What must be ensured is that the travel can be arranged in the shortest amount of time so that members of staff are not spending any more time than absolutely necessary in travelling. It is important to ensure that members of staff do not arrive late at a meeting. You should therefore build time into your itinerary to allow for transport delays.

Estimated cost

Travel is costly, as is accommodation. Although cost is an important consideration when making arrangements for travel and accommodation, it should be remembered that the members of staff have no alternative but to attend the meeting. For this reason, finding the most convenient method of travel and the nearest hotel are often more important than the cost.

With regard to accommodation, although members of staff would probably be quite happy to stay in a 5-star hotel, this is clearly not a cost-effective option. When making accommodation arrangements, you should select the most convenient and reasonably priced hotel. Very often, when members of staff visit the same area frequently, they have a preference with regard to their accommodation. This makes the arrangements easier, as you know the travellers will be happy with the hotel and their organisation will not find the rates too excessive.

STOPS

The travellers need to know why particular stops are being made, as they may wish to plan their activities (such as eating, sleeping or making phone calls home) around them. We will now look at the principal reasons for making stops during the journey.

Refreshment breaks

Most travellers welcome the opportunity to get out and stretch their legs and have the chance of seeing a slightly different environment. When large numbers of people are travelling, the person who is preparing the travel itinerary should forewarn the intended restaurant, café or service stations that the travellers will be arriving at a particular time. This means that the caterers can organise meals to be ready for the travellers so that time is not wasted.

Transport connections

When you are using forms of transport that are working to an inflexible timetable, such as aircraft or railway departures, all the other transport requirements will have to be centred around these. You must build in enough time throughout the itinerary to account for potential delays and ensure connections can be met. Additionally, you should make sure that you have allowed enough time to book in or collect tickets between different modes of transport.

Seeing places of interest

If the sole intention of the itinerary is to get to a particular destination in the quickest possible time, this may not be a consideration. However, many itineraries are flexible enough to include short refreshment breaks at places of interest and, if scheduled correctly, these can greatly enhance the travellers' overall enjoyment of the journey.

assignment

ELEMENT 6.3

PC 6.3.1–6
COM 1.1, 1.2, 1.3, 1.4
AON 1.1, 1.2 (if possible)
IT 1.1, 1.2, 1.3

In order to fulfil the requirements of this element, you will need to prepare two travel itineraries for two journeys to different major cities in the European Union, one of which could be in the UK.

| task | 1 | PC 6.3.1 |

Locate the travel destinations on a map and identify the country concerned.

| task | 2 | PC 6.3.2–4 |

Establish the travellers' needs, select suitable routes and means of travel, and identify dates and times of travel using a timetable.

| task | 3 | PC 6.3.5 |

Calculate the travel times and estimate the costs.

| task | 4 | PC 6.3.6 |

Prepare a travel itinerary for each destination, including necessary stops. Present them in an effective way, highlighting the relevant information and attaching additional material such as timetables.

Notes

You should make sure that you use the latest available timetable information, which can be obtained through travel agents, coach and rail travel centres, and local libraries. Your tutor may expect you to link this element with Element 6.2, where you carried out a simulated booking for a holiday or travel arrangement.

EXPLORING THE PROVISION OF TRAVEL AND TOURISM PRODUCTS AND SERVICES

element 7.1

INVESTIGATE THE PROVISION OF TRAVEL PRODUCTS AND SERVICES

Performance criteria

A student must:

1 Identify, with examples, the **main sectors of the UK travel industry**.
2 Describe the **chain of distribution** in the UK travel industry.
3 Describe different types of **travel products and services**.
4 Describe **sources of information** on **travel products and services**.
5 Match **travel products and services** with different **customer types**.

RANGE

Main sectors of the UK travel industry: retail travel, tour operations, transport (airlines, ferry companies, coach operators, rail operators), accommodation (hotels, motels, guest houses, self-catering, holiday villages)

Chain of distribution: producers (transport providers, accommodation providers, excursion providers), wholesalers (out-bound tour operators, in-bound tour operators), retailers (travel agencies, ticketing offices), customers

Travel products and services: package holidays, transport bookings (plane, train, ferry, coach), foreign currency, passports, visas, accommodation, catering

Sources of information: travel agencies, transport providers (railway stations, coach stations, airports, ferry ports), tourist information centres

Customer types: families, individuals, groups, young people, senior citizens, special interest groups, people with specific needs

7.1.1 *Identify, with examples, the main sectors of the UK travel industry*

MAIN SECTORS OF THE UK TRAVEL INDUSTRY

In this first performance criterion of the unit, we will be looking at the different parts of the UK travel industry:

▼ **retail travel (travel agencies)**
▼ **tour operators**
▼ **transport**
▼ **accommodation**

You will be able to see, as we develop the links, how the different parts work together to provide a whole service to the customer.

Retail travel

Travel agencies sell holidays on behalf of the following organisations:

▼ **tour operators**
▼ **airlines**
▼ **other transport companies**
▼ **hotel groups**

Travel agencies aim to help customers make informed choices about their holidays or mode of transport. They have a variety of different brochures to assist customers. They also have access to a great deal of information about travel and accommodation via their computer terminals. They use the terminals, known as computer reservation systems, to book holidays and transport. The database is able to tell them about the availability of transport and accommodation and they can confirm a booking for the customer by reserving a place on the transport or at the desti-

nation. This ensures that the customer gets the service that they have booked and that no other travel agency can sell the same seat or hotel room. In addition, customers will be able to use the vast experience of staff at the agencies. Once a decision has been made, the agency will make all the necessary booking arrangements for the customer.

The important thing to realise is that travel agencies do not 'stock' holidays. They do not buy any of the holidays or travel in advance. Agencies simply sell holidays or travel on behalf of the company providing them. They earn their money from what is known as commission. This is usually about 10 per cent of the total amount of the holiday or travel booking costs.

As we shall see later, travel agencies also provide the following services:

▼ **insurance**
▼ **currency exchange**
▼ **travellers' cheques**
▼ **guided tours**
▼ **tickets for entertainment events**

Tour operations

The names on the front of holiday brochures are usually the tour operators. These are the organisations who have put together the holidays featured in the brochure and had the brochures printed.

Europe has the largest and most influential tour operators. Some huge operators, like Thomson, sell as many as 3 million package holidays per year. Other tour operators may sell as few as 3–4,000.

As we will see later, there are basically three different types of tour operation. These are:

▼ *in-bound tour operators* **– who provide services for visitors to the UK**
▼ *out-bound tour operators* **– who provide services for UK residents abroad**
▼ *domestic tour operators* **– who provide services for UK residents visiting other parts of the UK (this includes Northern Ireland, the Isle of Man and the Isle of Wight).**

Fig. 7.1.1 *The AA offers a number of different packages and routes to the French Alps in its 'Ski Driveaway' brochure.*

Transport

The four main travel modes are air, sea, road and rail. Let us look at these in more detail.

Airlines

Air travel is extremely fast and reliable. There are only three things that can affect air travel:

▼ **bad weather conditions**
▼ **air traffic congestion**
▼ **flight-full zones over certain countries**

Wide-body jets, like the 747, allow more people to be carried on one flight and have reduced the cost per person enormously. Over London alone, more than 3,500 flights come in and out of the airports every day. About 85 per cent of all overseas travellers use airlines. Tour operators will use two different types of flight:

1   *charter flights* – which are sub-contracted aircraft used to help cope with high demand
2   *scheduled flights* – which are timetabled and will fly whether the aircraft is half full, full or nearly empty

Ferry companies

Ferry companies have come under some pressure recently with the opening of the Channel Tunnel, as cross-channel journeys are their most popular and profitable routes. In the new competitive climate, good ferry operators will survive and the poorer and more inefficient ones will fail. Many customers will continue to use cross-channel ferries despite the alternatives offered. There is still something to be said for getting out of your car, stretching your legs and having a break before facing a long drive to your next destination.

Ferries are also available for travel to the Isle of Wight, Northern Ireland, the Republic of Ireland, the Hebrides and the Shetland Islands. They form a vital link to these destinations for both tourists and business people.

Hovercraft and hydrofoils offer a faster (if bumpier) ride across the water. The main routes are to Belgium, France and the Isle of Wight.

Cruises represent a less-threatened aspect of the ferry companies' range of services. Cruises down the Nile in Egypt or around the Mediterranean or Caribbean, stopping off at exotic ports, are extremely popular.

Coach operators

Coach travel within the UK amounts to only 10 per cent of customers travelling to their destinations. Coaches are a relatively cheap alternative to rail travel. They have the following advantages:

▼ **they can provide very flexible pick-up and drop-off points**
▼ **they give the passenger good all-round views of the countryside and scenery**
▼ **most now have refreshments, toilets and videos (refreshments are supplied by stewards/stewardesses)**
▼ **they are comparatively safe as drivers have a specific speed limit and number of hours they can drive.**

There has been considerable debate regarding the safety of coaches, as there have been a number of horrific accidents which have caused fatalities. There are moves ahead to change the law so that all coach passengers must wear seat-belts and emergency exits are more clearly marked and numerous.

It is often said that coaches are the main culprits in congesting popular rural areas and cities in the summer months. Bear in mind, however, that coaches carry the same number of passengers as 30 or more cars. Taken as a whole, coaches still only provide 1 per cent of all transport needs of the UK.

Rail operators

Trains provide a fast and largely reliable service. They avoid the problems of parking and can take travellers right into the centre of a town or city.

Rail transport is in a state of major change in the UK. The nationalised service is gradually being sold off to private companies. Indeed, some of the new owners are coach operators. Interestingly the railways have played a large part in reviving tourism in areas where the rail network has been closed down. How can this be so? Well, private companies and charities have taken over these branch lines and put old-fashioned steam engines on them. They are very popular and you may already have visited one.

The Channel Tunnel and Le Shuttle link France and England (or London and Paris to be accurate). The trains run around the clock and are supposed to leave every 15 minutes; although in practice they have had some difficulties. On the first day of the service the train broke down, leaving all the passengers – including the owners of the company – stranded on the quayside.

Accommodation

There is a huge variety of accommodation available in the UK. These generally fall into five main categories: hotels, motels, guest houses, self-catering and holiday villages.

Hotels are basically overnight, furnished and serviced accommodation. The standard of accommodation will vary but, at the very least, they will all have a bed, wardrobe and table and chair. Some establishments may only have a handful of bedrooms, whereas others, such as the Dorchester Hotel in London, have hundreds of rooms and a staff of 600 or more. There are around 50,000 hotels, guest houses and bed and breakfast establishments in the UK, of which 40,000 have less than 10 rooms.

Motels are usually conveniently located alongside major transport routes. They tend to offer fairly basic facilities and are simply there to provide the opportunity for travellers to break their journey. They do, of course, cover a wide range of services and different standards of accommodation.

Guest houses are a cheaper alternative to conventional hotels. They are usually smaller than the average hotel with a handful of rooms. Normally, these are either people's homes or businesses in their own right. Accommodation is usually offered on a bed and breakfast or room only basis and the rooms will often be basic but pleasant. Many guest houses have regular customers who prefer the more friendly and family-orientated atmosphere.

Self-catering is less expensive than serviced accommodation and often appeals to tourists who wish to be more independent. There are

A Grade Cabin

D Grade Cabin

H Grade Cabin

J Grade Cabin

M Grade Cabin

Fig. 7.1.2 Aboard the QE2, there are a wide variety of different cabins available. This shows you do not have to be in a hotel to have a choice of facilities.

many different types of self-catering accommodation, and many of the facilities are privately owned and managed by companies on behalf of the owners. Typical examples of these would be

English Country Cottages, Hoseasons and Blakes Holidays.

Holiday villages provide a useful half-way service between hotels and self-catering. Whilst the visitors are able to cater for themselves in their own accommodation, they have all the services and facilities of a hotel on hand if they require them. Typical examples of holiday villages are those run by Pontins, Butlins and Center Parcs.

7.1.2 Describe the chain of distribution in the UK travel industry

CHAIN OF DISTRIBUTION

Organisations that make up the different parts of the UK travel industry form something known as the chain of distribution. This is really no different from the way in which all other products and services reach the high street for the customers to purchase.

The basic service, which is either transport, accommodation or excursions, is supplied by a provider. The provider sells its services to a tour operator, who, in turn, sells its services to the travel agencies. The travel agencies sell the package as a whole to the customer.

Obviously, each time the service is sold to the next part of the chain of distribution, the price of that service increases. The price that the customer pays is much more, therefore, than the price that the provider charged the tour operators.

We shall now look at the various layers of the distribution network. You will then understand the industry's structure and how the various travel products and services are provided to the customer.

Producers

Producers in the travel industry include transport providers, accommodation providers and excursion providers. When we consider the various parts of the chain of distribution, it is worth considering the fact that the majority of producers are members of associations which regulate their operations. The following are the major producer organisations:

▼ *International Air Transport Association (IATA).* This is a voluntary association, although 80 per cent of the world's airlines are members. It fixes fares on international routes and provides travellers with the assurance that tickets bought from its members will be valid and acceptable worldwide.

▼ *Civil Aviation Authority.* The Authority requires all British tour operators who sell package holidays to have an Air Travel Organiser's Licence. This, in turn, means that they have to lodge a bond or insurance policy against their business failing and leaving holiday-makers stranded.

▼ *Association of National Tourist Office Representatives.* This is a voluntary organisation, representing 80 different countries. It helps to promote different views about tourism worldwide.

▼ *British Incoming Tour Operators Association.* This represents tour operators that provide holidays, tours or other services in the UK for overseas visitors. There are currently around 100 members, which represents a quarter of all tour operators providing holiday services in the UK.

▼ *The Passenger Shipping Association.* This Association is approaching its 40th anniversary and was created to help face the challenge of airlines. It also offers up-to-date information and dispute settlement facilities for customers.

▼ *Association of British Travel Agents*

(ABTA). **This was formed just after the last war and is an independent self-regulating association with members drawn from travel agents and tour operators. Importantly, it has created codes of practice which it expects all of its members to adhere to.**

Wholesalers

The wholesalers in the travel industry are known as tour operators. When we think about tour operators, we tend to consider only the ones that provide holidays for UK residents. In fact, these are only part of the overall picture. **Out-bound** tour operators concentrate on providing holiday services for UK customers going abroad. They are able to provide the following:

▼ **short-haul tours (e.g. France, Belgium, Holland)**
▼ **medium-haul tours (e.g. Spain, south of France or Greece)**
▼ **long-haul tours (e.g. USA, South Africa, Hong Kong)**

In-bound tour operators, on the other hand, cater for visitors to the UK. They provide a variety of services, such as full package holidays, tours and other tourism services.

Retailers

Retailers in the travel industry include travel agencies and ticketing offices. As we have seen, travel agencies are convenient places for the sale of holidays and package tours. The agents receive a commission on the sales they make and are responsible for selling and promoting various products and services on the behalf of the tour operators. Some of the travel agencies are actually owned by tour operators, such as Lunn Poly, who are owned by Thomson holidays, and Thomas Cook, who have their own travel agencies nationwide. The large chains of retail travel agencies include:

▼ **Lunn Poly**
▼ **Going Places**
▼ **Thomas Cook**

▼ **A T Mayes**
▼ **Co-op Travelcare**

There are a number of shop outlets that provide ticket services for both entertainment (e.g. theatres and concerts) and travel (e.g. coaches, railways and airlines). They are usually reasonably competitive and offer a number of special deals. In fact, some special events only offer their tickets through these offices. You can find ticketing offices in Virgin Megastores, large department stores and as an additional service in travel agencies.

Customers

Customers are the final link in the chain of distribution. They are constantly looking for good value for money, a high level of service and a responsive approach from all parts of the distribution chain. Primarily, they deal with retailers, although on occasions providers deal directly with customers.

7.1.3 *Describe different types of travel products and services*

TRAVEL PRODUCTS AND SERVICES

In this performance criterion we will be looking at the specific products and services provided by the travel industry and associated organisations. The focus in this performance criterion is on the product or service as seen by and provided to the customer.

Package holidays

Package holidays are perhaps the most common form of travel product. A package holiday is very convenient as it includes:

▼ the cost of the travel to and from the destination
▼ all airport duties and taxes
▼ the cost of accommodation at the destination
▼ the cost of getting to the accommodation from the airport (and vice versa)

The package is, in fact, an all-in product. The customer does not have to worry about any aspect of the holiday, except, perhaps, for insurance. Normally the package will also include some of the following:

▼ breakfast
▼ mid-day meals
▼ evening meals
▼ child care
▼ excursions
▼ car hire

Fig. 7.1.3 Cunard offers all-inclusive package cruises aboard the Sea Goddess 1 *and 2 to the Caribbean, Mediterranean and Far East.*

Horizon was the first organisation to offer package holidays in the early 1950s. This development was made possible by the availability of jet aircraft.

Transport bookings

There are always booking conditions for all modes of transport (plane, train, ferry, coach), and these will be made clear to customers by the transport provider. Customers would normally be expected to:

▼ pay a deposit
▼ pay the balance within a specified time
▼ pay an extra fee if they make alterations to the booking

The transport provider will also provide information on refunds and mention the penalties that have to be paid if the customer makes a cancellation. Normally, the closer the cancellation is to the departure date, the less money the customer will receive back from the transport provider. According to the ABTA Code of Conduct, customers are entitled to compensation if there are major changes to their booking arrangements by the transport provider.

Foreign currency

Exchanging foreign currency can be very profitable to the service provider, as well as being convenient to the customer. The company will sell foreign currency at a higher price than they bought it for and this is how profit is made. Let us take an example to show how it works.

The customer wants to buy £100 worth of Greek drachma. The provider gives an exchange rate of 340 DR per £1 sterling. This means that the customer gets 34,000 DR for £100 (less, of course, the commission that will be charged on this transaction). The provider probably got the drachma at a rate of 350 DR per £1 sterling, which means that he or she spent only £97. The provider has made a profit of £3. When the provider buys back any unused drachma from the customer, there is another

BOOKING TERMS & CONDITIONS

Automobile Association Developments Limited trading as AA Motoring Holidays, is a wholly owned subsidiary of The Automobile Association Limited. These terms and conditions explain your rights and responsibilities and those of AA Motoring Holidays. Please read it carefully before completing the AA Motoring Holidays Booking Form. The word "you" means the client and the word "we" means AA Motoring Holidays.

HOW TO MAKE YOUR BOOKING

1. You must complete and sign an AA Motoring Holidays Booking Form. A deposit of £100 per party must accompany the booking form together with any additional deposit relevant to the booking.
2. A contract will exist only from the date shown on the confirmation invoice, which will be issued when a booking is made.

PRICES, SURCHARGES AND PAYMENTS

3. You must pay the balance of the total price not later than 8 weeks before the departure date. If not, we reserve the right to cancel the holiday and to treat it as if it were cancelled by you and the scale of cancellation charges shown in clause 6 will apply. If you book within 8 weeks of departure we will require full payment at the time of booking.
4. The price of your travel arrangements is fully guaranteed and will not be subject to any surcharges.
5. You should be aware that local taxes can be introduced in holiday areas at any time and payment would be your responsibility.

CANCELLATION OR ALTERATION

BY YOU THE CLIENT

6. Cancellation must be notified to AA Motoring Holidays in writing and will be effective from the date received. In the event of cancellation by you we will retain your deposit and in addition may apply cancellation charges up to the amount shown below.

Amount of notice you give us before the scheduled departure date.	
More than 56 days	Deposit
29-56 days	30%
15 - 28 days	45%
1 - 14 days	80%

No refunds are made by us for cancellations on or after the date of departure.

7. A late booking is a booking made within 8 weeks of the departure date and for which full payment of the total price is required on booking. In the event of you cancelling a late booking, you will indemnify us in accordance with the cancellation charges set out in Clause 6.
8. If after your booking has been accepted you wish to make any material change or alteration to your booking we shall do our utmost to satisfy your requirements. We do however reserve the right to charge an amendment fee of £15 per party for each change made and £30 per party for any change made after the Travel Documents have been issued. If you notify us within 8 weeks of your departure date that you wish to transfer to a new departure date then cancellation charges will apply as set out in Clause 6.
9. (1) Ferry tickets are issued as part of a total package and partial refund cannot be considered. (2) First nights' open hotel voucher is non-refundable. All other open vouchers incur £10 per party administration fee on refund.
10. We recommend that you take our holiday insurance to cover the difficulties that may be caused by your cancellation.

BY AA MOTORING HOLIDAYS

11. In normal circumstances we will make every effort not to cancel or make a material alteration to your holiday after the date when the balance becomes due unless it becomes necessary to do so as a result of hostilities, political unrest or other circumstances outside of our reasonable control.
12. If we cancel or make a material alteration to your holiday
(1) at any time prior to commencement of your holiday due to hostilities, political unrest or other circumstances outside of our reasonable control amounting to force majeure OR
(2) between the time a booking is made and the balance becomes due for any other reason then you will be notified without delay and offered the choice of a comparable alternative holiday, or one of a lower cost with a refund of the difference in price, or a full refund of all money paid. Such refunds will be made within 14 clear days of receiving your request for a refund.
13. In the unlikely event that we cancel or make a material alteration to your holiday on or after the balance becomes due for some reason other than as a result of unusual and unforseeable circumstances beyond our control or your default then, in addition to your rights under Clause 12 you will receive the following compensation per person.

Date of notification to your travel agent:

More than 56 days before departure:	Nil
56-43 days before departure:	£5.00
42-29 days before departure	£10.00
28-15 days before departure:	£15.00
Less than 15 days before departure	£20.00

FERRY AND TRANSPORT SERVICES

14. Your contract with AA Motoring Holidays is subject to the terms and conditions of carriage imposed by the ferry companies for the cross-channel service, and to the standard conditions of carriage imposed by the Societe Nationale des Chemins de Fer Francais for travel by rail within France. Copies of these terms and conditions are available on request. Tickets for travel within France are subject to the appropriate section of the French Civil Code and the Code de Commerce. Copies of these terms and conditions are available on request. Eurotunnel as owner/operator of Le Shuttle accepts no responsibility for the contents of this brochure. Changes to ferry and train service schedules are beyond our control and we cannot accept responsibility for any loss or inconvenience to you or your party as a result.

YOUR RESPONSIBILITY FOR THE HOLIDAY ACCOMMODATION

15. You must ensure that the accommodation, furniture and fittings are left clean and in good condition. You will be liable to pay for any damage (fair wear and tear excepted) or missing items.
16. The accommodation shall only be used by the persons indicated on the AA Motoring Holidays Booking Form. Subletting is not permitted. Assignment is not normally permitted and will usually be treated as a cancellation of the holiday. If you are unavoidably prevented from proceeding with your holiday and give reasonable notice of this prior to the departure date then you may transfer your holiday to a person who meets any conditions we may have imposed in relation to your holiday. Please note however that both you and the person to whom the holiday is transferred will be responsible for the payment of the holiday (or any balance) and for any additional costs or expenses incurred by us in making the transfer.

COMPLAINTS PROCEDURE, CONCILIATION AND ARBITRATION

17. If you are dissatisfied with your holiday accommodation, you are advised to contact the local agent at the earliest opportunity or phone AA Motoring Holidays (01256 814433) during the normal office hours shown in this brochure so that a speedy remedy can be sought. In any event, AA Motoring Holidays shall not be liable for any claim made with respect to your holiday as booked (including, but not limited to, travel arrangements, accommodation, or any services provided) unless we have received written notice from you within 28 days of the completion of your holiday.
18. Disputes arising out of, or in connection with this contract, which cannot be amicably settled, may (if the customer so wishes) be referred to arbitration under a special Scheme which, though devised by arrangement with the Association of British Travel Agents, is administered quite independently by the Chartered Institute of Arbitrators. The Scheme (details of which will be supplied on request) provides for a simple and inexpensive method of arbitration on documents alone with restricted liability on the customer in respect of costs. The Scheme does not apply to claims for an amount greater than £1500 per person or £7500 per booking form or to claims which are solely or mainly in respect of physical injury or illness or the consequences of such injury or illness. If you elect to seek redress under this Scheme, written notice requesting arbitration under this Scheme must be made within nine months after the scheduled date of return from the holiday but in special circumstances it may still be offered outside the period.
19. The information given in this brochure is believed to be correct at time of going to press. We attempt to give as full and accurate details as possible. However, amendment to the information can sometimes occur. In particular some of the facilities or services shown as available may not be available throughout the year. AA Motoring Holidays cannot take responsibility for any facilities that are not open as a result of seasonal influences where you are advised as to non-availability. "Please note that local amenities and facilities i.e. those not specifically attached to the accommodation booked and services which are not supplied by ourselves or our agents are outside of our reasonable control and do not form part of our contract with you. AA Motoring Holidays cannot be held responsible should they be unavailable
20. (1) AA Motoring Holidays accepts responsibility
(a) should the services we are contractually obliged to provide prove deficient or not of a reasonable standard.
(b) for the acts and/or omission of our employees, agents, sub-contractors and/or suppliers, save that, except as provided in Clause 20(2) below, no liability is accepted for death, bodily injury or illness.
(2) AA Motoring Holidays accepts responsibility for the negligent acts and omissions of
(a) our employees or agents and
(b) our suppliers, sub-contractors, servants and/or agents of the same, whilst acting within the scope of, or in the course of their employment in respect of claims arising as a result of death, bodily injury or illness caused to you and/or any other of the named persons on the booking form.
(3) AA Motoring Holidays liability under sub clauses 20(1) and 20(2) above shall be limited in the manner provided by any relevant international convention.
Note: AA Motoring Holidays will not be liable for any damage, loss or expense of any kind (including personal injury) suffered by you or any of your party which results from unusual and unforseeable circumstancess beyond our control (including the act of any third party) which we could not, with due care, have avoided or from an event which we or our suppliers could not, with due care, foresee or forestall.
(4) AA Motoring Holidays shall, where appropriate and subject to its reasonable discretion
(a) offer general assistance to you or any other person named on the booking form who, through misadventure, suffer illness, personal injury or death during the period of your holiday arising out of an activity which does not form part of your holiday or an excursion arranged through us.
(b) where legal action is undertaken by you in connection with 20(4)(a) above with our prior agreement the initial legal costs associated therewith shall be met by us, provided you request such assistance within 90 days from the date of the misadventure. The aggregate payable by us in relation to this Clause 20(4) shall not exceed a total of £5,000 per booking form. Furthermore, in the event of there being a successful claim for costs against a third party or there being a suitable insurance policy/ies in force costs actually incurred by us shall be recoverable from you.
(5) If any Payment is made by AA Motoring Holidays to you or to a person in your party in respect of any claim AA Motoring Holidays are subrogated to all the rights of recovery you or such member of your party may have in relation to that claim. AA Motoring Holidays shall be entitled to take action in relation to such claim at its own expense but in your name or that of the party member concerned.
21. In the event that any terms of the booking contract are unlawful or ineffective the remainder of the booking contract shall not be affected thereby.

WHICH LAW GOVERNS THIS CONTRACT?

22. This contract and all matters arising from it are governed by English Law and the courts in England shall have exclusive jurisdiction. This brochure is valid for travel 15th December 1994 to 15th January 1996.

Fig. 7.1.4 The booking terms and conditions for AA Motoring Holidays. They state clearly the rights and responsibilities of the AA when entering into a contract with the customer.

AA

Motoring Holidays

ABTA 65626

BOOKING FORM 1995

For Reservations
call 01256 814433

Agent's Stamp

Telephone Booking No.

Book at your local AA shop or send this form to:
AA Motoring Holidays,
Norfolk House, Priestley Road, Basingstoke RG24 9NY

Data Protection Act
The Automobile Association and its associated companies may use relevant information provided by you to supply you with details of their full range of services and products. The Association as a matter of policy does not sell, rent or exchange its lists with third parties.

Client's Name and Address

NAME

ADDRESS

POSTCODE

HOME TEL. NO. (STD CODE)

WORK TEL. NO. (STD CODE)

SELF-CATERING/BOATING HOLIDAYS

Choice of Resorts	Type of Accommodation/Resort name	Date of Arrival	Date of Departure	Number of Nights
First Resort				
Second Resort				
Third Resort				
Fourth Resort				

TRAVEL REQUIREMENTS (Please tick as appropriate) ☐ LE SHUTTLE ☐ FERRY ☐ HOVERSPEED ☐ MOTORAIL

Preferred Company				
Outward Route		Date and Time		Cabins/Seats
Inward Route		Date and Time		Cabins/Seats
MOTORAIL Outward Route		Date	Class	Type of Sleeping Accom.
MOTORAIL Inward Route		Date	Class	Type of Sleeping Accom.

VEHICLE DETAILS

	Model	Year	Reg. No.	Length	Height (if over 1.63M inc. roof rack)	Luggage or Boat Trailer		No. of Passengers		
						Length (inc. tow bars)	Height	Ad	Ch 4-13	Inf 0-3
1st Vehicle										
2nd Vehicle										

OVERNIGHT HOTEL RESERVATIONS

	Date	Number of Nights	Town	Hotel Group	Type and Number of Rooms Required each Night	
Pre Booked Hotel Reservations Required					Room Type	Number Required
					Single	
					Twin/Double	
					Triple	
					Family Room (Novotel/Mercure)	

AA FIVE STAR SERVICE

☆☆☆☆☆

AA Five Star Service

We believe that AA Five Star Service is essential to protect you, your family and your car when motoring abroad. Please enter the appropriate premium in the payment box below. Please note that. without Five Star Personal you will not be insured for cancellation or medical expenses.

MY INSURERS ARE (if not taking AA Five Star Personal)

Surname and initials of all the party	Male or Female	Ages of children under 16 on sailing date and date of birth

PAYMENT

Deposit £100 per party (or full payment if booked within 8 weeks of departure)	£
En route hotel booking deposit (£10)	£
Extra Motorail deposit (£60)	£

AA Five Star Service (see page 47 for additional premiums and cover)

Date leaving home _____ Date returning home _____

Vehicle Cover		Included
Vehicle cover premium for stays over 17 days	£	
Vehicle Plus Cover (vehicles under 15 years only)	£	
Personal Cover	£	

Cheque enclosed OR
I wish to pay by Access* ☐ or Visa* ☐ *(please tick appropriate box) £ _____
Please charge the above amount to my Card Account

Card Number ☐☐☐☐ ☐☐☐☐ ☐☐☐☐ ☐☐☐☐

Name and address of cardholder (if different from above) (BLOCK CAPITALS)

Expiry Date _____

Declaration
For myself and all persons named in this application form, I request the above holiday and facilities. I have the authority of all such persons to make the bookings on their behalf and to give the declarations on this page. I declare that I/we have read and accept the Booking Conditions on page 48 of the brochure. I warrant the truth of the above and that I am over 18 years old. I further declare I/we understand that no benefits can be afforded under this application if for any reason the foregoing does not represent the true position. In addition, I agree to accept and comply with the terms and conditions of AA Five Star Service as set out in the Five Star Service Handbook. I enclose payment as detailed.

Signature _____ Date _____

Cardholder's Signature _____ Date _____

Automobile Association Developments Ltd. Registered in England No. 1878835. VAT No. 363-3221-79. Registered Office: Norfolk House, Priestley Road, Basingstoke, Hants RG24 9NY.

Fig. 7.1.5 A booking form for AA Motoring Holidays. The customer's booking requirements are detailed on a single sheet in a clear and logical manner.

chance for him or her to make money. For selling the drachma, the customer may be quoted an exchange rate of 360 DR per £1 sterling. The customer would therefore now need 36,000 DR to get back the original £100.

Foreign currency will be available at:

▼ hotels
▼ banks
▼ building societies
▼ Bureaux de Change
▼ airports
▼ ferry ports
▼ post offices
▼ various supermarkets and larger shops on the continent

finding out

PC 7.1.3
COM 1.1, 1.2, 1.3

In pairs, find out the current exchange rate of the pound sterling for the currencies of the countries listed below:

• Holland
• France
• Germany
• Italy
• Portugal
• Japan

Passports and visas

If you are travelling overseas, you will require a passport and possibly a visa. But what are these and how are they used?

A passport is basically an identification card. It proves that you are who you say you are. You do not need a passport to travel around the EC, but it is a good idea to have one with you all the same. Passports are easily obtainable using a form available at all main post offices. You will need to fill in the form, provide photographs and other means of identification, enclose the fee and send it off to your local passport office.

Visas are printed or stamped into your passport by countries who restrict the entry of foreign visitors. The Passport Office will be able to tell you whether you need a visa to visit a particular country. Visas are available on request from the embassy of the country in question. The main types of visa are:

▼ tourist (the most common)
▼ transit (which means you are passing through the country)
▼ immigrant (for those who intend to stay for good)
▼ diplomatic (for representatives of other governments)

Accommodation and catering

We will now consider the different types of services available in hotels and other establishments. The star or crown system categorises hotels and accommodation by the quality and provision of additional services. The following types of rooms or suites of rooms available in hotels are:

▼ *single* – a room for one person
▼ *twin* – a room with two single beds for two people
▼ *double* – as for twin, but with one large bed
▼ *twin double* – a room with two double beds for three to four people
▼ *suite* – one or two bedrooms and a living room
▼ *duplex* – a two-storey suite connected by stairs
▼ *connecting rooms* – two or more rooms with private doors connecting the individual rooms
▼ *studio apartment* – any of the above with a kitchenette
▼ *cabanas* – rooms next to the swimming pool area, often separate from the main hotel building
▼ *en suite or private facilities* – the occupier has the sole use of a bathroom, shower and toilet facility

Turning our attention to catering, there are a number of different tariffs or levels of catering available. These are:

▼ *room only* – no meals included in the price
▼ *continental breakfast* – a roll or pastry, juice, coffee and/or tea
▼ *English breakfast* – a cooked breakfast, as well as cereal, toast, tea and/or coffee
▼ *half board* – breakfast and evening meal
▼ *full board* – breakfast, lunch and evening meal

7.1.4 *Describe sources of information on travel products and services*

SOURCES OF INFORMATION

In this performance criterion we return to the different sectors of the travel industry and look briefly at the kinds of information available to potential customers. If you need to be reminded about the nature of these sectors, you should refer back to Section 7.1.1.

We will be looking at the following sources of information:

▼ travel agencies
▼ transport providers (railway stations, coach stations, airports, ferry ports)
▼ tourist information centres

These sources are found throughout the UK. They have been selected as the most convenient for you to visit and gain information for the element assignment.

Travel agencies

Travel agencies are normally able to provide information on all the following:

▼ package and group tours
▼ holiday centres
▼ special interest holidays
▼ hotels
▼ theatres
▼ bargain breaks
▼ coach tours
▼ car rental
▼ car ferries

▼ **British and continental rail and motorail travel**
▼ **cruises**
▼ **airline reservations**
▼ **passport, visa and health requirements**
▼ **baggage and airport information**
▼ **insurance**
▼ **business travel**
▼ **complaints procedures**

Much of the basic information can be obtained by collecting brochures from a travel agency. However, it may be difficult to gauge the total range of facilities and services offered without actually asking a member of staff.

Transport providers

Railway stations, coach stations, airports and ferry ports are good sources of information about transport. At most stations and ports there will be leaflets and brochures available on the different services offered, as well as timetables and price lists. If you are close to a main line station where they have a manned ticket and booking office, you may be able to request further information which is not readily available in the racks or dispensers.

Tourist information centres

As we said in other units, tourist information centres provide one of the primary sources of information on local travel products and services. They routinely stock a wide range of different leaflets and brochures from most of the travel and tourism providers in the area. They are of particular use in advising visitors on accommodation, catering and local transport.

7.1.5 Match travel products and services with different customer types

CUSTOMER TYPES

This performance criterion asks you to match the different travel products and services with the various common customer types. This is an integral part of the element assignment and you will need to think very carefully about how you intend to suggest certain travel and tourism products and services to the customer. In this section we will look at the different needs of these customer types.

Families

Families are generally interested in package holidays which incorporate as many additional services and activities as possible. They need to be advised about appropriate accommodation, which may have facilities for small children and babies. It may also be useful for you to identify destinations which have baby care or child listening services, since these would greatly enhance a family's ability to relax whilst on holiday. In terms of catering, families need to know about eating establishments which welcome children as customers, and have child menus and high chairs.

Individuals and groups

People who are travelling on their own may wish to be informed of places they can visit in order to meet other people. Many specialised package holidays provide facilities which are ideal for the lone traveller. Club 18–30, for example, caters largely for individuals or small groups who wish to meet people of a similar age in a holiday environment.

Groups have varied interests and demands. The travel provider must ensure that the different demands of members within the group are addressed as well as possible. In many cases, however, this will be a question of compromise in terms of destination, facilities, activities and other services.

Obviously groups will attract a considerable discount; individual travellers, on the other hand, may be expected to pay single room supplements which could increase the overall cost of their travel and holiday arrangements.

Young people and senior citizens

There is a wide gulf between the interests and demands of these two groups of customers. If we assume that the young people are independent travellers and not part of a family group, they will be looking for travel products and services which are both interesting and exciting.

Senior citizens, on the other hand, may be looking for a relaxing break. Tour operators such as Saga Holidays provide a wide range of different cruises and coach holidays which cater for all their needs, including transport of luggage and organisation of excursions whilst at the destination.

Many thousands of senior citizens spend several months abroad each year in hotels in Spain, for example. They find that the cost of the travel and accommodation is far less than their heating bills would have been had they stayed at home.

Special interest groups

There are a huge number of travel providers who cater for special interest groups and offer some of the following:

▼ **battlefield tours**
▼ **adventure holidays**
▼ **pony trekking holidays**
▼ **cycling holidays**
▼ **arts and crafts activity holidays**
▼ **sports training camps**
▼ **murder and mystery weekends**

People with specific needs

It should not be assumed that all travellers are able to cope with the rigours of travelling without specific help. Tour, transport and travel providers have taken great steps in recent years to cater for people with specific needs, such as those who are blind and partially sighted, physically or mentally disabled, obese, or travelling with small babies. Some providers charge supplements in order to off-set the additional costs to them in providing these services.

assignment

ELEMENT 7.1

PC 7.1.1–5
COM 1.1, 1.2, 1.3, 1.4

In order to fulfil the performance criteria of this element, you will need to identify the main sectors of the UK travel industry; this will help you understand how the industry works. By matching the products and services to different customer types, you will be able to appreciate different customer needs for the various travel products and services.

| task | 1 | PC 7.1.1 |

Create a diagram which identifies the main sectors of the UK travel industry. You should include an example of each of the following sectors: retail travel, tour operations, transport, and accommodation.

| task | 2 | PC 7.1.2–4 |

Briefly describe the travel products and services and identify where you can obtain information about these. You should try to link your description to the chain of distribution in the UK travel industry.

| task | 3 | PC 7.1.5 |

Create a grid which matches at least two different travel products and services to three different customer types. You should use products and services mentioned in the range statement.

Notes
You could probably obtain the majority of information required for this element assignment by visiting your local travel agency.

element 7.2

INVESTIGATE THE PROVISION OF TOURISM PRODUCTS AND SERVICES

Performance criteria

A student must:

1 Identify, with examples, different **types of tourism products and services**.

2 Explain the **appeal** of tourism products and services to different **customer types**.

3 Suggest **reasons** for the relative popularity of different tourism products and services.

4 Describe **sources of information** on tourism products and services.

RANGE

Types of tourism products and services: tourist attractions (theme parks, national parks, resorts, heritage sites, galleries, theatres), accommodation (hotels, motels, guest houses, self-catering, holiday villages), catering, tourist boards, tourist information centres, guiding services, transport

Appeal: entertainment, culture, education, information, relaxation, health, recreation; cost, availablility, accessibility

Customer types: families, individuals, groups, young people, senior citizens, special interest groups, people with specific needs

Reasons: appeal, novelty value (of new products and services)

Sources of information: tourist boards (national, regional, local), tourist information centres, libraries, guiding services, accommodation providers, transport providers (railway stations, coach stations, airports, ferry ports)

7.2.1 *Identify, with examples, different types of tourism products and services*

TYPES OF TOURISM PRODUCTS AND SERVICES

In this part of the element we will, very briefly, go back over the different aspects of the industry and identify some of the key issues.

Tourist attractions

There is a diverse range of popular tourist attractions in the UK, including theme parks, national parks, resorts, heritage sites, galleries and theatres.

Theme parks

The major theme parks have had a marked impact on the tourist industry in the UK. They not only cater for UK residents, but also attract large numbers of overseas visitors. It is very big business, with new rides costing as much as £10 million to complete. Some of the theme parks have been built on new sites, such as derelict land (Thorpe Park) or old gravel pits (Alton Towers). Others have been constructed around stately homes (Beaulieu) or zoos (Chessington).

National parks

The national parks provide a firm foundation for the protection of the natural environment. They are huge areas of unspoilt landscape that appeal to thousands of people every year. They have proved to have long-term popularity, with visitors willing to pay nominal entrance fees to certain parts of the national parks. There are five national parks on the coast alone.

Resorts

Considering that the UK is made up of 6,100 islands, with 720 off the coast of England, there is little wonder that the resorts around the 3,240 mile coastline are popular. In 1994, British citizens took 24.5 million seaside holidays in the UK, 18.5 million of which were in England (that is nearly 4 in 10 of all holiday trips). They spent a staggering £4.1 billion. In addition, 110 million day visits to the seaside were made.

Heritage sites

The heritage aspect of the travel industry includes visits to:

▼ **historic cities**
▼ **cathedrals and churches**
▼ **castles**
▼ **stately homes and their gardens**
▼ **archaeological sites**
▼ **industrial heritage sites**
▼ **museums and galleries**
▼ **literary heritage sites**
▼ **traditional events and pageants**

Over 57 million visits are made to historic houses, castles and gardens in an average year. This accounts for 20 per cent of all of the visits to attractions. About 40 per cent of people in the UK visit at least one historic building every year. They are very popular with overseas visitors, 67 per cent of whom state that heritage visits are a key reason for coming to the UK.

Theatres

The theatre has suffered in recent years because people have found it difficult to afford this relatively expensive entertainment, although it does thrive in certain cities in the UK. One of the major problems that people encounter is the fact that they have to book many weeks in advance and so need to be informed about forthcoming attractions.

Accommodation

For information regarding this aspect of tourism, please refer to Element 7.1 where we discussed different forms of accommodation (hotels, motels, guest houses, self-catering and holiday villages) in some detail.

Catering

Again, please refer to Element 7.1 where the nature and provision of catering within the UK was discussed in some detail.

Catering also includes the many restaurants, public houses and cafés that are situated around the UK. You will notice that there are even more of these in areas that attract visitors. They may be a part of the tourist attraction itself, or situated close by so that they can attract visitors.

Tourist boards and tourist information centres

There are over 700 tourist information centres in the UK and they all have the following features:

▼ **they are free**
▼ **they are nationwide**
▼ **the staff are trained by regional and national tourist organisations**
▼ **they are well supplied with display materials, brochures and leaflets**

Manchester Youth Hostel

Potato Wharf, Off Liverpool Road, Manchester, M3 4NB
Tel: 0161 839 9960 · Fax: 0161 835 2054

The Youth Hostel

A brand new purpose-built Youth Hostel situated in the Urban Regeneration Park of Castlefield right in the heart of the city. The Hostel offers accommodation in ultra-modern rooms, mostly sleeping four – with *en suite* facilities – and there are specially adapted facilities for people with disabilities.

Museums, galleries, historic houses, shops, restaurants are all on the Hostel's doorstep, making it an ideal destination for an enjoyable city breaks for groups, families and individuals alike.

Opening Times · 24 hours a day, every day of the year. Reception is open between 0700 and 2300 hours daily.

Bedrooms

▲ accommodates up to 150 people
▲ bed breakdown: 31x4 beds, 4x6 beds, 2x4 bed (disabled)
▲ all bedrooms have *en suite* facilities, bedlights, secure luggage lockers and central heating
▲ there are additional toilets on every floor

Facilities

▲ a large lounge
▲ TV room
▲ well-equipped games room
▲ large, modern cafeteria
▲ self-catering kitchen
▲ three meeting/classrooms
▲ attractions booking service
▲ small shop selling souvenirs
▲ coin-operated laundry
▲ payphones
▲ parking for cars and coaches

Meals

▲ large restaurant seating 72
▲ licensed to sell beer and wine with meals
▲ breakfast, packed lunches and three-course evening meals are available
▲ self-catering kitchen

Accommodation at Manchester Youth Hostel

Attractions

Close to the Youth Hostel:
■ *Granada Studios Tour* · a valuable insight into the making of television programmes and films, including sets from Coronation Street, Downing Street and Hollywood
■ *The Museum of Science & Industry* · charts the progress of scientific discoveries and the development of industry particularly in the region
■ *Manchester United Football Club Museum and Tour Centre* · the Museum details the history of the club – stadium tours are available
■ *Salford Quays* · redeveloped dock area of Salford with a Heritage Centre exploring the history of the docks and Trafford Park
■ *Salford Mining Museum* · reconstructed coal mine tracing the history of mining
■ *Salford Museum and Art Gallery* · home to the Lowry collection and a recreated northern street of yesteryear at Lark
■ *river trips* · guided trips in glass-topped boats along the canals
■ *Jewish Museum* · outlines the calendar of Jewish events and festivals
■ *Tatton Park* · a working farm set in the era of the 1930s
■ *Quarry Bank Mill* · a working mill dating back to the 18th century

How to Book

To make a reservation, simply contact:
● *individuals and families* tel: 0161 839 9960 · fax: 0161 835 2054
● *groups* (educational/non-educational) tel: 0161 839 9960 · fax: 0161 835 2054
● *operators and travel agents* tel: 01727 845047 · fax: 01727 846170

Castlefield

How to Find Us

➤ *from Piccadilly and Victoria train stations and the bus station* · take the Metrolink and disembark at G-Mex station, or bus 33 route from Piccadilly
➤ *from the airport* · take the rail link to Piccadilly station, then Metro to G-Mex
➤ *by road* · follow signs for Castlefield/ Museum of Science and Industry and we are next door to the Castlefield Hotel

Fig. 7.2.1 Manchester Youth Hostel is ideally positioned for all the major attractions in Manchester city centre, including the Granada Studios Tour, the Manchester United Football Club Museum and Tour Centre, and the Museum of Science and Technology (courtesy of YHA and Hostelling International).

▼ they can answer questions about visitor attractions within a 50-mile or 80-km radius
▼ they are able to tell you about garages, restaurants and other facilities in the area

We will be looking at the nature of the national, regional and local tourist boards in Section 7.2.4.

Guiding services

Many areas with distinct attractions provide a range of guiding services so that visitors can experience all the facilities available. Typically, these guided tours will be either on foot or by coach or bus. Many of the guided tours are provided by local councils or local bus and coach operators.

Transport

The different modes of transport available include planes, trains, ferries, coaches and, at a local level, taxis, buses and underground provision. We have again looked at this aspect of travel and tourism in some depth in Element 7.1 and you will find all the necessary information there.

THE NEW FOREST ENCOUNTER

he New Forest Encounter offers the opportunity to experience the real forest in the company of people who have lived and worked there throughout their lives. Your host's recollections and anecdotes will bring the living history and heritage of the New Forest alive.

Every New Forest Encounter not only puts visitors in touch with the forest's spectacular landscapes but also its people and the characteristic way of life which sets this area apart as a unique survivor of England's Royal Hunting Forests.

All Encounters start at the New Forest Visitor Information Centre, where you meet your host and collect your welcome packs. You then travel by coach deep into the forest before disembarking for a gentle walk with your host while he explains and shows you just what makes the New Forest so special.

Additional options include a visit to the New Forest Museum to see the "Changing Forest" audio visual and forest life exhibition.

Prices for the New Forest Encounter start at £4.50 per person, bookings can be made through your accommodation provider or direct at the New Forest Visitor Information Centre, tel: (01703) 282269.

Fig. 7.2.2 The New Forest Encounter is just one of the many guiding services on offer in the Hampshire region (courtesy of South Hams).

7.2.2 Explain the appeal of tourism products and services to different customers

APPEAL

In this performance criterion you will be expected to choose four tourism products or services and assess the appeal of them to at least two different customer types. We have offered some suggestions as to how you might go about this. By using the companion volume to this book, *Foundation Leisure and Tourism*, you will find that Unit 2 has covered many of these aspects already.

Entertainment: cost, availability and accessibility

In this rather broad category, you should consider the travel and tourism products and services that are designed simply for entertainment and enjoyment. In any given area, you are likely to find a huge variety of different forms of entertainment to suit all pockets. You can generally gain access to them fairly freely, although the more popular events may be booked up well in advance of the event date.

Culture: cost, availability and accessibility

Ballet, opera and classical music are some of the tourism products and services that are claimed to be culture. Whether they have any artistic merit at all is debatable. In any event, they are far too old-fashioned and dated to be of any great relevance to the majority of the population. Of much greater importance now in terms of influence on the UK are the architectural culture, modern culture and impact of other cultures.

Access to the ballet, opera and classical music performances is limited as the price of the tickets excludes the overwhelming majority of the population. The availability is also limited to larger and more select venues around the UK. In the case of more important cultural activities, they often attract greater subsidies and are far more open to the general public as a result.

Education: cost, availability and accessibility

Some attractions have designed educational materials to encourage educational visits and other interested parties. These educational materials are normally free, but the visitors still have to pay an entrance fee (often reduced for students). The educational material is usually well written and designed for a particular age or interest group. Typical examples of attractions which offer educational materials are the Granada Studios Tour and Pleasurewood Hills.

Most museums offer very comprehensive educational facilities and activities. Many of them

Fig. 7.2.3 The Granada Studios Tour offers specific educational opportunities, including pre-prepared packs for GNVQ Leisure and Tourism (courtesy of Granada Studios).

have staff dedicated to catering for educational visits and others have produced educational material that can be used during and after the visit.

Information: cost, availability and accessibility

The majority of information is available free and in a wide variety of different sites. The cost and availability of information is governed by the providers of the products and services, who are keen to attract as many customers as possible. Accessibility can only be measured in terms of how clearly the information is laid out and written. Most information material can be picked up easily and at no cost (or at most the price of a telephone call). Customers are generally expected to pay for souvenir guides or booklets, however, which provide more detailed information about the attraction or activity.

Relaxation: cost, availability and accessibility

Some users of facilities, products and services are looking mainly for an opportunity to relax and escape the normal pressures of life. Basic relaxation on beaches does not cost any more than the cost of transport to the beach, but there are other, more expensive, facilities that offer relaxation and quiet holidays, such as Center Parcs and other holiday villages. Obviously, the sort of relaxation preferred by the customer will determine the location. The accessibility or availability may be more difficult if the customer wishes to travel to a specific location for this relaxation. The most costly form of relaxation must be cruises; a relaxing cruise around the Greek islands or the West Indies can cost the customer thousands of pounds.

Health: cost, availability and accessibility

The general availability of health clubs, farms and other facilities has increased greatly over the past few years. The cost is high, but the benefits are supposed to outweigh the price that is paid for the services. Access and availability is high as most areas have health clubs and other facilities that offer some of the following:

▼ **saunas**
▼ **steam rooms**
▼ **massage**
▼ **aromatherapy**
▼ **body toning**
▼ **manicures and pedicure**
▼ **mud baths**
▼ **stress management**
▼ **relaxation techniques**
▼ **yoga**
▼ **aerobics**

Recreation: cost, availability and accessibility

Recreation is a very broad category that covers a multitude of sports and other activities. In any area there are a number of facilities and activities on offer. A principal characteristic of recreation is that it can be undertaken at a number of levels. You do not have to attend a particular facility or centre in order to take advantage of sports or other recreational activities. Access and availability is therefore high and the cost is as low as the participant needs it to be.

CUSTOMER TYPES

As we indicated in Element 7.1, there are different customer types who have different needs and interests. Just as different travel modes cater for different customer types, so too do the various tourism products and services. In this part of the element you will be expected to match tourism products and services against the different customer types and see if there are any conclusions you can draw from this.

Families, individuals and groups

If you refer back to Section 7.1.5, you will find many of the reasons why particular products and services appeal to different types of customer. Remember that every group or individual will be looking for something slightly different, so a good product or service should appeal to the majority rather than the minority.

Young people and senior citizens

The tourism products and services demanded by the young are usually very different to those used by senior citizens. There is an obvious difference in the abilities of these groups to participate in particular forms of entertainment and recreation, which sometimes causes misunderstandings between the young and old. One thing these groups do have in common is that they can often get considerable discounts from the various attractions on the basis of their age.

Special interest groups and people with specific needs

The appeal of different tourism products and services will very much depend on the nature of people's basic interests. When we consider that groups of people enjoy different things, we can begin to realise that products and services will attract some and not others. For example, national parks and areas of outstanding beauty will be natural attractions for walkers and ramblers. Equally, resorts which are well-planned and have identified coastal walks will appeal to them too.

People with specific needs will look for areas which offer a comprehensive range of additional services to match their specific needs, particu-

larly in terms of access and acceptance within the various attractions and facilities.

7.2.3 Suggest reasons for the relative popularity of different tourism products and services

REASONS

In this part of the element you are asked to consider the main reasons for the relative appeal of different tourism products and services. Some of them have long-term appeal (perhaps they are traditional entertainments and a part of the local community) and others will have novelty value (they are new and exciting).

Appeal

One of the major reasons why certain tourism products and services have more appeal than others is the fact that they cater for a number of different customer types. In this way they are not bound to any one age group or interest group. Universal appeal, whilst being difficult, is something that most facilities aim for.

Novelty value

Many tourism products and services enjoy great popularity in the first few weeks or months of opening due to their novelty value. This is no different from any products and services that we buy.

The media plays an important role in making new products and services popular; customers are heavily influenced by seeing a product or service on television, video or in the cinema. Disney is one of the most successful companies at doing this. Each of their new cartoons or movies is supported by a huge range of products such as cuddly toys, stationery and books. Their cartoon characters feature in new rides and entertainments at Disneyland Paris, Disneyland and Disneyworld. Customers become familiar with these characters on screen and this is a very powerful way of selling products and services. In the UK, for example, the recent films by Nick Parks (featuring his plasticine heroes 'Wallace and Gromit') have meant that over 200 different products have been created so that customers can have the characters in their own homes.

New and popular ideas, usually from television or film, influence the choice of entertainment offered by new attractions such as theme parks which, in turn, increases their appeal. New sports made popular on TV also feature heavily in leisure centres and sports facilities. If it was not for Channel 4's screening of American Football, for example, this sport would probably never have taken off in the UK.

7.2.4 *Describe sources of information on tourism products and services*

SOURCES OF INFORMATION

In this performance criterion we will be discussing the following sources of information:

▼ **tourist boards**
▼ **tourist information centres**
▼ **libraries**
▼ **guiding services**
▼ **accommodation providers**
▼ **transport providers**

Whilst we have covered many of these sources in other units, there are some further considerations to look at here.

Tourist boards

Tourist boards operate at a national, regional and local level. They are a good source of information about the popularity of different tourist attractions.

National

As you may have already realised, a tourist destination is only as good as its ability to attract customers. Most countries who wish to attract overseas visitors will have a national tourist board. The British Tourist Authority fulfils this role in Britain; it was set up in 1969 and is based in London. The major tasks that it undertakes are:

▼ **to increase the number of overseas visitors to Britain**
▼ **to encourage visitors to spend more money once they have arrived there**
▼ **to encourage visitors to go to places in Britain that are 'off the tourist path'**
▼ **to promote London as the premier destination**
▼ **to encourage visitors to come to Britain all year round and not just in the summer**

The national organisation incorporates three tourist boards which look after the interests of the different countries in Britain: the English Tourist Board (based in London); the Scottish Tourist Board (based in Edinburgh); and the Wales Tourist Board (based in Cardiff). These boards are responsible for running promotional and advertising campaigns, publishing annual guides to holidays in their country, and giving financial assistance to tourism businesses in their country in the form of grants.

In Northern Ireland the situation is a little different. The Northern Ireland Tourist Board was set up in 1948 and is responsible for the following:

▼ **developing tourist facilities**
▼ **improving tourist facilities**

▼ **developing tourist amenities**
▼ **improving tourist amenities**

It has offices in the UK, the Irish Republic, Frankfurt and New York.

Regional

Regional tourist organisations are smaller and more localised. They are responsible for promoting particular parts of the country. In England, these are:

▼ *Cumbria*
▼ *Northumbria* – **Cleveland, Durham, Tyne and Wear, and Northumberland**
▼ *North-west England* – **Cheshire, Greater Manchester, Lancashire, Merseyside, and the high Peak District of Derbyshire**
▼ *Yorkshire and Humberside* – **North, South and West Yorkshire and Humberside**
▼ *Heart of England* – **Gloucestershire, Hertford and Worcester, Shropshire, Staffordshire, Warwickshire and the West Midlands**
▼ *East Midlands* – **Derbyshire, Leicestershire, Lincolnshire, Northamptonshire and Nottinghamshire**
▼ *Thames and Chilterns* – **Bedfordshire, Berkshire, Buckinghamshire, Hertfordshire and Oxfordshire**
▼ *East Anglia* – **Cambridgeshire, Essex, Suffolk and Norfolk**
▼ *London*
▼ *West Country* – **Avon, Cornwall, Devon, Somerset, Western Dorset, Wiltshire and the Isles of Scilly**
▼ *Southern England* – **Eastern Dorset, Northern Dorset, Hampshire and the Isle of Wight**
▼ *South-east England* – **East Sussex, Kent, Surrey and West Sussex**

These regional organisations were set up by the English Tourist Board in the 1970s. They are funded by the English Tourist Board, the county and district councils, and the membership fees charged to tourism operators. They are responsible for publishing regional guides, inviting travel

agents and the press to visit the region, advertising, and attending travel shows.

Scotland has 32 area tourist boards which promote regions. These are:

▼ **Angus**
▼ **Aviemore and Spey Valley**
▼ **Ayrshire**
▼ **Banff and Buchan**
▼ **Caithness**
▼ **City of Aberdeen**
▼ **City of Dundee**
▼ **Clyde Valley**
▼ **Dumfries and Galloway**
▼ **Dunoon and Cowal**
▼ **East Lothian**
▼ **Edinburgh Marketing**
▼ **Forth Valley**
▼ **Fort William and Lochaber**
▼ **Gordon District**
▼ **Greater Glasgow**
▼ **Inverness, Loch Ness and Nairn**
▼ **Isle of Arran**
▼ **Isle of Skye and Southwest Ross**
▼ **Kincardine and Deeside**
▼ **Loch Lomond, Stirling and the Trossachs**
▼ **Moray**
▼ **Orkney**
▼ **Perthshire**
▼ **Ross and Cromarty**
▼ **Rothesay and Isle of Bute**
▼ **Scottish Borders**
▼ **Shetland**
▼ **St Andrew's and North East Fife**
▼ **Sutherland**
▼ **Western Isles**
▼ **West Highlands and the Isle of Argyll**

Wales has just three regional tourist councils, covering:

▼ **North Wales**
▼ **Mid Wales**
▼ **South Wales**

Local

On an even smaller scale, there are local tourist boards that cover towns, cities and districts. They are supported by their local authorities and not

THE NEW FOREST
VISITOR INFORMATION i

Make the most of your stay in this very special corner of England by visiting one of our Information Centres. Meet our friendly staff who will be more than happy to help with your enquiries and provide detailed holiday and visitor information along with a wide variety of free leaflets.

Whether you are looking for any type of Accommodation, a night out at the Theatre, or a day at a Rural Show, We can book them all for you.

All centres sell a wide range of maps and guide books. From the excellent value New Forest Map to Ordnance Survey maps and atlases. From leaflets on short walks to books with routes that will keep you out walking for a day (or more).

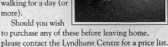

Should you wish to purchase any of these before leaving home, please contact the Lyndhurst Centre for a price list.

Tourist information points provide a wealth of ideas on what to see and do in the New Forest. They also have details of places to eat and drink as well as accommodation lists.

Locations - Lyndhurst TIC; Lyndhurst Police Station; Lymington; Ringwood; Fordingbridge; Brockenhurst; Burley and New Milton.

The New Forest Encounter Walk and Encounter Tour can also be booked through the information centres. *Further details of these can be found on page 8 of this guide.*

Purchase an Explorer Bus ticket and see the area without using your car. Transport tickets are at present only available from Lyndhurst and Ringwood TICs.

Details of public transport to and around the district can be obtained from all New Forest Tourist Information Centres.

New Forest Tourist Information Centre (open all year)
High Street, Lyndhurst,
Hampshire, SO43 7NY
Tel: (01703) 282269 Fax: (01703) 284404

Seasonal Tourist Information Centres (Easter to Sept.)
Lymington, tel: (01590) 672422
Ringwood, tel: (01425) 470896
Fordingbridge, tel: (01425) 654560

This publication is printed on paper produced from trees planted in sustainable forests.

Fig. 7.2.4 The New Forest Tourist Information Centre is open all year round and offers a comprehensive range of services (courtesy of South Hams).

by central government. There are several hundred local tourist boards in existence and their role is to attract businesses as well as tourists. Many of them have been successful in attracting tourists to an area, particularly areas that have not been associated with tourism in the past.

Tourist information centres

As we mentioned in Element 7.1, tourist information centres (TICs) are useful sources of information about their local area. In terms of tourism products and services, TICs can also offer:

▼ **local bed-booking services – the TIC will make reservations for you at a local hotel or guest house; it will find you a suitable place to stay and do all the hard work**

▼ **book-a-bed-ahead services – the TIC will phone a TIC in another area and book a bed at your next destination. This is ideal for touring holidays**

TICs are extremely popular and deal with 10 million enquirers nationwide every year.

Libraries

Libraries provide a wide range of information for both the casual user and those who wish to look at information in more depth. It is standard policy for the majority of libraries to stock a wide range of different leaflets and other materials, but you would have to use their archive services to look at information from the past.

Guiding services

Guiding services are not available in all areas of the UK, but are generally found in areas which have specific attractions. Areas which have an interesting historical background, hold current interest or are associated with celebrities or notorious murderers (such as the Jack the Ripper tours in the East End of London) will have a variety of guiding services available through the local council or transport providers.

Accommodation providers

Accommodation providers are usually only too happy to let you have information regarding the various services they offer. They will be able to give you material about the accommodation itself and hold stocks of leaflets and other information about the local area.

Transport providers

As we have already discussed the availability of information from transport providers (railway stations, coach stations, airports and ferry ports) in Element 7.1, you should refer back to page 100.

assignment

ELEMENT **7.2**

PC 7.2.1–4
COM 1.1, 1.2, 1.3, 1.4

In order to fulfil the performance criteria of this element, you will need to investigate the provision of tourism products and services.

| **t a s k** | **1** | PC 7.2.1–4 |

Write a brief report that outlines in general terms the provision of tourism products and services. The report should:

- *identify the different types of tourism products and services, and give one example for each of the four main categories selected from the seven listed in the range statement*

- *explain the appeal of four selected tourism products and services to two different customer types. The four selected products and services can be the same ones as you used in the first part of the report*
- *suggest reasons for the relative popularity of the four selected products and services*
- *describe the sources of information on tourism products and services*

Notes
Tourist boards and tourist information centres are good sources of information for the whole of this assignment.

element 7.3

INVESTIGATE THE LOCAL PROVISION OF TRAVEL AND TOURISM PRODUCTS AND SERVICES

Performance criteria

A student must:

1   Identify **local providers** of travel and tourism products and services.
2   Identify **local sources of information** on travel and tourism products and services.
3   Describe **information materials** on travel and tourism products and services provided by local sources.
4   Extract prices of **key travel and tourism products** and services from **information materials**.

RANGE

Local providers: travel agencies, tour operators, tourist attractions (theme parks, national parks, resorts, heritage sites, galleries, theatres), accommodation (hotels, motels, guest houses, self-catering, holiday villages), catering, tourist boards, tourist information centres, guiding services, transport (airports, railway stations, coach stations, ferry ports)

Local sources of information: local tourist boards, tourist information centres, libraries, guiding services, accommodation providers, transport providers (railway stations, coach stations, airports, ferry ports), travel agencies

Information materials: brochures, leaflets, timetables

Key travel and tourism products: package holidays, transport (air, sea, rail, road), accommodation, entrance fees (theme parks, galleries, heritage sites), theatre bookings, guided tours

7.3.1 *Identify local providers of travel and tourism products and services*

LOCAL PROVIDERS

Now that we have looked, in general terms, at the provision of travel and tourism products and services across the UK, you must consider your local area and see how it addresses the particular needs of the customers and visitors.

By following all the performance criteria and range statements in this element, you will be able to provide a comprehensive view of the provision in your area. Remember that the focus in this element is on local providers and you should discuss with your tutor what is understood by **local**. This may mean the county in which you live, the city, the borough or just the town or immediate area. Some of you may have to look further afield than others in order to cover all the different providers, products and services identified in this element.

The following headings cover the major providers that you will have to look at, and you should try to identify those that are applicable to your area. Bear in mind that some will not be appropriate, such as ferry ports for landlocked areas.

Travel agencies and tour operators

The *Yellow Pages* or a similar directory could prove to be of great value here. There will be a large number of travel agencies in most areas and you can easily identify them. It would be useful to make a distinction between those which offer local services and those which offer a more global service to the customers.

There may not be any tour operators actually based in your area, but there may be tour operators that offer holidays or services in the locality through travel agencies. Again it is worth making this distinction, as it is likely that tour operators based in your locality are sizeable employers and make a positive contribution to the local economy.

Tourist attractions

The local tourist boards or tourist information centres are probably the best place to start with this aspect of your research. You will need to get a comprehensive list of all the tourist attractions in your local area. If you are stuck and cannot find enough information, then most public libraries will have a list of tourist attractions and will also stock many of the leaflets and brochures that are printed by the tourist attractions free of charge.

Try to organise your collection of information into the following categories:

▼ **theme parks**
▼ **national parks**
▼ **resorts**
▼ **heritage sites**
▼ **galleries**
▼ **theatres**

You may find that some of the attractions fall into more than one category; this is quite acceptable. Remember that some of the theme parks or galleries, for example, will be an integral part of a resort; do not think about resorts as being only beach-based.

Accommodation

Again, the *Yellow Pages* or a similar directory would be a good starting point in trying to collate details of the accommodation (hotels, motels, guest houses, self-catering and holiday villages) available in your local area.

It is important to consider the fact that quite a lot of accommodation works on a small scale and therefore may not be able to advertise widely; this is particularly true of guest houses. The

Royal Botanic Gardens Kew Richmond Surrey TW9 3AB Tel.01 940 1171

Fig. 7.3.1 The Royal Botanic Gardens are home to an amazing collection of plants, trees, bushes, shrubs and flowers from around the world. Local areas have their own smaller versions of the facilities and attractions offered here (courtesy of the Royal Botanic Gardens, Kew).

larger facilities, such as hotels and holiday villages, may have information sheets, leaflets and brochures available in your local library. Many local tourist boards publish brochures that cover the different accommodation providers and this could save you a great deal of research work.

Catering

Many providers of accommodation offer additional catering services to customers other than those staying with them. The larger hotels, in particular, do significant business in providing a wide range of catering services. This would include the following:

▼ **bar food and snacks**
▼ **restaurant meals (breakfast, lunch and evening meals)**
▼ **catering for meetings and conferences**
▼ **catering for weddings and other functions**
▼ **outside catering for events off the premises**

Tourist attractions, too, have a wide range of catering facilities for visitors or those who are staying at the attraction. The range of catering services offered includes fast-food facilities so that visitors do not have to use up time queuing and sitting down to eat a meal. Snack facilities are also very common, offering hot and cold food as well as drinks.

The majority of catering services offered in any area would be provided by the following:

▼ **restaurants**
▼ **cafés**
▼ **bars**

Local directories, such as *Yellow Pages*, are good sources of information about the catering services available in your local area.

Tourist boards and tourist information centres

Referring back to Element 7.2, you will find that all the main areas of the UK have a tourist board. The scope and nature of the work that each

tourist board undertakes will differ from area to area. Tourist information centres tend to be located close to the major attractions or in resorts and will be listed in the local directories. If you are lucky, your tutor will have already established links with the local tourist board and tourist information centres. You can also contact the local council, who will be able to tell you how to get in contact with them.

To fulfil this performance criterion, you will need to say where these facilities are in the local area. The kinds of information they can offer to the visitor will be covered later in this element.

Guiding services

There may be guiding services in your area which provide the opportunity for visitors to take a comprehensive tour of local travel and tourism facilities or a particular site.

Tour or special event guides are normally contactable through the local tourist boards or tourist information centres. They will also advertise in the tourist information brochures and be fairly prominent at centres that are popular with visitors. For example, the seafronts of most resorts have guide services available which offer tours of the local area (scenic routes on open-topped buses, trips out to sea or visits to tourist attractions outside the main resort). In cities and larger towns, guide services are commonly available so that visitors can see and enjoy the various attractions of the area.

Transport

You need to look at the different types of transport available in your local area, including airports, railway stations, coach stations and ferry ports. If you refer to Unit 2 (in the companion volume *Foundation Leisure and Tourism*), you will find that a great deal of the work has already been done for you in relation to airports and ferry ports.

You probably already know where your local railway stations are and, as you will discover, they provide a wide range of valuable informa-

Fig. 7.3.2 This tram offers an interesting guided tour of the facilities at the North of England Open Air Museum (courtesy of the Museum and Galleries Commission).

tion. Coach stations, if applicable, will also be of great use to you in the collection of data.

Obviously, the availability of these different forms of transport will influence how visitors arrive in your local area. Still, the majority will probably make the journey by car. It is unlikely that domestic travellers will use the airports or ferry ports; these are more likely to attract overseas visitors. Railway and coach stations will provide the alternative means of transport into your area for UK visitors.

7.3.2 Identify local sources of information on travel and tourism products and services

LOCAL SOURCES OF INFORMATION

As we have seen in the first part of this element, there are a number of different travel and tourism providers that operate in any given area of the UK. In this performance criterion we will suggest sources and types of information that you are likely to find on the different products and services offered locally. Bear in mind that we will only be able to make some generalisations here; you should refer to Elements 7.1 and 7.2 for greater detail.

Local tourist boards

Local tourist boards operate as the central point of information for the local area. They have comprehensive information regarding the following:

▼ **local attractions**
▼ **travel within the area**
▼ **travel to areas nearby**
▼ **accommodation**
▼ **special events**
▼ **theatre events**

Additional information that may be available includes:

▼ **prices of various attractions (theatres, galleries, etc.)**
▼ **opening times (day and seasonal)**
▼ **approximate number of visitors to the area**

- ▼ source of the visitors (where they have come from)
- ▼ information about plans to enhance the local attractions
- ▼ an overall marketing plan to promote the area

Tourist information centres

These operate as the primary point of contact for tourists once they have arrived in the locality. As we mentioned in Element 7.2, they provide a number of very useful services for the visitor. They also operate as a key source of leaflets and other information materials for the visitor. Tourist information centres are extremely popular and valuable resources; visitors know they can obtain information and unbiased help and assistance regarding all the attractions, events, services and accommodation in the area.

Libraries

As a part of the local council's provision for the inhabitants of the area, the library offers comprehensive services for the collection of information about the locality. Bear in mind that visitors to a particular attraction are likely to include local inhabitants as well as those who have specifically travelled there.

A typical library will have a rack of leaflets and other information that can be taken away for later reading. You will find leaflets and booklets about all the major attractions and services, as well as coach, bus and rail timetables. Libraries will also be able to give you more in-depth information from their archives of newspapers, books about the local area and other collections of materials.

Guiding services

Guiding services will generally be provided by the following:

- ▼ the local council, if it provides the coach/bus services and has decided to

take an active part in the promotion of the area
- ▼ local bus or coach companies that offer guided tours as an integral part of their overall services
- ▼ other private providers who have specialised knowledge regarding certain aspects of the local area
- ▼ specific attractions, offering guided tours to visitors in the facility

All these are likely to have leaflets and brochures describing their services.

Accommodation providers

Essentially, there are two main types of providers in the local areas. These are:

1 *hotel and motel chains* – they generally advertise widely; they offer a comprehensive information service and can often make bookings for other service providers in the area
2 *smaller or local accommodation providers* – they advertise on a smaller scale, but are happy to give you information about their facilities and may be able to help you find out information about the other facilities in the area

Again, the local tourist board and tourist information centres will have information about the accommodation providers in the area. Each of the accommodation providers will also have racks of leaflets regarding local attractions.

Transport providers

Railway stations, coach stations, airports and ferry ports are good sources for the following types of information:

- ▼ timetables
- ▼ links with other transport services (such as coaches/buses from an airport or ferry port)
- ▼ links to accommodation in the area
- ▼ links to tourist attractions in the area

They will be able to offer you information about the nature and availability of transport services throughout the locality, as well as providing a comprehensive collection of leaflets about other services available.

Travel agencies

Local travel agencies can, of course, be a very valuable source of information. It is likely that the agencies (particularly if they are independent) will be aware of all the activities and amenities available in the locality. It is advisable that you approach these carefully; do not descend on them and take all their brochures. It is far better to get your tutor to approach them first and request permission for you to visit. They will be only too happy to help, in most cases, but will not take too kindly to being bombarded with questions and requests for information. Bear in mind that they are a business and need to sell holidays and services in order to survive.

7.3.3 Describe information materials on travel and tourism products and services provided by local sources

INFORMATION MATERIALS

As you will have seen throughout this book and its companion volume *Foundation Leisure and Tourism*, there are only certain ways of providing information. Information materials that can be given to the potential customer are restricted to three main types:

▼ **brochures**
▼ **leaflets**
▼ **timetables**

It is intended that visitors will keep these materials and read them in their own time. Other forms of information materials are not necessarily designed for customers to take away.

Brochures

Local sources of information, such as tourist information centres and travel agencies, will carry stocks of brochures regarding a huge variety of different travel and tourism products and services.

Bear in mind that although these products and services are being offered locally, they may be located elsewhere. For example, a travel agency in Bridport, Dorset, may offer a diverse range of products and services, including package holidays to Gouves in Crete and tickets and travel to an event in Dorchester. It is not the location of the product or service that is important, but the location of the provider.

Brochures are ideal for extracting a comprehensive view of the nature of the products and services offered in a locality. Remember, however, that brochures are created by the tour operators and are only supplied to the local providers as booking agents.

Leaflets

Leaflets form an integral part of the information materials available in a particular locality. You will find a wide variety of leaflets in a number of different locations around your local area. They will tend to fall into the following categories:

▼ **local attractions**
▼ **local events/special events**
▼ **regional facilities/events**
▼ **national facilities/events**

Leaflets tend to be more general than brochures and may not carry as much information about a specific product or service. Remember that leaflets are normally designed to attract people's attention to a travel and tourism product or service and may be supported by additional information on request.

Timetables

Timetables do not relate only to travel services; they may also include timetables of events and special activities.

Timetables do not tend to include prices and other details; they are designed to inform the customer of the availability and timing of services. They are sometimes supported by the inclusion of a map showing the various routes covered by the travel service around the local area.

You will find that the coach and railway stations also have regional or national timetables showing the availability of transport in and out of the locality. These timetables will be of great use to visitors and local residents alike. Additional information regarding prices and other aspects of the service will be available on request from the stations or via their telephone services.

7.3.4 Extract prices of key travel and tourism products and services from information materials

KEY TRAVEL AND TOURISM PRODUCTS

In this final part of the element, you will need to make use of the information materials you have collected throughout the unit. The subject of this performance criterion is the pricing of the key travel and tourism products and services.

As the element assignment explains, you will have to construct a grid and look at six travel and tourism products and services which should include some of the following:

▼ **package holidays**
▼ **transport (air, sea, rail, road)**
▼ **accommodation**
▼ **entrance fees (to theme parks, galleries, heritage sites)**
▼ **theatre bookings**
▼ **guided tours**

We look briefly at these aspects in this section, but you will find further information in Elements 7.1 and 7.2.

Package holidays

Calculating the costs of package holidays is not as easy as it may first appear.

The brochures use codes to identify the different accommodation offered and these need to be cross-referenced with a particular month or departure date. Obviously you will have to decide which month or departure date you will be using as the example in your grid.

There may be discounts available, so you will need to look at the stickers on the cover or displays in the travel agency before calculating your final price. Do not forget that certain departure sites attract surcharges and you will also have to consider insurance.

Your tutor will tell you how many people you need to quote a price for; if it is one, there may be a single person supplement to add to the basic price.

Transport

Transport costs can be obtained from a variety of different sources. Equally, transport can be booked through different providers. Bear in mind that the price may differ depending on whether you book the transport directly from the provider (operator) or through an agency (the booking agent).

Be careful when calculating the transport costs as the structure of the pricing may be complicated and unclear. There may be discounts and other cost factors to take into account when you are thinking about the price of the transport.

Accommodation

Accommodation can, again, be booked through a variety of different providers. These would include the following:

▼ **the accommodation itself**
▼ **a centralised booking system for hotel/motel chains**
▼ **the tourist information centre**
▼ **the local travel agency**
▼ **a national travel agency**

The pricing structures can be complicated and you will need to be aware of the quality and service offered by the accommodation provider. The star system gives you guidance on the level of service you can expect.

Entrance fees

This information is reasonably easy to obtain and understand. Attractions will be happy to let you know the entrance fees and you can obtain this information from leaflets or by telephoning the site. Bear in mind that there may be concessions for families, groups, older people, disabled people, students and children. Although this complicates the matter slightly, entrance fees are perhaps the easiest cost to sort out.

Again, the cost will depend on the location of the attraction. If it is local, you will normally pay at the door. If the attraction is further afield, you may find that ticket or travel agencies charge an additional fee over the entrance price to make a booking on your behalf. This price may be part of an overall service which would include travel to and from the attraction.

Theatre bookings

If the theatre is a local one, you will be able to purchase tickets at the ticket office. Leaflets and posters around the local area will tell you all the information you need to know about prices.

Alternatively, theatre bookings can be made via ticket agencies or travel agencies who may charge an additional 'booking fee' on top of the ticket price. Normally, these agencies offer travel to and from the venue as an additional service.

Theatre tickets can also be purchased by credit card over the telephone. The tickets are then either posted to you or can be picked up on the day of the performance. The telephone booking service would serve as an ideal way of discovering the pricing and availability of tickets.

Guided tours

Guided tours are offered by the following providers:

▼ **local councils**
▼ **travel agencies**
▼ **private guide companies**
▼ **coach and bus companies**
▼ **individuals with special knowledge**
▼ **English Heritage and other agencies responsible for the site**

Prices should be easy to obtain and will usually depend on the number of individuals in the group. The larger the party, the less each individual pays for the guided tour. Leaflets, brochures and posters should be available to help you track down the guided tour providers.

ADMISSION CHARGES 1995
For the Royal Botanic Gardens, Kew and Wakehurst Place

ROYAL BOTANIC GARDENS KEW

Adults	£4.00
Concessions for Senior Citizens, Students, Unemployed and those eligible for Social Security Benefits (see over)	£2.00
Children aged between 5 and 16	£2.00
Children under 5	free
Family Ticket (any 2 adults and up to 4 children)	£10.00
Last hour of admissions (**Kew only**)	£2.00

Entry is **free** for the blind, partially sighted and wheelchair occupants. Attendant at appropriate rate (as above)

Entry to Wakehurst Place is **free** for National Trust members

SEASON TICKETS AND FRIENDS MEMBERSHIP
Valid for one year from the date of issue
Available from the Ticket Offices

Standard Season Ticket	£17.00
Concession Season Ticket	£10.00
Family Season Ticket	£33.00
Concession Family Season Ticket	£16.00
Individual Friend	£32.00
Senior Citizen Individual Friend	£21.50
Student Friend	£16.00
Family Friend	£43.00
Senior Citizen Family Friend	£32.00

Please see over for more details

MADAME TUSSAUD'S

WHERE THE PEOPLE MEET THE PEOPLE.

LONDON PLANETARIUM

ADMISSION PRICES

	WITH EFFECT FROM	
	1 April 1995	1 April 1995
	INDIVIDUAL	GROUP
MADAME TUSSAUD'S		
Adult	£8.35	£6.85
Child (Under 16)	£5.25	£4.35
Senior Citizen	£6.25	£5.20
Family Ticket	£21.95	
THE LONDON PLANETARIUM*		
Adult	£4.75	£3.95
Child (Under 16)	£2.95	£2.50
Senior Citizen	£3.65	£2.95
Family Ticket	£12.45	
COMBINED TICKET		
Adult	£11.25	£8.95
Child (Under 16)	£6.95	£5.75
Senior Citizen	£8.50	£6.65
Family Ticket	£29.45	

Group rates apply to 10 or more persons.
*Children under 5 not admitted.

THE TUSSAUDS GROUP LIMITED
Marylebone Road, London, NW1 5LR
Telephone: 0171-935 6861
Fax: 0171-465 0862

ALL PRICES ARE SUBJECT TO CHANGE

Fig. 7.3.3 These leaflets outline the admission prices for the London Planetarium and Royal Botanic Gardens. Considerable discounts are offered to groups and people eligible for concessions (courtesy of Madame Tussaud's and the Royal Botanic Gardens).

assignment

ELEMENT 7.3

PC 7.3.1–4
COM 1.2, 1.4
AON 1.2, 1.4

The focus of this element is the local provision of travel and tourism products and services. In order to address the performance criteria of this element, you should undertake the following assignment.

task	1	PC 7.3.1–2

List the local providers and sources of information on travel and tourism products and services.

task	2	PC 7.3.3

Briefly describe the information materials on travel and tourism products and services provided by local sources.

task	3	PC 7.3.4

Create a grid which details six travel and tourism products and services, indicating the price for each of them.

Notes
Remember that the focus of this element is on local providers and local sources. You do not have to concentrate on local products and services – these may be offered locally but located elsewhere. You should use the information materials collected to extract the prices of the travel and tourism products.

EXPLORING RECREATIONAL ACTIVITIES IN LEISURE AND TOURISM

element 8.1

INVESTIGATE RECREATIONAL ACTIVITIES IN LEISURE AND TOURISM

Performance criteria

A student must:

1 Identify the **needs** of different **client groups**.
2 Suggest **suitable recreational activities** which meet the **needs** of different **client groups**.
3 Identify the **benefits** of **recreational activities** for the health and well-being of different **client groups**.
4 Describe, with examples, **common barriers** to participation in **recreational activities**.
5 Explain, with examples, **how common barriers** can be **overcome**.

RANGE

Needs: for physical activity, for social interaction, for intellectual stimulation; for a new experience, for a challenge, for personal satisfaction

Client groups: children, adolescents, older people; families, groups; from different cultural backgrounds, with physical disabilities (sight, hearing, mobility), with obesity

Suitable according to: age, physical condition, gender, cultural background, budget

Recreational activities: physical, social, intellectual

Benefits: physical, social, intellectual; providing a new experience, presenting a challenge, providing personal satisfaction

> **Common barriers:** cost, access, location, transport, availability of activities, lack of specialist equipment, lack of specialist staff
>
> **How to overcome:** concessions, adapting facilities, finding alternative source of activities, improving transport links, adapting programme of activities, installing specialist equipment, deploying specialist staff

8.1.1 Identify the needs of different client groups

NEEDS

We will begin our look at recreational activities by considering the different client groups and their needs. As we will discover, the range of needs is quite wide and it is often difficult to provide all these. The different client groups make various demands on the providers of recreational facilities, and you will see how difficult it is to make sure that all these groups are catered for at all times.

Needs for physical activity

We were all forced to take part in physical activities at school, whether we enjoyed them or not. For some, an interest in a sport or physical activity began here; for some, it ended here too. The 15 most popular physical activities include:

- ▼ walking
- ▼ cycling
- ▼ golf
- ▼ running and jogging
- ▼ soccer
- ▼ tennis
- ▼ fishing
- ▼ swimming
- ▼ bowls
- ▼ watersports
- ▼ cricket
- ▼ horse riding
- ▼ field sports
- ▼ sailing
- ▼ hockey

Of these, swimming is the only indoor activity; the others are all played outdoors. For many people, physical recreation offers the following benefits:

- ▼ **it is fun**
- ▼ **it allows you to socialise with friends**
- ▼ **it allows you to meet new people**
- ▼ **it allows you to escape from routine**
- ▼ **it can provide physical exertion**
- ▼ **it can enable you to excel**
- ▼ **it can enable you to relax**
- ▼ **it can allow you to be competitive**

Many of the reasons for non-participation, as we shall see later, are to do with the fact that it is difficult to play certain sports in particular localities.

FIGURE IT OUT

PC 8.1.1
COM 1.1, 1.2

00:10

As a group, try to figure out some other reasons why you and other people enjoy sports activities. Write a list of your thoughts and keep them, as you will need to refer to them for Element 8.2.

Stradbroke Pool, Wilby Road, Stradbroke, Suffolk IP21 5JN
Telephone (01379) 384376, Fax No. (01379) 388375

Mid Suffolk MID SUFFOLK DISTRICT COUNCIL

Mid Suffolk **Leisure**

Fig. 8.1.1 This leaflet offers canoe courses at different skill levels for individuals aged 8 and over.

Needs for social interaction

For many people, recreational activities offer their only chance to socialise with friends and meet new people. Regardless of the fact that we may be at school, college or work all day, we tend to have a different circle of friends when we engage in recreational activities. Many recreational activities are team sports and are often enjoyed more because of this. Most recreational activities are followed by a degree of social activity and interaction and provide the chance to develop new friendships and interests.

Needs for intellectual stimulation

Recreational activities may fulfil a need for intellectual stimulation. There are hundreds of different recreational activities which stretch the mind and demand great levels of intellectual thought and concentration. These include the following:

▼ **archaeology**
▼ **board games**
▼ **card playing**
▼ **drama**
▼ **genealogy**
▼ **heraldry**
▼ **ornithology**
▼ **photography**
▼ **quizzes**
▼ **war gaming**

FIGURE IT OUT

PC 8.1.1
COM 1.1, 1.2

 **00:10**

*A*s a group, try to list another 10 intellectually stimulating leisure or recreational activities. Again, you should keep this list for reference in Element 8.2.

Needs for a new experience or a challenge

When we consider new experiences and challenges, we tend to think about the more dangerous recreational activities such as:

▼ **abseiling**
▼ **bungey jumping**
▼ **caving**
▼ **parachuting**
▼ **paragliding**
▼ **parascending**
▼ **skiing**
▼ **windsurfing**

There is no doubt that these sports offer both a challenge and a very new experience to those considering taking them up. Less 'exciting' sports and recreational activities can, however, also fulfil these needs. Starting anything new is both exciting and interesting. A great many people will try a wide variety of different sports and recreational activities before they settle upon one or two that really suit them. Others will continually chop and change, always looking for new experiences and the challenge of trying something different.

Needs for personal satisfaction

Even when you have been enjoying a recreational activity for a number of years, there is still a great deal of personal satisfaction to be had by improving your own ability or performance. It is only when you do not get any personal satisfaction from a recreational activity that it becomes boring and you will begin to look for something new. For some, taking up a new recreational activity is all about attaining a certain level of ability in that activity. This is how some people achieve personal satisfaction that cannot be obtained in other aspects of their lives.

CLIENT GROUPS

In previous units we have referred to the individuals who visit various leisure and tourism facilities as customers, or visitors. Another way of describing customers or visitors is **client groups**; this is simply a slightly broader description of different types of customers. We will now look at the major different client groups and identify how certain recreational activities meet their needs.

Children, adolescents and older people

Clients needs and interests will be influenced by their age; activities which are popular with younger people may not appeal to older ones. It should not be assumed, however, that the more active recreational pursuits will be unpopular with older people (although they are probably less likely to try newer sports, such as in-line skating or stunt skiing). Many older people have the experience and skills necessary to perform well in a wide variety of different recreational activities.

Any leisure or tourism facility would be wise to make sure it caters for all age groups and can offer alternatives, particularly for members of a group or family.

Families and groups

As you saw in Units 1 and 2, families and groups make up the bulk of visitors to many of the visitor attractions in the UK. Whether this is true for leisure facilities will depend on the range and availability of activities offered. Bearing in mind that families are made up of people of different ages and needs, the facility needs to offer services which are appealing to both parents and children.

Groups include schools, clubs and other organisations which make regular visits to leisure facilities. They may use the same facilities and services on a weekly basis, such as a swimming pool. Some football clubs, for example, who do not have their own pitch or training facilities will routinely use the leisure services provided by a local centre.

Booking Form for Party Hire

Please fill in details and return the form with payment to the pool

Name of Hirer _____
Address _____
Phone Number_____
Date of Party _____ Time _____
Reception Required: YES☐ NO☐ *(time based on 1/2 hr period)*

	Adults	Children
Total No. of People Attending: Swimmers	_____	_____
Non-Swimmers	_____	_____
Spectators	_____	_____

* Parties with over 20 swimmers will require an extra lifeguard in accordance with health and safety recommendations at a cost of £5.00 for every extra 20 swimmers (includes adults and children)

Type of Reservation (please tick box)
Birthday☐ Social Club☐ Family Gathering☐
Name _____ Age _____ (if applicable)
Will you be using a camera or video equipment: YES☐ NO☐

Booking Type Required (please tick box)
1 hr Pool with Play Equipment	£42.50	☐
1 hr Pool with Small Inflatable	£47.50	☐
1 hr Pool with Large Inflatable	£52.50	☐
1 hr Pool with Play Equipment + 1/2 hr Reception	£52.50	☐
1 hr Pool with Small Inflatable + 1/2 hr Reception	£57.50	☐
1 hr Pool with Large Inflatable + 1/2 hr Reception	£62.50	☐
1 hr 30 mins Pool with Play Equipment	£63.50	☐
1 hr 30 mins Pool with Small Inflatable	£67.50	☐
1 hr 30 mins Pool with Large Inflatable	£75.00	☐

Cancellation of the booking is required 14 days prior to the date or full payment will be required

Sign _____ Date _____

Fig. 8.1.2 Swimming pools can sometimes be hired for birthday parties or other social gatherings. This booking form shows the range of additional services and facilities available.

Client groups from different cultural backgrounds

In areas where there are a variety of people from different cultural backgrounds, there will be a need to provide a range of recreational activities to cater for their needs. The majority of sports, in particular, are universally popular, but there may be a demand for specific cultural activities such as:

▼ **Greek, Turkish or Indian dancing**
▼ **specialist sports (e.g. Kabaddi)**
▼ **ethnic cookery courses**
▼ **cultural activities (history teaching, music, etc.)**

Client groups with physical disabilities

As mentioned in Units 1 and 2, facilities would be wise to incorporate features which enable people with physical disabilities (sight, hearing or mobility) to make full use of the different activities available. This goes far beyond ensuring that disabled people can gain access to the facility. Facilities should be designed or adapted to allow disabled people, once inside, to gain access to any part of the building and use changing rooms, toilets, refreshment areas and any other services. It should not be assumed that disabled people will only wish to take part in recreational activities with other disabled people. The facility should make sure that people with disabilities are given equal opportunities and able to mix freely and easily with able-bodied client groups.

Client groups with obesity

It is believed that by the end of the century over 20 per cent of the population will be considered to be obese. This simply means that the individuals concerned weigh more than the recommended weight for their age and height. There are, of course, degrees of obesity and there is no reason to believe that individuals who are overweight will not wish to involve themselves in recreational activities.

8.1.2 Suggest suitable recreational activities which meet the needs of different client groups

SUITABILITY

The vast majority of leisure and tourism facilities attempt to cater for all age groups, both sexes and individuals from a variety of different backgrounds. In this performance criterion we will look at the needs of different client groups and try to identify the recreational activities that would suit them.

Suitability according to age

As far as most recreational activities are concerned, age on its own is not a barrier. Whilst there should be no form of barring as a result of age, there are obviously some recreational activities which elderly people would be unwise to get involved with. Veteran or senior versions of sports have sprung up to cater for people who have still got a great interest in a sport, but are not really fit enough to compete against younger individuals.

At the lower end of the age scale, there are always junior clubs or versions of a sport or recreation. Whilst these less complete versions of a recreational activity are not true reflections of the activity as a whole, they do allow younger people to gain a valuable insight into the area itself.

Some facilities, mainly due to insurance considerations, do bar young people from using certain equipment or services. You will all have been to funfairs or theme parks when you were younger, for example, and discovered to your annoyance that you were too short to be allowed on the best rides.

FIGURE IT OUT

_PC 8.1.2_
COM 1.1, 1.2

00:15

In pairs, list at least five recreational activities that young people would be ill-advised to take part in. Also list five recreational activities that old people would find difficulty with. Compare your lists with those of the rest of the group.

Suitability according to physical condition

In many respects physical condition is related to age, but not necessarily in all cases. Certain recreational activities have definite hazards or potential dangers. Individuals who wish to use gymnasiums are often required to provide a medical certificate pronouncing them fit and then be assessed by trained staff before being given their programme of exercise.

Gentle aerobic exercise, whether this is dance, exercise or water based, should be fine for most people, although anyone who has a physical condition which could be aggravated by a particular form of exercise should always consult their doctor before beginning the programme. This is particularly important for people who suffer from back problems.

Suitability according to gender

There should be very few cases when gender actually matters or determines who may get involved in a recreational activity. Certain sports bodies insist that they make a division between male and female, but fortunately these are becoming the exception rather than the rule. Some swimming pools do set aside special sessions for females only, pregnant women or women with small children.

There are some sports which doctors believe women are ill-advised to take part in. Long-distance running, weightlifting and other sports which put a strain on the female anatomy can cause physical difficulties in the future if not strictly monitored.

Suitability according to cultural background

Centres providing recreational facilities in a multi-cultural environment obviously need to be aware of the demands of ethnic minorities and people from different cultural backgrounds. In many cases, assuming there is no funding available from central or local government, these activities need to attract sufficient individuals in order to make them viable. Fortunately, since people from different cultural backgrounds are underrepresented, there is usually funding available to support and promote activities for them. This also has the advantage of giving other individuals the opportunity to experience different cultural activities and broaden their outlook.

Suitability according to budget

Given the fact that a great number of centres which provide recreational activities are privately owned, it is alarming to consider that those which remain in local government hands are under pressure to pay for themselves, and may even be under threat from privatisation. This means that previously cheap and freely available recreational activities are becoming more and more expensive. Consider, for example, that swimming pools used to be known as public baths and were designed so that people who did not have bathing facilities at home could visit the local baths for a small fee.

Some centres deliberately set their prices high in order to keep their membership select. Typical examples of these would include golf clubs. In most cases you not only have to be put forward as a member, but also have to pay a subscription fee of at least £500 per year.

Other centres insist that certain sports clothing is worn at all times and will not allow individuals to use the facilities unless they have footwear which does not damage the flooring, and knee and arm pads for protection. Obviously some recreational activities, such as judo and karate, attract clothing costs. For the most part, however, involvement in a recreational activity should only require you to wear conventional sports clothes, such as shorts, shirts, tracksuits and trainers. Many recreational activities require you to use specific equipment, which can be expensive in some cases, but most centres do have the equipment for hire by the hour.

On top of any additional costs, there will be a set price for taking part in a recreational activity; for most sports the charge is by the hour or session. Ideally the centre will set the price at a level that can be afforded by the majority of potential users.

8.1.3 *Identify the benefits of recreational activities for the health and well-being of different client groups*

RECREATIONAL ACTIVITIES

By now you should have a fair idea what is meant by recreational activities. There is an enormous spread of different pastimes and sports which suit people's needs. In this performance criterion we will be looking at the benefits of the different types of recreational activity and how they suit the different client groups.

Physical activities and benefits

Physical activities are not restricted to those which can be undertaken indoors. They cover a wide range of different activities which extend from hill walking and swimming to yoga and aerobics. The following two lists look at the most popular outdoor and indoor physical activities.

Outdoor
▼ **walking, rambling and hiking**
▼ **swimming**
▼ **football**
▼ **golf**
▼ **track and field and jogging**
▼ **fishing**
▼ **cycling**

Indoor
▼ **snooker, billiards and pool**
▼ **swimming**
▼ **darts**
▼ **keep-fit and yoga**
▼ **squash**
▼ **badminton**
▼ **bowls and tenpin bowling**
▼ **gymnastics and athletics**
▼ **table tennis**

Although these are the most popular in terms of different people participating in them, there are a number of other outdoor activities which could be included:

▼ **tennis**
▼ **horse riding**
▼ **field sports**
▼ **sailing**
▼ **rugby**
▼ **climbing**
▼ **pot-holing**

The most obvious benefit of physical exercise is increased fitness. However, this is not necessarily the main or only reason for people to get involved

Fig. 8.1.3 *This modern adventure playground provides a variety of different physical activities which are suitable for young children (courtesy of the National Playing Fields Association).*

in physical activities. As we mentioned at the beginning of this element, people enjoy the social interaction, challenge and personal satisfaction of taking part in physical sports.

Social activities and benefits

Social activities include playing bingo, taking part in team activities and attending parties and functions. Also in this group we could include:

▼ **film and cinema**
▼ **theatre and drama**
▼ **concerts**
▼ **opera**
▼ **dance**
▼ **cabaret**
▼ **variety shows**

An important benefit of these activities is the opportunity for social interaction with other individuals which they provide. People who take part in the activities have a shared basis upon which to interact and communicate with each other. The provision of many of these recreational activities is dependent on the availability of suitable venues within a particular area. However, in recent years there has been an increase in the number of smaller venues catering for no more than two hundred or so people, who are either **club members** or pay an annual subscription as **friends** of the venue. In this way the costs of running the venue are underwritten by the membership.

Social interaction through recreational activity means that individuals will improve their communication skills and encounter many people from different walks of life who share a common interest.

Intellectual activities and benefits

Intellectual activities include the following:

▼ **coaching**
▼ **learning sports tactics**
▼ **chess and bridge**
▼ **attending day or evening classes**

Within this area, the variety of different activities is even more immense than the others we have already discussed. There is a tendency for individuals to want to learn new things so they can pursue a more active and interesting life.

Providing a new experience, presenting a challenge and providing personal satisfaction

Any centre which takes its job seriously and aims to provide a wide range of interesting and challenging recreational activities, will also be aware that only a limited number of people will ever use the centre. To this end, a well-managed and organised centre will develop a range of recreational activities which can be enjoyed at a variety of different levels. For the newcomer, a recreational activity will present both a fresh experience and a challenge. To an individual who has mastered the basics of the activity, there is the challenge of developing to a higher level in

Fig. 8.1.4 Hockey is becoming increasingly popular among young people in Scotland (courtesy of the National Playing Fields Association).

order to obtain personal satisfaction. Even the most experienced individual will embrace the possibility of excelling at a particular activity and will always strive to improve his or her performance in some way.

8.1.4 **Describe, with examples, common barriers to participation in recreational activities**

COMMON BARRIERS

When we consider the common barriers which prevent or dissuade individuals from participating in recreational activities, we should think about the following:

▼ **the cost of the activity, including the price of participation and any other related expenses**

▼ the ease of access to the activity, including provisions for elderly people and people with disabilities, as well as any tests or conditions which may prevent participation

▼ the location of the venue and whether it is within a reliable transport network

▼ the availability of the activity, which may be limited if the activity is not very popular or only run on a seasonal or annual basis

▼ the lack of specialist equipment available at the venue, which will apply, in particular, to recreational activities which require the use of expensive equipment

▼ the lack of specialist staff available at the venue, which may prevent the activity from being offered if participants need to be trained and supervised or monitored during the activity

Cost

Some centres deliberately set their prices at a level which they know many people cannot afford, in order to restrict membership. These centres maintain that they would not be able to cope with the demand for the facilities that would be generated by charging lower prices. Although this is unfair to those who cannot afford to use the facilities, it is felt that this policy protects the facility from overuse.

Expenses related to certain activities can also put people off participating in them. Take, for example, the high costs involved in purchasing clothing and equipment for scuba diving.

Access

As we mentioned earlier, access does not just mean the ability to get into a venue. Certain sports and recreational activities deliberately limit access by imposing high membership charges or very strict guidelines about who can be a member. You would normally think that any recreational activity would benefit from an increase in participation, but some governing

bodies prefer to limit the number as there may be a lack of sufficiently trained staff to teach the activity. In some cases there is a financial reason behind it; by limiting the number of people who

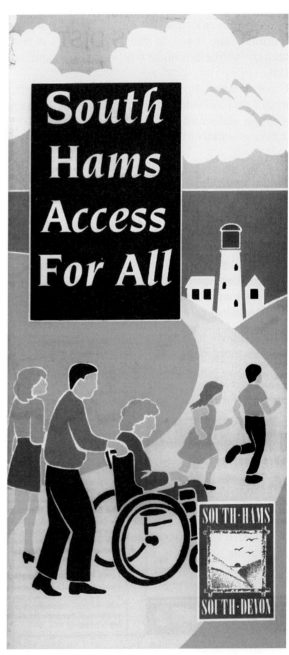

Fig. 8.1.5 South Hams takes active measures to make its facilities accessible to all people, including those with disabilities. Provisions include wheelchair access, tactile surfaces and Braille cards.

take part in a certain activity, the price charged can remain high.

Access can also refer to the provision for disabled customers at a facility. Some of the more old-fashioned facilities may not have adequate access for wheelchair users or those with mobility problems. The inclusion of wheelchair lifts and ramps is expensive, but it does ensure that the disabled are not disadvantaged and effectively barred from using the facility.

Location

Although there are literally thousands of centres around the UK which offer a broad range of recreational activities, it is inevitable that the one activity you wish to participate in will not be available locally. Bear in mind that centres generally only offer the most popular recreational activities. If a particular activity is not offered locally, it is always worth approaching a centre to see whether it would be prepared to lay on the necessary equipment and expertise if you could guarantee a certain number of participants.

In rural locations, the problem of remoteness and non-availability of recreational activities is much more obvious. In many cases it is a question of 'do it yourself'. Centres are open to suggestions as naturally they wish to make the best use of their facilities. They would much rather have a room or hall at the facility in use on a particular evening than leave it locked and empty.

Transport

Again, in rural areas, transport can be a big problem; public transport is almost non-existent after a certain time. In urban areas, despite the fact that public transport is available on virtually a 24-hour basis, the infrequency and unreliabilty of that transport may stop individuals venturing out to enjoy recreational activities. In most cases, it is a question of relying on those with cars of their own to provide the transport to and from the venue. This leads to another major problem – parking the car – which has been ignored by many venues.

Availability of activities

If you look through the list of activities offered at any venue, you will see that a great number of them are available only at certain times of the day, week, month or year. Some of the recreational activities are aimed at those who have considerable amounts of leisure time and are, therefore, scheduled during the day. The busy times for most venues are in the evenings. This is when the maximum amount of pressure is placed on the venue to provide facilities for a wide variety of different activities. In these cases, only the most popular ones will win.

Even when it appears that a recreational activity is available at a time to suit you, it is often the case that the facilities are booked up well in advance. This is particularly true of badminton and squash courts, for example, where a centre may only have one or two courts available at any time of the day or evening.

Lack of specialist equipment

This is often a tricky problem for a venue. Laying on facilities for a new recreational activity can, of course, involve considerable investment. The centre needs to be sure that it will be able to attract sufficient customers in order to justify the expense. However, if it does not buy the specialist equipment, it will lose these customers. Many smaller centres are under very strict financial limits, which may prevent them from purchasing specialist equipment and thereby expanding their range of recreational activities. In such cases it falls upon the customer to organise the purchase of specialist equipment which may be used at the venue; the centre will be happy to store the equipment whilst it is not being used. Good examples of this are judo mats, badminton nets and table tennis tables.

Lack of specialist staff

You will have realised by now that individuals who work in a venue or leisure centre are experienced and professional people. They have particular expertise in a limited number of recreational activities. It should not be expected that a swimming coach, for example, would be able to train people in karate or judo. Centres tend to look for specialist staff who they can employ on a part-time or 'as-and-when' basis in order to provide specialist tuition and guidance.

It should not be assumed, however, that these specialist individuals will automatically be available on demand. It may be impractical for someone who lives a considerable distance away to justify supervising a one-hour session, for example. Specialist members of staff will also be unavailable on occasions due to illness, holidays or other commitments. In such situations, the centre is faced with the prospect of having to either replace that person or cancel the activity.

If the activity attracts disabled people or those with special needs, a suitably experienced individual will be required who not only knows about the recreational activity, but also has experience regarding the needs of the participants.

8.1.5 *Explain, with examples, how common barriers can be overcome*

OVERCOMING COMMON BARRIERS

Many people, as we have seen, cannot enjoy recreational activities because of factors far beyond their control. In this performance criterion, we will look at the ways in which a centre or venue could address the most common barriers in a practical and effective way.

Concessions

Typically, concessions are available to the following groups:

▼ children
▼ disabled people
▼ unemployed people
▼ students
▼ senior citizens
▼ local residents
▼ regular users
▼ local companies
▼ groups

When we consider concessions, we are referring to reduced prices. The individuals involved will have to provide proof that they are eligible for the discount and may be restricted in the use of the venue or centre to off-peak times.

Adapting facilities

Increasingly, modern centres and refurbished centres are becoming multi-use venues. Whilst main sports halls are marked out with five-a-side football, basketball, netball and badminton courts, they are also used for many other different recreational activities. Standard rooms, such as those at the Michael Sobel Sports Centre in London, are multi-purpose and, indeed, can be enlarged by pulling aside partition walling. This level of flexibility means that the facilities can be adapted to almost any use. The principal problem remains where to store the equipment that may be needed for the different recreational activities.

Finding an alternative source of activities

If a venue is unable or unwilling to offer a particular recreational activity, the potential participants have no alternative but to seek a different venue. In many communities, less physical recreational activities are often held in public houses, village halls and local colleges and schools. Bearing in mind that these alternative venues are happy to receive the income that is generated from the hire of the facilities, there should be no reason why a site cannot be found for any kind of recreational activity. At the end of the day, it is the existing centre's loss and the new site's gain.

Improving transport links

When local authorities act in partnership with local centres, they can often put pressure on bus companies to offer a service to the venue. If the demand for public transport is sufficient and brought to the attention of local service providers, they will be able to assess whether to reconsider laying on additional transport.

Sometimes the centre itself will have its own transport, usually in the form of a mini-bus or small coach. For a nominal fee the centre will pick up and drop participants as a vital part of the overall customer service it provides. This additional service can mean the difference between success or failure for remote venues.

Adapting the programme of activities

If it is found that the programme of activities does not suit the needs of the customers, the centre needs to reconsider its options. If it has prepared a programme of activities based on the assumption that certain activities will be popular during the day, for example, and subsequently discovers that they are not, it will need to adapt the programme as quickly as possible. The centre will have a wide range of possible activities that could be included. It should always take an informed and practical approach to adapting its programme, as an activity that looks very good on paper may not work in practice. Above all, it must consider the needs of its customers.

Installing specialist equipment and deploying specialist staff

When we consider these two methods of overcoming potential barriers, we must not forget that they will cost money. For many small centres, funding is a major problem. There are countless cases of centres raising money through their customers to invest in new equipment and staff training in order to provide a wider range of recreational activities to the local community. Stradbrooke Swimming Pool in Suffolk, for example, was built on the proceeds of a will left to the local community from an avid swimmer and public-spirited individual. It is now run by the local council on behalf of the community.

assignment

ELEMENT 8.1

PC 8.1.1–5
COM 1.1, 1.2, 1.3, 1.4

In order to fulfil the performance criteria of this element, you will need to compile a brief report. Remember that much of the basic information in this element and assignment will also be useful for Element 8.2.

| task | 1 | PC 8.1.1–3 |

Choose four different client groups from:

- *children*
- *adolescents*
- *older people*
- *families*
- *groups*
- *people with different cultural backgrounds*
- *people with physical disabilities*
- *obese people*

Identify their needs in relation to recreational activities, suggest suitable activities and describe the benefits they would get from them.

| task | 1 | PC 8.1.4–5 |

Describe the common barriers to participation in recreational activities and explain how these barriers can be overcome. You should identify four different barriers and four different ways of overcoming them. They could be linked to the client groups identified in Task 1.

Notes
You could interview different client groups, particularly from your own class or family.

element 8.2

SURVEY PARTICIPATION IN RECREATIONAL ACTIVITIES LOCALLY

Performance criteria

A student must:

1   Identify and describe the **provision** of **recreational activities** at local centres.
2   Identify the main **client groups** participating in **recreational activities** at local centres.
3   Identify the main **characteristics of clients** participating in **recreational activities** at local centres.
4   Describe the **patterns of use** of a local centre by different **client groups**.
5   Identify the **benefits** of **recreational activities** to clients using a local centre.
6   Describe **barriers** to client participation at a local centre.
7   Explain **how barriers** to participation in **recreational activities** at a local centre can be **overcome**.

RANGE

Provision: type of activity offered, when activity is offered, location

Recreational activities: physical, social, intellectual

Client groups: children, adolescents, older people; families, groups; from different cultural backgrounds, with physical disabilities (sight, hearing, mobility), with obesity

Clients' characteristics: age, physical condition, gender, cultural background, budget

Patterns of use: type of activity, frequency (of using the centre, of participating in the activity), time spent on each activity

Benefits: physical, social, intellectual; providing a new experience, presenting a challenge, providing personal satisfaction

Barriers: cost, access, location, transport, availability of activities, lack of specialist equipment, lack of specialist staff

How to overcome: concessions, adapting facilities, finding alternative source of activities, improving transport links, adapting programme of activities, installing specialist equipment, deploying specialist staff

8.2.1 *Identify and describe the provision of recreational facilities at local centres*

PROVISION

This whole element is a two-part survey of the use of local centres. The first part of the survey looks at the general provision in your local area (this means the type and nature of the facilities within your local area). Specifically, you will need to:

▼ **identify and describe the provision of recreational activities at local centres**
▼ **identify the main client groups and their characteristics**

In the second part of the survey, you will need to concentrate in depth on one selected centre providing recreational facilities (probably one which you already know or use regularly). You have to:

▼ **describe the pattern of use of the centre by different client groups**
▼ **identify the benefits of the recreational activities to clients using the centre**
▼ **describe any barriers to client participation at the centre**
▼ **explain how these barriers could be overcome**

We will now look at some of the issues that you should consider and make suggestions which may help you in your survey.

Type of activity offered

To cover this aspect of the assignment, you will have to list all the activities offered by the different facilities in your area. You should consider this to be a key part of the survey, as it will help you in choosing a suitable centre to describe in greater depth. It is a good idea to choose a centre that offers you positive help and encouragement in the collection of your information.

Remember that this element focuses on recreational activities (physical, social and intellectual). You should restrict your research and survey to centres which offer these kinds of recreational activities.

When the activity is offered

For this aspect of the survey, you should study the pre-planned timetables and schedules that form an integral part of all centres. You need to determine exactly when the activities are on offer. You may wish to consider the following questions:

▼ **What activities are offered during the day?**
▼ **What activities are offered in the evenings?**
▼ **What activities are offered throughout the whole day?**
▼ **What activities are offered seasonally?**
▼ **What activities are offered only when weather permits?**

Location

As we said in Element 8.1, the availability and range of activities may be restricted as a result of the location. In rural areas the location is a key factor, whereas in cities it may not be as important. Bear in mind that local residents may be given preference over those who have to travel from outside the area to make use of the facilities. It may be helpful to consider the following questions:

▼ **How accessible are the recreational activities?**
▼ **Are they close to main centres of population?**
▼ **Are there groups of clients that find it difficult to get to the recreational facilities?**

RECREATIONAL ACTIVITIES

As we have already mentioned, you will need to make a list of the recreational activities (physical, social and intellectual) offered by the various centres in your locality. This can be done by creating a simple table. A list down the page should be made of all the different recreational activities that fall under the three main headings given above. Along the top, as column headings, should be the names of the main centres in your area that offer these recreational facilities. This means that you will only have to put a tick or a cross in each of the places that are relevant on the table.

Fig. 8.2.1 The National Playing Fields Association aims to provide recreational facilities in areas where they are most needed.

8.2.2 Identify the main client groups participating in recreational activities at local centres

As we have already discussed, the main client groups are:

▼ **children**
▼ **adolescents**
▼ **older people**
▼ **families**
▼ **groups**

In addition, you should consider client groups who come from different cultural backgrounds, have physical disabilities or are obese. Again, it will be useful to create a table which cross-references the different types of recreational activity available with the main client groups who take part in these activities in your locality.

8.2.3 Identify the main characteristics of clients participating in recreational activities at local centres

Having identified the main client groups and the specific activities that they engage in, you must now try to identify the main characteristics of these client groups. You need to consider the following:

▼ **age**
▼ **physical condition**
▼ **gender**
▼ **cultural background**
▼ **budget**

You will already have some idea about age, as you considered this aspect in the previous performance criterion.

Physical condition may be more difficult to identify, but this could be worked out by looking at the number of activities aimed at older people, or activities that do not require a great deal of physical exertion.

Gender should be fairly straightforward and for some activities you will find that the vast majority of participants are of one gender or another.

Cultural background should also consider the fact that certain individuals have different activity needs and this should be looked at in addition to strictly cultural differences based on race, religion or nationality.

Finally, the budget aspect is important. Council-run centres will be affordable to a wider range of people than centres which are privately owned.

8.2.4 *Describe the patterns of use of a local centre by different client groups*

PATTERNS OF USE

This performance criterion begins the second part of your study, where you have to concentrate in depth on one selected local centre. To identify patterns of use, you need to consider:

▼ **What type of activity is generally used by the client groups?**
▼ **How often do individuals use the centre?**
▼ **How often do individuals participate in a particular activity?**
▼ **How much time is spent on each activity?**

This is important information, as the centre will need to be able to assess the probable demand for a particular activity and try to make plans for the future as a result.

In assessing the patterns of use you may wish to observe the general use of a facility over a number of days, or perhaps return to the facility for a set period of time at the same time each week.

Type of activity

This requires you to look in more depth at the specific activities offered by your local centre. You will have to assess the overall availability of these activities and try to work out how much they are used over a period of time. The centre may be able to help you with this as it should have details about the number of clients that have entered the premises over a period of time.

It is important that you try to get accurate figures, as the rest of your deductions about patterns of use will depend upon having assessed this correctly.

Frequency

There are two parts of this aspect of pattern of use which need to be addressed. The first is frequency of using the centre. Many clients will use the facility again and again and become **regulars**. They may, of course, have paid a membership fee, so they will be looking for good value for money and will use the facility as often as possible. The main point is that they use the facility; in this respect it is not important what they actually do when they get there. They may participate in a lot of different activities and make full use of the facility.

The other aspect to look at is frequency of participating in the activity. Some clients only use the facility for one activity or the same range of activities. A group of people may regularly do an exercise class and then use the swimming pool, for example. Others will only ever attend certain classes, events or use particular equipment. This is important information for the centre as it needs to know who uses the facilities and for what reasons if it is going to consider expanding the range of activities available.

Time spent on each activity

Certain activities are offered for set periods of time only. This means that the 40-minute or 1-hour classes in a particular recreational activity are fairly easy to monitor. Sometimes clients book a facility for a short period, such as a squash court or five-a-side football pitch, which will also help you analyse the time spent on the activity.

If you take this information together with the frequency of use, you can work out how long individuals spend on a particular activity over a given period of time. Do not expect this aspect of your survey to be easy. You should restrict your research to a single activity or group of individuals.

8.2.5 Identify the benefits of recreational activities to clients using a local centre

In Element 8.1, we discussed the general benefits of recreational activities. You should now identify these and mention any specific benefits of using the centre you have chosen. A good way of identifying specific benefits is to interview individuals and see what they actually get from particular activities. Each individual will be looking for slightly different things and will achieve different levels of satisfaction from what they do.

8.2.6 Describe barriers to client participation at a local centre

Depending on the area, the spread of the population, the spending of the local council and the level of unemployment, each locality is going to have its own set of barriers to client participation.

One way of finding out about barriers is to try to find individuals who do not regularly (or ever) use the local centre for their recreational activities. You can then interview them and try to assess why they do not use the local facilities. The other line of enquiry that you could use is to ask customers of the local centres what problems they encounter in using the facilities.

Many of the more common barriers have been discussed in Element 8.1; these will be a good starting point for your research into this aspect of the assignment.

8.2.7 Explain how barriers to participation in recreational activities at a local centre can be overcome

Having established the main barriers to participation, you will now have to come up with some ideas as to how these could be overcome. Again, in Element 8.1 we discussed the possible strategies that could be used in the majority of cases.

Your locality may have specific problems that you have identified as key concerns. It will be a

Table 8.2.1 *This table, produced by the National Rivers Authority, shows access to its sites for land-based activities.*

Type of access	Restricted	Permit	Open	Total
Activity				
bird watching	1	2	103	106
cycling/mountain biking			32	32
horse riding			17	17
model boating	1	1	2	4
motor sports			2	2
orienteering			1	1
jogging/running			41	41
hunting/shooting	9			9
walking	1		372	373

vital part of your research to suggest solutions that would actually work given the local barriers.

It will be valuable in this part of the assignment to interview individuals who have specific requirements, such as access, timing or coaching needs, and find out how they cope with the lack of suitable facilities in the local area.

element 9.1

PROCESS INCOMING PAYMENTS

Performance criteria

A student must:

1 **Describe**, with examples, **common methods of payment**.

2 Explain the **importance** of maintaining accurate records of payments received.

3 Suggest **secure systems** for handling received payments and their records.

4 **Calculate** accurately **the amount** to be paid by customers.

5 **Process incoming payments** accurately.

RANGE

Describe: what the transaction method is used for, how the payment is processed

Common methods of payment: cheque, cash, vouchers, credit card, debit card, direct debit, standing order, bank transfer, credit note

Importance: responding to customers' enquiries, calculating income, providing data for management, providing documents for VAT inspection, providing documents for audit inspection

Secure systems: for cash payments, for card payments, for cheques, for vouchers; alarm systems, freestanding safe, built-in safe, regular emptying of tills, time-delay locks, practical drills for staff, illuminated overnight storage

Calculate the amount: items, quantity, basic price, discounts, VAT, totals

Process incoming payments: preparing a bill, giving change, issuing receipts, recording amount received, recording type of income, recording VAT, preparing summaries of payments received

9.1.1 *Describe, with examples, common methods of payment*

DESCRIBE WHAT THE TRANSACTION IS USED FOR

The survival of a leisure and tourism facility will depend on its financial state of health. In order to find out whether an organisation is spending more than it is earning, it is important that the series of financial transactions undertaken routinely by the facility are controlled in a strict and logical way. In this element we will be looking at the various inward and outward transactions which need to be processed by a leisure and tourism facility in the normal course of its activities. We will also see how some recent developments in payment methods have made many of these activities easier. Despite the use of new technology, there is still a need to check all transactions manually and for this reason we will be looking at many of the documents involved. The final part of this element considers the measures which a leisure and tourism facility can take to ensure that the records are accurately maintained.

DESCRIBE HOW THE PAYMENT IS PROCESSED

Dealing with and monitoring inward transactions is as vital as handling outward transactions. Leisure and tourism facilities need to keep complete records of all income received. This is not only an important legal requirement, but is also necessary to ensure that the facility's creditors (organisations or individuals that owe money to the facility) have paid the correct

amount at the right time. Some leisure and tourism facilities employ a credit controller to make sure that purchasing organisations do not exceed their credit limit or are late in paying their outstanding bills. These transactions can be dealt with using information technology, as we will see later in this element.

COMMON METHODS OF PAYMENT

In this part of the performance criterion, we are going to look at the main or most common ways of making payments. There are obviously many ways of doing this, but at this stage you only need to know the most popular ones. Some of them may be obvious to you, such as **cash** or **cheques**, others you will become more familiar with, such as **debit** or **credit cards**. The single method of payment that you may not have come across so far is **bank transfer** (also known as electronic transfer of funds). This method is used by organisations and banks and does not directly involve the customer or the facility.

Although you will encounter all these forms of payment in leisure and tourism facilities, the emphasis is likely to be on cash, card or voucher transactions.

Cheque

It is much safer to carry a cheque book than to carry cash. The reason for this is that once the cash is gone it cannot be replaced, whilst a cheque can be 'stopped' by a bank or building society if it is stolen or lost.

In many ways it is better for a supplying organisation to receive payment by cheque. The customer will not need to be issued with a receipt as the cheque book counterfoil is evidence of the payment, although in most cases a till receipt is supplied. The customer will also receive a bank statement which will itemise the transactions and show that the cheque has been cashed.

Another advantage of paying by cheque is that this method of payment can be sent through the post quite safely. If a cheque gets lost whilst in the post it is of no use to anyone except the

FIGURE IT OUT

PC 9.1.1
COM 1.1, 1.2

00:20

*D*iscuss in pairs, and then write down, what you would do if you had your cheque book stolen.

payee, unlike cash (which is of great use to everyone!).

When an individual opens a current account at a bank or building society, he or she is issued with a cheque book and a cheque guarantee card. The cheque book will contain a number of cheques, each of which are identical in every way, except for the serial number printed on them.

It is almost impossible nowadays to pay by cheque unless it is accompanied by a cheque guarantee card. This card virtually guarantees that the bank or building society (the drawee) will honour the cheque on behalf of the person writing the cheque (the drawer). Once a cheque guarantee card has been used, it is impossible to 'stop' the cheque.

A crossed cheque is one which has two lines drawn or printed down the centre, and the words 'account payee' written between these lines. This means that the person receiving the cheque will have to pay it into their bank account and cannot 'cash' it anywhere else. By doing this, the banks and building societies are making it more difficult for people to steal cheques and cash them.

Many facilities pay their bills using a cheque book. In larger leisure and tourism facilities, certain named people will be the only ones allowed to sign the cheques.

Cash

There is no way that the carrying of cash can be described as safe. Despite this, many people still pay for products and services by cash. In some ways it is more convenient to carry cash, and it is certainly less irritating to the person behind you in the queue if you pay by cash instead of writing a cheque.

Many facilities have concerns about payment by cash. It has become increasingly necessary for facilities to use ultra-violet machines to check whether bank notes are forgeries. It will not be long, however, before the forgers figure out a way of getting round this system, and another method of checking will have to be designed. It is certainly true that most facilities would prefer their customers not to pay in cash. It is far more convenient for the facility to receive payment by a credit or debit card, which not only cuts down on the paperwork but also guarantees (to some extent) that the payment will actually be made.

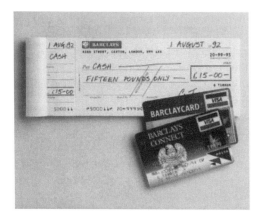

Fig. 9.1.1 A Barclays Bank cheque book and supporting cheque guarantee cards.

Fig. 9.1.2 *This voucher allows one person to enter Pleasure Island Theme Park free if accompanied by two adults paying the full entrance fee (courtesy of Pleasure Island Theme Park, Cleethorpes).*

Vouchers

As part payment (or sometimes as full payment), the customer may offer a voucher. These vouchers usually come from the following sources:

▼ **leaflets and brochures that the attraction, facility or centre have produced**
▼ **advertising or sales promotions that have been created by the attraction, facility or centre (e.g. on the back of a parking ticket)**
▼ **a joint promotion with another business in the area (e.g. MacDonalds offering 'money-off' vouchers for Pleasurewood Hills and other visitor attractions)**
▼ **general discount vouchers that have been given out by the attraction, facility or centre to certain individuals**

Credit card

Not too long ago, it was unusual to see someone paying for goods with a credit card. Today, however, they are commonly used and most people

feel quite happy about buying and using something that they have not really paid for yet. In fact, credit cards are very useful, although in the wrong hands they can be dangerous. Someone who is irresponsible could use a credit card to run up debts which he or she has little chance of being able to repay.

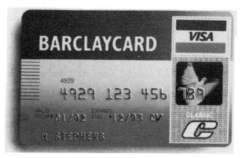

Fig. 9.1.3 *A Barclaycard – an example of a credit card.*

Each individual, or organisation, issued with a credit card is given a credit limit. This is the amount that they are allowed to spend using the card. Each month they will receive a statement from the credit card company, showing them the transactions that they have made using the card, the balance they owe the credit card company and the minimum amount they need to pay that month. If the owner of the card pays the amount owed in full, no interest is charged to the account. If, however, he or she can only pay a small amount, the interest charged can be high.

It is easy to see which facilities and businesses, both in this country and abroad, will accept credit card payments, as they display the fact in the window or near the counter of their premises.

Offering a credit card in payment does not necessarily guarantee that the facility will accept it. The facility will have a limit to the amount they can accept from a customer. This is called the **floor limit**. Anything above this has to be authorised directly from the credit card company. The facility will telephone the credit card company in order to receive an authorisation code. This code is then entered onto the sales voucher. If the credit card company will not issue an authorisation code (maybe because the limit of the card has already been reached, or the owner of the

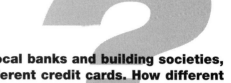
card has missed payments), the facility will not accept payment by credit card.

Increasingly, authorisation can be obtained using a special terminal linked directly to the credit card companies. These are easy to use for the retailer and quick for the person making the purchase. Many of these terminals will also print the sales voucher for the facility, although sometimes the sales assistant will complete the sales voucher by hand. The voucher is made up of four copies and is distributed as follows:

▼ **the top copy is given to the customer as the receipt**
▼ **the second copy is sent to the credit card company**
▼ **the third and fourth copies are kept by the retailer for its records**

Debit card

The need to carry around a cheque book with a cheque guarantee card is becoming a thing of the past. Increasingly, banks and building societies are adopting a card which looks and operates very much like a credit card, but simply and immediately debits the current account of the holder for the amount of the goods purchased. Once the bank has accepted the card, the retailer is then guaranteed payment within three days. **Switch** and **Connect** are the most common examples of this debit card method of payment. Some banks and building societies now also pro-

vide a multi-function card, which acts as a cheque guarantee card, a debit card and a cash dispenser card all in one.

Direct debit

For those making regular payments, it is often convenient to set up a direct debit. This means that the person or organisation receiving the money from you knows that the money will be paid on a particular day of the month. When setting up a direct debit, you will normally have to fill in a form or, perhaps, tell your bank or building society the amount to be paid and the date of payment, as well as the account number and details of the person to receive the money. Should the person or organisation need to change the amount which you pay, they will inform you before the next payment is due and this will be amended by the bank or building society.

Fig. 9.1.4 A Barclays Connect card – an example of a debit card.

In pairs, contact or visit your local banks and building societies and find out what their debit cards are called. What can these debit cards do? How many different places can you use them in? Is it easy to obtain cash from cash dispensers around your local area with these cards?

Standing order

Standing orders are ideal ways of dealing with regular payments. They differ from direct debits as a standing order is an agreement to pay the same set sum every month or quarter. This is used by a number of facilities and centres for monthly payments from their customers. It is particularly useful for the collection of membership fees and regular donations to charities and sanctuaries, such as those run by the various zoos.

We talk more about standing orders in the following section, as it is a form of bank transfer.

Bank transfer

The banks' automated clearing system (BACS) is used for both direct debit and standing order payments, as well as salary transfers. It reduces the amount of paperwork involved in each transaction. The necessary information is supplied to the bank on magnetic tape or disk and is processed via the BACS computer centre. Once the information has been processed, the necessary payments are made automatically.

In the case of direct debits, regular payments can be made from one account to another using this system. The customer informs the bank of the date and amount of payment, and the bank transfers the funds. With a direct debit, the facility receiving the money can vary the amount, although it is required to inform the customer before taking this action.

With standing orders, regular payments can be made using this system. A customer can tell his or her bank to pay by standing order on a certain date for a fixed amount. The facility receiving the money cannot change the amount unless the customer informs the bank of the change in advance.

In the same way that BACS can transfer money from one account to another, the Electronic Data Interchange (EDI) system can transfer information from one organisation to another. Immediate electronic data interchange can be made through a series of menus and sub-menus. It is rather like browsing in a library, but on screen. The data can be transferred to the computer of the person requesting the information, no matter where that terminal may be, and it can also be printed with the same speed.

Credit note

A credit note will be issued if a facility has overcharged a customer or has had faulty goods returned by the customer. A credit note from one facility to another would be much the same as one you might receive if you took goods back to a shop and asked for a refund. If, for some reason, this was not possible, the shop would issue you with a credit note. This means that you can spend the credit note at a later date or use it in part-payment for something more expensive.

Focus study

Electronic Data Interchange

The market researchers Internet Info calculated that in mid-1994 some 38 per cent of the top 2,000 US companies had some kind of link with Internet. Indeed, the Internet Society also figured out that 24 per cent of all the Internet hosts (these are separate directories which can be accessed via the Internet) were US organisations. The UK, by the same stage, accounted for some 5 per cent.

On a commercial basis, the Internet can provide information on demand for a price. You can also buy items via the Internet which are not necessarily information but products. Organisations have realised that making EDI available on the Internet allows them to provide a useful direct link with existing customers in providing back-up information for their products or services.

finding out

PC 9.1.1
COM 1.1, 1.2

  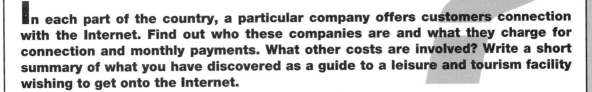

In each part of the country, a particular company offers customers connection with the Internet. Find out who these companies are and what they charge for connection and monthly payments. What other costs are involved? Write a short summary of what you have discovered as a guide to a leisure and tourism facility wishing to get onto the Internet.

```
                  CREDIT NOTE



 TO                          NUMBER

                             DATE

 ORDER NUMBER                INVOICE NUMBER


┌──────────┬──────────────┬────────┬────────┬──────┐
│ QUANTITY │ DESCRIPTION  │ UNIT   │ TOTAL  │ VAT  │
│          │              │ PRICE  │ PRICE  │      │
├──────────┼──────────────┼────────┼────────┼──────┤
│          │              │        │        │      │
│          │              │        │        │      │
│          │              │        │        │      │
│          │              │        │        │      │
│          │              │        │        │      │
│          │              │        │        │      │
│          │              │        │        │      │
│          │ Gross Value of Goods  │        │      │
│          │ LESS Trade Discount   │        │      │
│          │ Net Value of Goods    │        │      │
│          │ PLUS VAT @      %     │        │      │
│          │ CREDIT NOTE TOTAL     │        │      │
└──────────┴──────────────┴────────┴────────┴──────┘
```

Fig. 9.1.5 A blank credit note.

9.1.2 *Explain the importance of maintaining accurate records of payments received*

IMPORTANCE

It is important that a facility records *all* transactions, either manually (this means written in a book) or using a computer. These records will be kept for various reasons but, whatever the reason, they must always be kept accurately. Some of the main reasons for recording payments are:

▼ **so that there is a record which can be found if there should be any query from the customer**
▼ **so that the success or failure of the facility can be monitored**
▼ **so that the department responsible for paying the bills of the facility can find out if it has enough money to do so**
▼ **so that all the money owed to the facility is collected**

Importance in responding to customers' enquiries

Without records of transactions and monies received from customers, it would be impossible to deal with their enquiries. These enquiries may take a variety of different forms:

▼ **customers may wish to confirm that a payment has been received by the organisation**
▼ **customers may wish to know whether a standing order or other bank transfer has been made**
▼ **customers may wish to make changes to the regular payments made to the organisation**
▼ **customers may wish to make sure that the organisation has an up-to-date version of their address, bank details and other information**

Importance in calculating income

In order to prepare the accounts, a leisure and tourism facility needs to keep a clear, accurate and easy-to-find set of documents which relate to its payment transactions. The information within the documents will be copied into relevant ledgers and from these ledgers the facility will be able to:

▼ **identify the amount of money coming into the facility**

▼ **identify the amount of money being spent by the facility**
▼ **produce the accounts of the facility**
▼ **produce the accounts of the customers of the facility**

A facility needs to record its payments so that it can check its cash flow (that is, the money the facility needs to buy stock). Stock is used to produce goods, which are then sold. More cash is then fed into the facility. You can see that this cash flows around the facility.

As well as the cash flow situation of the facility, it is also very important that the facility makes a regular check on the profit or loss it is making. It would be very unwise for a facility to trade without checking whether it is making a profit or not. If it is making a loss, this might lead to the facility being forced to stop trading due to lack of money or bad debts.

Importance in providing data for management

The management of a facility will need to know whether the incoming payments that were expected over a particular time period have been received. Financial information is very important, as this forms the basis of many business decisions that have to be made. The management will not be able to make new financial commitments without knowing they have the money to hand. Obviously, the money received by the facility, or at least some of it, will have to be spent on ensuring that sufficient products and services are made available for the future.

Importance in providing documents for VAT inspection

As we have already mentioned, a leisure and tourism facility needs to keep accurate records of its financial transactions so that accounts of the business can be prepared. The accounts or finance department takes all the information from either the ledgers or computer files and processes it. This processing of financial data is necessary

in order to give an accurate idea of the way the facility is progressing. Company accounts have to be produced by law and the information contained in them is required by the following organisations:

▼ *the Inland Revenue* – **so that the correct amount of tax is worked out for the facility to pay**
▼ *the Customs and Excise Department* – **so that the correct amount of VAT is worked out for the facility**

Importance in providing documents for audit inspection

Nearly all organisations, particularly those that are limited companies, are required to have an independent audit inspection on a yearly basis. This audit inspection is required by the government to ensure that all the records of the organisation are correct and in order. The organisation will have to account for all incoming and outgoing payments and show where the remainder of the money is.

The organisation has to allow the auditors access to all the documents that relate to payments, so that they can be assured the records are a true reflection of all the transactions made over the period in question.

9.1.3 **Suggest secure systems for handling received payments and their records**

SECURE SYSTEMS

It is essential that all organisations have clearly defined methods of handling and recording various transactions. Not only do they need to account for each and every transaction (for tax purposes, for example), but they may also have to track a transaction back if there is a problem with payment or a query from the customer.

In this performance criterion, we will investigate the various ways in which organisations can maintain and record all of these transactions. In addition to the completion of their records, organisations need to take steps to ensure that all of the transactions can be accounted for and that none of the money received has been stolen or mislaid.

Secure systems for cash payments

In the course of a normal day, the organisation will take in a number of cash payments. If the facility is one that has regular arrivals of people (such as a theme park, museum or leisure centre), the customers will probably be paying entrance fees. They will also spend money on souvenirs, products and equipment or refreshments.

In a travel agency, for example, the typical products that could be paid for by cash are:

▼ **package holidays (deposits and full amounts)**
▼ **hotel reservations**
▼ **car rentals**
▼ **insurance**
▼ **theatre bookings**
▼ **airline tickets**
▼ **coach tickets**
▼ **ferry tickets**

All members of staff who handle cash should be responsible for ensuring that no mistakes are made. Each till or cash register should have only one key in daily use. The manager will hold another key in a secure place. Cash should be banked on a daily basis and a record of all cash transactions should be kept. The till roll in a cash register will do this.

Secure systems for card payments

Depending on the cardholder's income, the card will have a limit. It is important to check the following to ensure that a secure system is used in handling card payments:

▼ **that the expiry date on the card has not elapsed**
▼ **that the card has been signed**
▼ **that the signature is the same on the voucher as it is on the card**
▼ **that an approval code has been obtained from the card company if the amount is large**
▼ **that the customer has checked the details on the voucher and is happy with the information**

Secure systems for cheques

Just because someone has paid by cheque, does not mean that the facility or company is guaranteed payment. The bank receiving the cheque for payment into the facility's account might have problems in 'clearing' the cheque. The bank or building society may refuse to accept the cheque for a variety of reasons, including:

▼ **if there is not enough money in the account of the person writing the cheque**
▼ **if the cheque is more than six months old (this is known as a 'stale' cheque)**
▼ **if the cheque has not been dated**
▼ **if the cheque has been postdated (written for a future date)**
▼ **if the amount written in words is different from the amount in figures**
▼ **if the name of the payee (the person receiving the cheque) is incorrect (e.g. it may have been misspelt)**
▼ **if any corrections or alterations have been made on the cheque and have not been initialled by the drawer (the person writing the cheque)**
▼ **if the cheque has not been signed**
▼ **if the signature on the cheque does not**

match that on the cheque guarantee card
▼ **if the cheque guarantee card has expired (become out of date)**

All the above items have to be checked either at the counter or with the drawer's bank before the bank will clear the cheque.

Because the processing of a cheque can take so much time, it is important for the facility to have a record of these transactions. The facility would use the counterfoil of the cheque book as its record of the transaction until the bank statement arrives.

If you pay for something by cheque, there is no need to request a receipt for your own records. The counterfoil (cheque stub in the cheque book) should be completed showing the date, the amount paid and the person to whom the cheque was made out. This is your record of the payment. It is not, however, proof of payment and a till receipt should be kept in case the goods need to be replaced or a refund requested. In addition to the counterfoil, the bank will send a bank statement which shows the transactions that have taken place during the period. This bank statement is also a record of the payments you have made.

Secure systems for vouchers

When vouchers are offered as payment or part-payment for the products or services, a number of checks should be made:

▼ **that the voucher is valid in terms of the products and services requested by the customer**
▼ **that the voucher is valid in terms of the date and expiry of the offer**
▼ **that the customer is actually purchasing products and services that relate to the voucher**
▼ **that any rules about the use of the voucher are correct (such as two paying customers with a voucher allow a third to get into the facility free)**

Alarm systems

A facility must have an adequate alarm system that is positioned to protect the cash and staff who use the cash registers. If threatened with violence, staff should always hand over the money rather than risk injury. However, a secure area that is alarmed will act as a good deterrent against attack.

All side and rear doors should be alarmed in order to alert staff to any unauthorised entry into the premises or site. This will be part of the alarm system that protects the whole of the facility once it is closed for the night. Some facilities need to have more extensive alarm systems to include the following:

▼ **panic buttons to call for help if in trouble**
▼ **mechanical shutters to close if attacked**
▼ **pressure pads and sensors to pick up movement in unobserved areas**
▼ **regular patrols to check the alarms and sensor systems**

Freestanding safes and built-in safes

It should be standard practice for money to be taken from tills at regular intervals to be stored in a safe. In any case, tills and cash registers should be empty overnight, so there is definitely a need to have a secure place to keep the money.

Some facilities will have their safe situated in a location that is freely visible from the outside of the building. This is to ensure that if anyone is trying to break into the safe, then they can be observed. These freestanding safes are very heavy and the location has to be carefully considered before a final decision is made. Other facilities may have a more traditional wall-mounted or built-in safe. This will be located in a secure area of the building well away from the gaze of passers-by.

Regular emptying of tills

This is a vital task of the manager or supervisor. The regular emptying of the tills will ensure that the minimum amount of cash is vulnerable to theft. The system used will depend on the facility. Some supervisors have to empty the tills hourly or at least a few times during the day. This is sometimes called a 'pick up'. The money is taken from the till, stored in sealed bags or containers, and totalled at the end of the day.

Time delay locks

This is an expensive addition to the safe or other areas that house the cash that has been collected. It is not very common in leisure and tourism facilities. The time delays mean that the safe can only be opened at times that have been agreed by the management of the facility. This ensures that the safe cannot be opened out of hours, even if a member of staff is being threatened by potential robbers. If the time delay locks are tampered with, an alarm will be set off.

Practical drills for staff

Any member of staff that is expected to handle cash will have to be trained in the security measures that have been recommended by the management. In many cases, the centre will have consulted the local police to learn the best ways of securing its premises and cash. Regular updates and refresher courses are used to ensure that the staff understand the procedures and functions of the security systems.

Illuminated overnight storage

In situations when payments are stored overnight within the premises, it is important to make sure that the safe or other secure unit is in clear view of security or police. In these cases, the room (or perhaps foyer) which houses the safe should be illuminated once the building has been locked and the alarm set. Not only will this serve as a deterrent (anyone attempting to gain access to the safe will be clearly visible), but it also removes the necessity of having full-time security staff on duty throughout the night. It should be pointed out, however, that it is unwise to keep large sums of money in overnight storage on the premises, regardless of the security systems used.

9.1.4 Calculate accurately the amount to be paid by customers

CALCULATIONS

Whenever numbers are concerned, it is always important to ask someone else to check your work. Making accurate calculations is probably one of the most important duties that the facility will expect of its staff. If an error is made in making calculations, it could have the following effects:

▼ **customers will become annoyed, which is not good for the facility. A facility wants its customers to remain happy and to recommend it to their friends and family so that sales increase**
▼ **any error made in a calculation will be transferred to further documents, creating a 'knock-on' effect. When the accounts are finally drawn up, they will not give a true picture of how well the facility is doing**
▼ **you will be causing work for someone else who has to trace the error back through the documents to find out where it was made**
▼ **if the mistake is serious enough, it could be brought to the attention of senior members of the management team and this would not be good for your career**

FIGURE IT OUT

PC 9.1.4
COM 1.1, 1.2

00:20

In pairs, copy out the following dates. Swap your papers so that your partner can check your work for legibility and accuracy.

25 January 1950

3 February 1955

6 April 1994

24 April 1958

15 June 1972

27 June 1970

1 August 1975

24 August 1921

17 November 1992

21 December 1920

Using a calculator may be helpful, but you should not assume that your figures are correct. You may have pressed a wrong key or missed out one of the figures. By producing the wrong calculations, it could mean that the facility has the following problems:

▼ *customers are overcharged* – **this will mean that the facility loses its reputation for being efficient and customers may think that the facility is trying to get more money out of them deliberately**

▼ *customers are undercharged* – **this will mean that when the owners or managers of the facility find out, you will be disciplined. Some facilities will deduct the money lost from your wage or salary**

▼ *the accounts do not balance* – **this will mean a lot of additional work for somebody else who has to trace the source of the error**

Even if you are using a spreadsheet package for calculations, the machine will only carry out the instructions it is given. If you input the wrong information, the computer will make the wrong totals. Again, everything you do should be checked thoroughly.

Cross-checking is a skill which is used commonly in office situations. It really means that you double-check everything you have done so that you do not miss any mistakes. Cross-checking is particularly useful when dealing with numbers because, although it is easy to see that a word is misspelt or missing, it is not so easy to find a mistake in column upon column of numbers.

Items

When filling out an invoice (see Figure 9.1.6), the 'description' column refers to the goods the customer has actually received. This information will help the customer to check the goods to which the invoice relates. If this information is not included, it may delay the customer in making payment. The description of items sold may relate to any of the following:

▼ **information from your facility catalogue (this may include a reference number)**
▼ **information transferred from the order the customer sent to your facility**
▼ **information transferred from the delivery note which was sent with the goods to the customer**

In addition to the description column, the 'quantity' column would be completed showing the number of each of the items that have been sent to the customer.

Quantity

As mentioned above, it is important to note the quantity of the products or services that the customer requires. In other cases, the term quantity can apply to the number of visitors; for example, you may have to calculate the total cost of entry for a number of individuals of different ages.

Basic price

The 'unit price' column shows the current price of the goods the customer has ordered. This is the price quoted to the customer when he or she made the order, even if the price has been increased since that date.

Discounts

Sometimes a customer is allowed a discount. The discount allowed could be either trade, cash or prompt payment discount. In the case of trade discount, this is allowed to the customer because they have bought a large quantity of goods, or because they regularly purchase from the facility. The trade discount is normally shown as a percentage on the invoice and is deducted from the total price of the goods before any VAT is added.

VAT

VAT is a government tax that is added to the normal price of most products and services. The current rate of VAT is 17.5 per cent.

Totals

The 'total price' column would be the price per item column multiplied by the quantity column. When the total price of each item ordered is added together, this is the **gross value** of the invoice. This means it is the grand total before any discounts are taken off and any VAT is added on.

Once the gross value, less any trade discount, has been calculated, this gives the **net value** of the invoice. The VAT is then added to the net value of the invoice, which gives the **invoice total**. This is the amount the customer has to pay.

9.1.5 *Process incoming payments accurately*

PROCESS INCOMING PAYMENTS

Payment processing methods can be completed either manually using written records or automatically using a till or computer-based system. The income received should be classified under appropriate headings. For example, in a

```
                    INVOICE

  +-----------------------------------------------+
  | TO                      NUMBER                |
  |                         DATE                  |
  |                         TERMS                 |
  | YOUR ORDER NO           DISPATCH DATE         |
  +----------+-------------+------+------+--------+
  | QUANTITY | DESCRIPTION | UNIT | TOTAL| VAT    |
  |          |             | PRICE| PRICE|        |
  |          |             |      |      |        |
  |          |             |      |      |        |
  |          |             |      |      |        |
  |          | Gross Value |      |      |        |
  |          | LESS Trade Discount |   |         |
  |          | Net Value of Goods  |   |         |
  |          | PLUS VAT @      %    |   |         |
  |          | INVOICE TOTAL       |   |         |
  +----------+-------------+------+------+--------+
  E & O E
```

Fig. 9.1.6 A blank invoice.

leisure centre it might be for a swim or sports goods; in a heritage centre it might be for entrance or purchase of a guide book. Again, it is vital that payments are recorded accurately. Anything which is incorrectly recorded in the ledger will give an incorrect figure when the accounts are prepared.

Preparing a bill

Bills are either handwritten or created automatically by a cash register or till. In order to make sure that the amount on the bill is correct, you should make the following checks:

▼ that the quantity of the items is correct
▼ that the items are correct
▼ that the price is correct
▼ that any discounts have been included
▼ that the VAT (if applicable) has been included, although this will probably be part of the basic price
▼ that the total is correct

These are fairly easy to check as the till will show a display before you press the key to finally print the bill.

FIGURE IT OUT

PC 9.1.4
COM 1.2, 1.4

00:15

*C*opy and complete the invoice form given in Figure 9.1.6 using the following information:

Brian Forbes, 124 Chedworth Road, Barking, Dorset ordered the goods below (order no. 1346) on 24.6.19 – . He is a good customer and always receives 2.5 per cent discount. His goods were dispatched the same day and you are sending the invoice at the end of the month. He received the following:

- *10 badminton rackets (ref. no. 45) at £24.99 each*
- *10 pairs of shuttlecocks (ref. no. 24) at £3.50 each*

Make sure your figures are neat and the whole invoice is legible.

Giving change

Making sure that the correct change is given is not as easy as it may seem. This is particularly true of situations when the cashiers are under pressure with a queue of people waiting to pay. Most modern tills make this process easier, as follows:

▼ **the cashier enters the amount tendered (given) by the customer**
▼ **the cash register then displays how much change the cashier must give to the customer (if appropriate)**
▼ **the register prints out a receipt, showing the total price, the amount tendered and the change to be given**

You should always count the change into the hand, or in clear view, of the customer. In cases when the till is old-fashioned or the transaction is carried out without a till, you should keep the money tendered by the customer in sight until the transaction has been completed. This will remind you how much was tendered by the customer and how much you will have to give in change. There

can be no dispute if the money that was given has not been put away until the customer has received the change and is happy with the transaction.

Issuing a receipt

A receipt is a document which confirms that a certain amount of money has been paid. This

```
A.E KERRIDGE+SONS LTD.STATION GARAGE.
DARSHAM SAXMUNDHAM SUFFOLK.

V.A.T. REG. NO 105 6763 74.
             DATE               17/04/95
             PUMP NUMBER              6
             PENCE PER LITRE       54.9
             LITRES               47.35

     PRICE INC. 17.5% V.A.T.     £26.00
```

Fig. 9.1.7 A till receipt proving that a purchase has been made using cash.

could be from one individual to another, such as when you go shopping and receive a till receipt, or from one business to another. Someone buying petrol may ask for a receipt because they can claim the purchase on their expenses.

Receipts take many forms, but in all cases they will state the amount of money involved and the date the transaction took place. They will be made out in duplicate (two copies) so that each person involved in the transaction has a copy.

Most people are familiar with the way in which a receipt works. Here is a summary:

▼ **when you buy goods from a shop, you usually receive a printed till receipt**
▼ **in some smaller shops, the assistant will write a receipt by hand**
▼ **if you have a cheque book, the counterfoil (cheque stub) can act as a form of receipt or record of what you have spent and who you have paid it to**
▼ **when you pay money into a bank account using a paying-in slip, the counterfoil acts as a form of receipt or record of how much you paid in**
▼ **if you receive a bank statement, this lists all the monies paid in and taken out of your account, and acts as a receipt for the amount you have in balance**
▼ **if you travel by bus or train you will receive a ticket. This is your receipt that you have paid the fare**

▼ **when you take clothes to the dry cleaners, the assistant will issue a receipt which you have to present when collecting the goods**

Receipts are normally quite simple to complete, and are usually made up of the following items:

▼ **the name of the business issuing the receipt**
▼ **the date of the transaction**
▼ **the name of the person making the payment**
▼ **the amount of the payment**
▼ **the reason for the payment**

Recording amount received

It is important that a facility keeps all till records for the following reasons:

▼ **so that it can keep a record of the total sales for the shop**
▼ **so that it can identify the sales for individual items**
▼ **so that it can identify the sales for individual members of staff**
▼ **so that it can keep a record of any refunds that have been given**

Many large facilities have electronic tills which read the bar codes from items being sold. The tills are programmed with information about any special offers the facility may have, as well as any

Fig. 9.1.8 A recorded delivery receipt, proving that a package has been sent by Royal Mail.

> CASH RECEIPT
>
> Number ...... NUMBER .... DATE ....
> Date .... RECEIVED FROM ....
> From ....
> ....
> .... THE SUM OF ....
> ....
>   £   p   £   p

Fig. 9.1.9 A blank cash receipt.

FIGURE IT OUT

PC 9.1.5
COM 1.1

00:15

In pairs, using Figure 9.1.9, decide why each of the headings are necessary and who would make use of the information written beside each.

discounts available. The till will automatically adjust the bill to take these special offers and discounts into account and the total of the bill is amended accordingly.

```
PLEASE KEEP THIS FOR YOUR RECORDS

   ASDA STORE GREAT YARMOUTH

EPS NO. 6542
DELTA

EXPIRY DATE 07/96
AUTHORISED    067302
      CARD              84.18
      CHANGE            20.00
TOTAL NUMBER OF ITEMS SOLD =  59
6/04/95 17:47 0756 12 0094 411

      POCKET THE DIFFERENCE
```

Fig. 9.1.10 A till receipt which has been produced by an electronic till.

Recording type of income

A **payments received sheet** is completed if the facility does not have a till. A market trader might use a payments received sheet to log the sales during the day, for example, and a washing machine repair person might use one to log the payments customers have made in the course of the day.

The payments received sheet needs to allow for the various methods of payment to be logged, as not everybody pays by the same method. Obviously, it would not allow for debit card payments as these are computerised and require an electronic terminal link.

By using a payments received sheet, the facility can transfer the payments made straight into the cash book. It can also be used for completion of the paying-in slip if the money is paid into the bank account of the facility.

Recording VAT

It is very important to make sure that the VAT component of the payment is recorded. The Customs and Excise Department requires organisations to provide quarterly returns on all the VAT received and spent. The organisation therefore has to make sure that the following are carried out:

▼ **all incoming payments of VAT are recorded**
▼ **all incoming payments of VAT are totalled**
▼ **all outgoing payments of VAT are recorded**
▼ **all outgoing payments of VAT are totalled**
▼ **if more VAT has been received than spent, a cheque for the balance is sent to the Customs and Excise Department**
▼ **if more VAT has been spent than received, a claim is sent to the Customs and Excise Department for a refund of the overpaid VAT**

PAYMENTS RECEIVED SHEET

DATE	DETAILS OF PAYMENT RECEIVED	AMOUNTS RECEIVED		
		CASH	CHEQUE	CREDIT CARD

Fig. 9.1.11 A blank payment received sheet.

PAYMENTS RECEIVED SHEET

DATE	DETAILS OF PAYMENT RECEIVED	AMOUNTS RECEIVED		
		CASH	CHEQUE	CREDIT CARD
1 May	Repairs to machine at 14 High Street	£27.50		
1 May	Service to machine at 47 Silver Road		£55.00	
1 May	Repairs to machine at 12 The Elms, Bracton		£57.00	
1 May	Replace water pump to machine at 1 North Road			£69.60

Fig. 9.1.12 A completed payment received sheet.

Preparing summaries of payments received

Each facility has its own way of accounting. A computerised system allows all the information to be collated and summarised at the push of a button. Payments received sheets and other summaries are useful in recording information that will be used to monitor the sales and activities of the organisation.

Whatever system you use, it is important to make sure that all the details of every transaction have been accounted for on the summary sheets. The following details should be included:

▼ **the dates of the payments**
▼ **the amounts of the payments**
▼ **the methods of payment**
▼ **the nature of the payments**

It is important to keep track of the various payments, as this will provide accurate information on the current financial situation of a facility, attraction or centre.

FIGURE IT OUT

PC 9.1.5
COM 1.1, 1.2, 1.4

00:15

*Y*our parents are paying for you to have a new hairstyle for your Christmas present. They want you to pay in cash and then give them a receipt so that they can refund you the money. Unfortunately, when you ask the receptionist at the salon for a till receipt, you are told that they do not have a till. What should you do? Write down your thoughts and then compare them with those of the rest of your group.

assignment

ELEMENT 9.1

PC 9.1.1–5
COM 1.2, 1.4
AON 1.1, 1.2, 1.3

*I*n order to complete this element, you will need to show that you understand how and why incoming payments are processed, focusing on the methods most common to leisure and tourism facilities.

| **task** | **1** | PC 9.1.1–5 |

Write brief notes on the common methods of payment and security of payments. Your notes should describe each of the following:

- *cheques*
- *cash*
- *vouchers*
- *credit cards*
- *debit cards*
- *direct debit*
- *standing orders*
- *bank transfers*
- *credit notes*

You must specify what transactions each is used for and how each type of payment is processed. Include an example of each of the following:

- *cash payment*
- *card payment*
- *cheque payment*
- *voucher transaction*

| **task** | **2** | PC 9.1.1–5 |

Explain why incoming payments should be recorded accurately and stored securely. Give suggestions for secure systems for cash, card, cheque and voucher payments.

| **task** | **3** | PC 9.1.1–5 |

Your tutor will provide you with some information to prepare bills for six customers. Each bill will have to include calculations for at least three items. Two of the bills will include discounts and two will involve the calculation of VAT. You will have to fill in the appropriate documents to record these transactions.

Performance criteria

A student must:

1 Describe **payments commonly made** by leisure and tourism organisations.

2 List the main **items** a selected leisure and tourism facility would need to buy to operate effectively.

3 **Process documentation** prior to making payments.

4 Match different **methods of payment** with different **purposes**.

RANGE

Payments commonly made: wages, salaries; goods bought, services bought

Items: goods, services, expertise, other

Process documentation:

check   quantity, price, VAT, totals, discounts, other calculations

record   invoices, credit notes, payments; breakdown of expenditure, summaries of payments

Methods of payment: cheque, cash, vouchers, credit card, debit card, direct debit, standing order, bank transfer, credit note

Purposes (of payment): for regular staff, for occasional staff, for regular suppliers, for occasional suppliers, small irregular payments

9.2.1 Describe payments commonly made by leisure and tourism organisations

PAYMENTS COMMONLY MADE

In the relevant performance criteria and other sections of this element we will be looking at the main ways payments are made and the processing methods used. The procedures followed and documents used will differ from organisation to organisation. However, there are a number of similarities found regardless of the type of organisation, its purpose or its size. As we mentioned earlier, routine payments can now be made using information technology, although it is still common to find manual systems in operation.

Taken together, these inward and outward financial transactions are used to create company accounts, including balance sheets, profit and loss accounts and cashflow statements. Although we will not be looking at these within this programme of study, you will learn about these gradually as you progress into GNVQ Intermediate and Advanced Business.

All organisations have a budget. Whether the organisation is large or small, it will have an objective which it must try to meet. It would be impossible for managers to monitor the performance of the organisation if documents relating to the amount of money spent and the amount of money coming into the organisation were not readily available and accurate.

Obviously, the larger the organisation, the more documents it will generate. In addition to this, a larger organisation is more likely to purchase goods on a credit basis. This means that it will order and receive goods when the need arises, and pay for them on a monthly basis or after an agreed period of time. Such an organisation is likely to generate its documents by computer software packages, although it is not unusual for an organisation to still be handling some transactions manually.

Because so many transactions are dealt with, mistakes such as the following could easily occur unless the organisation records all transactions:

▼ **goods being sent to the wrong customer**
▼ **incorrect goods being dispatched to a customer**
▼ **delay in payments for goods**
▼ **complaints being received from customers**
▼ **loss of business because of confusion with customers**

Although the activities of different organisations may vary, all organisations use the business documents they generate to plan and control the way the organisation is performing. The documents may either relate to the day-to-day work of a small number of workers, or it may relate to a specific job of the production line.

Whatever the activity, the accounts department would need to be informed of every financial transaction that takes place within the organisation. Because so much credit is offered nowadays, the accounting team need copies of each document received or sent out from the organisation so that it can generate the accounts of the business.

Wages and salaries

Despite the day-to-day fortunes of a facility, wages and salaries still have to be paid. Wages are usually paid by cheque or sometimes in cash on a weekly basis, and are normally processed by the facility itself. Salaries are usually paid by bank transfer on a monthly basis, and may be handled by the facility or its bank.

The facility may also be paying out the following kinds of wages and salaries:

▼ **hourly pay to instructors, coaches and trainers, which may be paid on receipt**

of a claim from them or regularly as a salary or wage
- ▼ occasional payments for staff filling in for permanent staff who are ill or on holiday
- ▼ seasonal payments for staff who are taken on at times when the facility is busy

Goods and services bought

Depending on the nature of the facility, this may be a consideration that is complex or quite simple. The fact that all facilities have to buy in some goods and services means that they will have to have mechanisms in place to cope with the paperwork.

Most of the goods and services will be paid for on receipt of an invoice. This means that the facility will have some time to pay for the goods and services after they have been supplied.

Facilities have their own procedures and methods of dealing with invoices. These include the following:

- ▼ some pay immediately on receiving the invoice
- ▼ some pay at the end of the period stated on the invoice
- ▼ some pay at the end of the month in which the invoice was presented
- ▼ some pay when they have been reminded that the invoice is outstanding

In the final case, the facility is trying to get the most out of the supplier. The facility is not refusing to pay, it is just waiting until the last moment to pay. This is quite common practice in business generally. In such cases, suppliers will be keen to make sure that the facility is reminded as often as possible that invoice payment is still due.

9.2.2 *List the main items a selected leisure and tourism facility would need to buy to operate effectively*

The list of items a leisure and tourism facility would need to buy to operate effectively will depend on the exact nature and scope of the facility. You should consider goods, services, expertise and any other items that will be required. A swimming pool, for example, would need the following:

- ▼ dispensers for refreshments and food
- ▼ drinks and food for the dispensers
- ▼ cleaning materials
- ▼ inflatables and other pool equipment
- ▼ staff uniforms
- ▼ safety equipment
- ▼ publicity materials, leaflets and fliers
- ▼ pool cleaners
- ▼ specialist instructors for particular events and activities

9.2.3 *Process documentation prior to making payments*

PROCESS DOCUMENTATION

We all need money of some sort daily, and, depending on our circumstances, we pay for the goods we buy in a variety of different ways. To some extent, the same applies to business organisations. There are six main ways in which a facility may choose to pay for the goods or services it has bought. As we have seen, these are:

▼ **cheque**
▼ **cash**
▼ **credit card**
▼ **debit card**
▼ **direct debit or standing order**
▼ **bank transfer (electronic transfer of funds)**

Although cash, cheque and debit card are different methods of payment, they are all still regarded as being 'cash' payments because the supplier receives the money for the goods or services on an immediate basis. A credit card payment gives the supplier the money instantly, but the credit card company may not receive the money from the purchasing organisation or customer for some time.

You will need to be able to do the following basic calculations when processing documentation:

▼ **Items have to be *added* together when more than one item is listed on the invoice. The VAT also has to be added to the net value of the invoice**
▼ ***Percentages* have to be calculated when working out the trade discount the customer is entitled to and the VAT that has to be added to the net value of the invoice**
▼ **You have to use *subtraction* to take the trade discount away from the gross value of the invoice**
▼ ***Multiplication* has to be used when working out the total price of each item if more than one has been ordered**

Checking quantity

This is extremely important, as the facility needs to be sure that the quantity quoted on the invoice and delivery note is the same as the number of items it has received.

When the invoice is being looked at prior to payment, the original order needs to be checked against the invoice to make sure that the quantities are the same. The supplier may have sent too many or too few items. This may just be an error, but there may be a reason that will need to be followed up.

Checking price

In order to ensure that the facility has not been overcharged for a product or a service, it must check that the price quoted on the documentation accords with the agreed purchase price. Again, there may be a reason for the difference in the price, but this needs to be checked and the reasons behind the change agreed with the person who originated the order.

Checking VAT

If there is a VAT payment that is part of the overall price of the product or service, this needs to be checked for accuracy. It is not the easiest thing in the world to add 17.5 per cent to any figure, so mistakes regarding this could have been made. It is essential that the facility has been neither over nor undercharged VAT, as this will have to be made clear to the Customs and Excise Department who collects this tax on behalf of the government.

Checking totals

Checking totals can be a reasonably simple task with the aid of a calculator or computer. On more straightforward invoices this may be done manually. Whichever method is used, it is important to make sure that all the sub-totals and the overall total are correct. If there has been an error made somewhere in the calculations, this will affect the totals. For example, if the price or VAT was not worked out properly by the person who prepared the invoice, the final total will not be accurate.

Checking discounts

If the facility is entitled to a discount, it should be easy to identify where this has been mentioned on the invoice. Sometimes, however, the situation is less clear. For example, if the discount has already been taken off the price of the products or services before the amount has been entered onto the invoice, it may not be clear whether the discount has been calculated correctly. Equally, if the discount is in the form of free or bonus products on the invoice (the facility may receive one extra product for every ten that has been purchased), this may throw up what seem to be incorrect quantities or totals.

Generally the discount is shown clearly at the end of the invoice. The facility may also be entitled to a further discount known as **early settlement**. This means that if the facility pays the invoice quickly, it will be able to claim a further discount – usually somewhere between 2.5 and 5 per cent.

Checking other calculations

Special items like early settlement discounts could fall into this category. Also, if the invoice includes a payment for delivery, this should be checked against similar deliveries by the same supplier to make sure its calculations and totals are correct.

Recording invoices

A sales invoice is a document which is sent out to the purchaser of the goods or services. As always, the information should be correct, neat, and contain all the details required. It is to the advantage of the supplier to send out its sales invoices quickly so that it can receive payment for the goods or services as quickly as possible. Obviously, any sales invoice which is sent out containing errors or with something missing will have to be changed or amended, and this could cost the supplier money and valuable time.

How quickly the facility pays the supplier for the goods or services it has received will depend on the terms under which it ordered them. This is an arrangement made between the organisation selling and the organisation buying, which includes the time limit for payment. The facility buying the goods may wish to take advantage of any prompt payment discount (money off the total of the invoice if it pays quickly) it has been offered by the seller. On the other hand, it may be entitled to cash or trade discount. Cash discount is allowed if the bill is paid in cash and trade discount is allowed if the facility regularly orders from the supplier or if it always orders large amounts.

FIGURE IT OUT

PC 9.2.3
COM 1.2

00:10

*C*an you remember the types of discount we have discussed? Write down the difference between trade, cash and prompt payment discounts.

Recording credit notes

If you buy something from a shop which is faulty in some way, or which proves to be unsuitable, you may return the goods and ask for a refund or

a replacement. Refunds will only be given if you can prove that you have bought the goods from the store or from one of the branches of the chain store involved.

If, when you made the purchase in the first

```
                        INVOICE

  TO                          NUMBER

                              DATE

                              TERMS

  YOUR ORDER NO               DISPATCH DATE

  QUANTITY   DESCRIPTION    UNIT    TOTAL    VAT
                            PRICE   PRICE
```

	Gross Value			
	LESS Trade Discount			
	Net Value of Goods			
	PLUS VAT @ %			
	INVOICE TOTAL			

```
  E & O E
```

Fig. 9.2.1 A blank invoice.

place, you bought several other items as well, the till receipt will be amended to show the refund on the single item.

If you paid for the item in cash, the shop will refund in cash. If you paid by cheque or debit card, then, provided enough time has passed so that the transaction has 'cleared' the bank, the shop will refund in cash.

If you paid by credit card, a different system of refund is used. The shop will complete a **refund voucher**. This voucher simply informs the credit card company that the amount you paid on your credit card has to either be cancelled or paid back into your account. It is not normal for a shop to refund in cash when the first payment method was by a credit card.

finding out

PC 9.2.3
COM 1.1, 1.2

In pairs, try to find out from a store what would happen if the following situation arose:

> You purchase four items using a credit card. Three days later you need to return one of the items because it is not suitable. You have your receipt, but the store refuses to refund you in cash because you paid by credit card.

It would be good if each pair used a different store. When you have made your enquiries, discuss as a group what the outcomes were from the different stores.

Recording payments

Your receipt is your proof of payment. In a similar way, facilities need proof of payment for many different transactions. If someone requires petty cash, for example, a receipt for the goods purchased must be provided to the petty cashier. Facilities require evidence from their employees that they have spent money on behalf of the organisation. To comply with this, sales representatives request receipts for any money they spend on behalf of the business. These are then passed onto the accounts department who record the income (money coming in) and expenditure (money being spent) of the facility.

FIGURE IT OUT

PC 9.2.3
COM 1.1, 1.2

00:15

*S*ales representatives need to produce receipts for the money they spend on behalf of the organisation. Make a list of items they can 'claim back' then compare your list with those of the rest of your group.

Recording breakdown of expenditure

In order to keep track of the expenditure of the facility, it is important to make sure that all payments are correctly and accurately recorded. Remember that all the records of individual transactions will be used to make up the overall record of the facility's financial dealings. The breakdown of expenditure, usually under the headings of the different departments or areas of the facility, will have to be compared with the expected expenditure for that particular time period. By doing this, the facility can make sure that it is not spending more than it was expecting to spend during a particular period of time. This information will find its way onto the summary of payments and eventually the cash flow itself.

Recording summaries of payments

Suppliers usually send statements of account to their customers once a month, at the end of each month, and these list the transactions that have taken place between the two companies. They show the totals of each of the sales invoices sent to the customer, plus any payments made by the customer during the month. The balance shown at the end of the statement is the amount of money still to be paid by the customer to the supplying organisation.

Statements of account are important to an organisation for two reasons:

▼ **to keep a check on what a customer still owes**
▼ **to keep a check on what has been sent to the customer**

STATEMENT

TO

Sutherland Sportswear
124 South Street
LONDON
SE2 4DC

DATE 28.2.19..

NUMBER 32

TERMS   2.5%

DATE	DETAILS	DEBIT	VAT	CREDIT	VAT	BALANCE
10/2	Balance					£120.60
15/2	Goods	£519.40	77.91			£717.91
18/2	Returns			£171.50	£25.73	£520.68
20/2	Cheque			£220.68		£300.00

PAYMENTS RECEIVED AFTER THE END OF THE MONTH WILL NOT BE SHOWN ON THIS STATEMENT.

Fig. 9.2.2 A statement of account.

9.2.4 *Match different methods of payment with different purposes*

METHODS OF PAYMENT

As we have seen in Element 9.1, there are various methods of making payments. Different methods of payment are appropriate for different purposes. For example, salaries for regular staff are often paid by bank transfer, but occasional staff would be paid wages by cheque. In this performance criterion, we will look at the purposes of the different methods of payment.

Cheque

Cheque payments are the most common method used by facilities. Many people also have a cheque book which they use for some of their household bills. Paying by cheque is much safer than using cash. Debit cards have more recently begun to replace the cheque book, but leisure and tourism facilities do not use these as much as individuals do when they are out shopping. In order to own a cheque book or a debit card, the person or organisation has to have a current account with the bank or building society concerned.

FIGURE IT OUT

**PC 9.2.4
COM 1.1, 1.2**

00:15

*I*n pairs, write a list of the types of bills your chosen facility has to pay. For each of the items, write in those that are paid by cash. Why do you think cash is used in these circumstances? Discuss your list with those of the rest of your group.

Cash

Cash is quick and easy to handle and is generally used for any small amounts of money that have to be paid.

Vouchers

When a facility accepts a voucher in part or full payment for a product or service, it may be accepting the voucher on behalf of another business. If, for example, a customer offers a voucher for a bag of crisps (Walkers Crisps often have this type of promotion), the facility has given the crisps to the customer in return for the voucher and not cash. The voucher is worthless in the sense that it cannot be taken to the bank. The facility collects all the vouchers and sends them off to the business that supplied them. The business concerned then sends the appropriate amount to the facility. More commonly, it would issue a credit note to the facility so that this can be used against any outstanding or future invoices.

Credit card

Customers might pay by credit card when they want to clear the bill straight away but would like time to find the money. The credit card company sends them a statement once a month. The cus-

tomers can either pay the full amount when the statement is received, or the minimum amount shown on the statement. If they only pay the minimum amount required, they will have to pay interest on the outstanding balance.

Some facilities have accounts with credit card companies and issue senior members of staff with these cards so that they can pay bills on behalf of the facility. If this is the case, the credit card company will send the monthly statement to the facility rather than the individual and it will pay. Members of staff, such as sales representatives or those who travel on behalf of the facility, might be issued with company credit cards. They would use the credit cards for paying such things as fares, meals and hotel bills.

Debit card

A facility may use a debit card to pay its invoices instead of a cheque book if it is linked to a system which allows the transfer of money to be done electronically. For this system to be used, the organisation has to be linked by a computer terminal.

Even if the facility does not always pay its invoices using a debit card, it may be that its customers will want to do so. For this reason, the facility may choose to use the electronic transfer of funds system for its customers to pay their bills.

FIGURE IT OUT

PC 9.2.4
COM 1.1, 1.2

`00:15`

*I*magine that you work for a large leisure and tourism facility. You have been issued with a company credit card. List the items that you might use the card to pay for. Compare your list with those of the rest of your group.

finding out

PC 9.2.4
COM 1.2
IT 1.1, 1.2, 1.3

Using the leaflets and brochures you have collected from local banks and building societies, you must now prepare a memorandum to your tutor. This memorandum should state the rules and regulations required by the bank or building society for anyone requesting a debit card. Your memorandum should be word processed and should include information from two different banks or building societies.

Direct debit

Another alternative is to set up a direct debit as detailed in Element 9.1. In this way the facility is able to pay a regular amount to another person or organisation on a particular day of the month. Direct debits are used mainly to pay an agreed amount which is normally the same each month. It is possible to amend the amount being paid, but the person or organisation paying the direct debit has to be notified in writing before the amount of money can be changed.

Standing order

It may be convenient for the facility to arrange a standing order to pay a regular sum to a supplier or hirer. This is particularly useful if the payments are the same amount each week, month or quarter. The facility then knows that the amount will be paid automatically, provided that there is enough in the account to cover the standing order total.

Bank transfer

Electronic transfer of funds, as we have seen, is another good way of reducing the amount of time that has to be spent in organising regular payments. Although the totals may be different at each payment date, the bank will have the details of all the destinations of the payments and will transfer the amounts as directed.

Credit note

Handling credit notes as payment should be viewed in exactly the same way as cash. The only major difference is that change is not always given if the credit note is for more than the amount spent. As we are considering business to business payments, this restriction does not necessarily apply. The use of the credit note is in the hands of the facility that has been issued one by the supplier. It may be used immediately or at any time to cover part or full payment of an invoice. Sometimes a physical credit note will not be issued or required to confirm that the credit is being used. The supplier will simply reduce the outstanding balance owed by the facility by the amount that is to be credited, just like a payment.

PURPOSES OF PAYMENT

In this final section of the element, we look at the various purposes of payment and try to identify the ways in which these payments could be made. We only offer some solutions; you will have to complete the list yourself.

Payment for regular and occasional staff

Salaries for regular staff are generally paid by bank transfer. Wages for occasional staff are usually paid by cheque or sometimes in cash.

Payment for regular and occasional suppliers

Regular suppliers are usually paid by cheque, or occasionally cash. Sometimes, to make things easier, a standing order or direct debit is used.

If the facility is unknown to the supplier, it may insist upon cash. Company cheques will not be acceptable until the facility has proved it can pay its bills or has supplied references. Credit cards and debit cards would also be acceptable forms of payment for occasional suppliers.

Small irregular payments

These are usually made in cash using the petty cash system. Occasionally a cheque may be acceptable. Other payments may be made by credit or debit card.

---

 assignment

ELEMENT 9.2

PC 9.2.1–4

To fulfil the performance criteria in this element, it is necessary for you to check a series of documents to make sure they are accurate. If they are not, you need to make a note of any mistakes that you find and then correct them. Your tutor will provide you with additional documents to check, but we have supplied one set in this assignment so that you can practise. As well as the documents, we have included some cheques which have been incorrectly completed for you to check.

When checking the documents, you should make sure that you take note of the following:

Words

Check that all the details are written correctly and legibly and make sure the spelling is correct.

Amounts

Check the calculations to make sure that no errors have been made. Also, make sure that the figures are legible and easy to read, and that figures have been copied from one document to another without error.

Dates

Make sure the dates are correct, including the year. At the beginning of a new year it is easy to forget that we have moved into January and to continue using the previous year on a cheque. All correspondence should be dated so that it can be filed correctly and also so that the date can be quoted in the future.

Totals

When checking totals, make sure that additions, subtractions, percentages and multiplications have been correctly calculated.

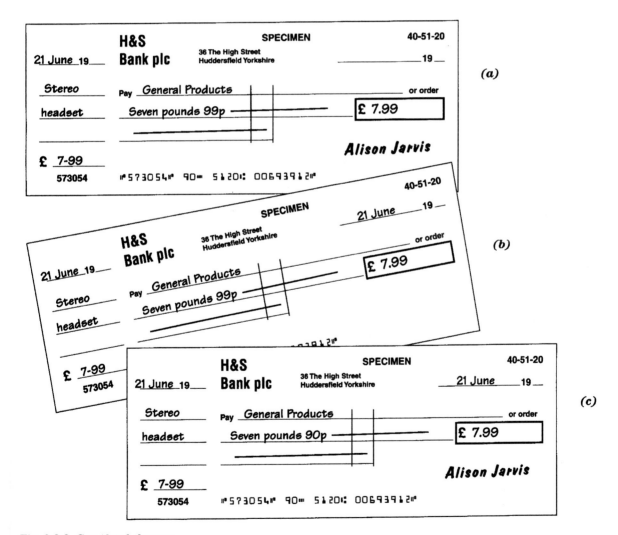

Fig. 9.2.3 Completed cheques.

In order to complete this assignment, there are some final things to consider:

1 Provide a brief set of notes that describe the payments commonly made by leisure and tourism organisations.
2 Include in your notes the main items that a selected leisure and tourism facility would need to buy to operate effectively.
3 Match the five purposes of payment (regular staff, occasional staff, regular suppliers, occasional suppliers and small irregular payments) with the most appropriate payment methods.

FIGURE IT OUT

PC 9.2.4
COM 1.2, 1.4
AON 1.1, 1.2, 1.3

00:30

*L*ook at the three cheques in Figures 9.2.3(a)–(c). There is a mistake on each which will mean that the bank will not accept them. Thinking about all the reasons why a cheque needs to be accurate, write a list of the mistakes you can find.

ORDER FORM

TO Sutherland and Canwell		ORDER NUMBER ST448		
		DATE 25 January 19..		

DELIVERY ADDRESS		SPECIAL INSTRUCTIONS		
		None		

REF NO	QUANTITY	DESCRIPTION	UNIT PRICE	AMOUNT
A4 154	14	Reams of white A4 paper	£3.01	£42.03
D11	10	Packs of D11 size envelopes	£2.00	£20.00

Fig. 9.2.4 A completed order form.

```
                    GOODS  RECEIVED  NOTE
```

NO	DATE RECEIVED	ORDER NO	DELIVERED BY
367	30 January 19..	ST448	Company van

QUANTITY	DESCRIPTION	NUMBER OF PACKAGES	STORES REF
A4 154	Reams of white A4	10	Bay 56
D11	Packs of D11 envelopes	10	Bay 55

RECEIVED FROM	ENTERED INTO STOCK		RECEIVED BY
	DATE	INITIAL	
SUPPLIER			STOREKEEPER

Fig. 9.2.5 A completed goods received note.

```
                    INVOICE
```

TO			NUMBER	5/149/dec
Sothereland and Conwell			DATE 28/2/..	
			TERMS 2.5%	
YOUR ORDER NO ST445			DESPATCH DATE 30/1/..	

QUANTITY	DESCRIPTION	UNIT PRICE	TOTAL PRICE	VAT
14 reams	A4 A54 white A4 paper	£3.01	£42.03	£7.35
10 boxes	D11 envelopes	£2.00	£20.00	£3.50

Gross Value	£62.03	
LESS Trade Discount	£1.55	
Net Value of Goods	£60.48	
PLUS VAT @ 17.5%	£10.85	
INVOICE TOTAL	£71.33	

E & O E

Fig. 9.2.6 A completed invoice.

FIGURE IT OUT

PC 9.2.3
COM 1.1, 1.2, 1.4
AON 1.2, 1.3

00:45

*I*ndividually, *compare the completed order form, goods received note and invoice given in Figures 9.2.4, 9.2.5 and 9.2.6. Do all the documents agree? Make a list of the mistakes that you can find and then, using blank forms, write out a correct copy of each document.*

element 9.3

PREPARE A BASIC CASHFLOW BUDGET FOR A LEISURE AND TOURISM EVENT

Performance criteria

A student must:

1 Describe given **parameters** for a leisure and tourism event.
2 Identify **sources of income** for the event.
3 Estimate expected income from the event.
4 Identify **items of** necessary **expenditure** for the event.
5 Estimate expected expenditure for the event.
6 Prepare a **basic cashflow budget** for the event.

RANGE

Parameters: needs and demands for the event, potential customers, activities for the event, estimated numbers attending, financial targets

Sources of income: entrance fees, souvenirs, programmes, refreshments, sponsorship, grants

Items of expenditure: staff, equipment, venue, publicity, materials, insurance, other

Basic cashflow budget: estimated income, estimated expenditure, statement on the need for an advance of income

9.3.1 Describe given parameters for a leisure and tourism event

PARAMETERS

These parameters, or restrictions, will be determined by your tutor. The exact nature of the proposed leisure and tourism event will be set as a result of a discussion and agreement between both you and your tutor. It may be possible for you to be able to work as a member of a group on this assignment; the whole of the element is practical and you will need to have a variety of different skills.

This assignment ties in well with the requirements of Units 5 and 6, so you may be able to link these to give you ideas for the proposed event.

Needs and demands for the event

You need to establish why you are proposing to put on the particular event and whether there is any demand for it. You do not have to think about a very complex event as it will probably be staged at your centre. You could, for example, propose to run a tournament or competition in order to raise money for a charity or your own centre. This would be the ideal type of event, as it has very definite needs and you can probably be assured of a certain level of demand for it.

Potential customers

Having covered some of the mandatory and optional units, you will now be in a position to understand that events are only as good as their ability to attract customers. If you are proposing to put on an event in your own centre, the majority of the potential customers are likely to be of the same age and background as you. If you are proposing a sports event, for example, you will know what is the most popular sport. If you are proposing to create an event for older age groups, then probably the staff will be your potential customers. Remember that there will be fewer of them and you will have to do a little bit of research to find out whether they would be interested in the kind of event you are proposing.

Activities for the event

The key point here is not to be overambitious. It is far better to restrict the range of activities, bearing the following thoughts in mind:

▼ **What facilities are available for the event?**
▼ **Where is the event to be staged?**
▼ **What equipment is available at the venue?**
▼ **Do you have the necessary skills to stage and supervise such an event?**
▼ **Will the venue owners/supervisors/ managers allow this event to take place?**

It is wise to restrict your event to things you can be sure about. You should not rely on external help or promises as a key part of the event. Trust your own judgement here, but make sure that you can come up with the necessary equipment, skills and facilities you require before making any hard and fast decisions.

Estimated numbers attending

Be pessimistic about this. Do not think that your event is going to attract hundreds or thousands of people. Bear in mind that a lot of people who would like to come, may not be able to on the day. Budget for the worst situation. You need to know how many people have to attend to make the event a success. You may wish to measure this in terms of money received from entrance or participation fees. Alternatively, you may wish to consider the event a success if you can attract more than you were expecting to attend.

Financial targets

We have emphasised throughout this unit that a facility needs to record its transactions so that it can find out whether or not it is making a profit. The amounts of money recorded from these transactions are transferred to the accounts of the facility and these show either the **gross profit** or the **net profit**. We will explain these in a little more detail here:

▼ *gross profit* – **this is worked out by taking the total sales for the year and deducting what it cost the facility to make the goods. Any goods held in stock would also be taken into consideration**

▼ *net profit* – **this is the gross profit of the facility, less any expenses incurred in the running of the business. Expenses could include rent, rates, telephone bills, advertising costs and wages of staff**

9.3.2 Identify sources of income for the event

SOURCES OF INCOME

In this performance criterion we will look at the most common sources of income for a leisure and tourism event, but bear in mind that others may be added depending on the type of event planned.

Entrance fees

Again, you need to be sensible about this aspect of the event. If you charge too much, you will put people off. If you charge too little, you run the risk of not covering all the expenses of the event – even if many people attend it. Here are some suggestions to help you think about this aspect:

▼ **consider what your average potential customer could afford**
▼ **make sure you have a range of entrance fees, including concessions for elderly and disabled people**
▼ **make sure you have organised a float for the entrance ticket staff, as they may have to provide change**
▼ **try to set your entrance fees as round figures; this will avoid confusion and the need to give out a lot of change**

Souvenirs

This may take a lot of preparation, but a simple souvenir of the event will be attractive to the customer and may supply another useful source of income for the event. A good idea would be to provide badges or stickers. These should be easy to produce and you could sell them for a reasonable price and make a good profit.

Programmes

Programmes do not have to be very large or complicated. They can either be given to the customer as part of the entrance fee (they can also serve as a receipt if you do not have a till), or they can be sold at the entry point and around the event. They should be prepared well ahead of the event and probably printed under the guidance of your tutor.

Refreshments

Simple refreshments such as chocolate bars, canned drinks and other pre-prepared items are probably the ideal things to provide. You could, of course, make your own refreshments such as tea, coffee, sandwiches and cakes. This does require more planning and effort, but you would make more money from these than refreshments bought in for the event. Again, keep it simple and make sure that you have not overstocked. You do not want to be left with masses of food and drink that you can not sell. It is not worth providing refreshments if visitors can easily obtain refreshments from other sources in the immediate vicinity of the event.

Sponsorship

It may be possible for you to obtain sponsorship money from a local provider of leisure and tourism. Whilst the amount may not be large, this is not important. It could be enough to make sure that the event covers its costs. Also, the fact that you have obtained sponsorship from an organisation may mean that the event will be considered more important and credible by potential visitors or customers.

If you wish to approach a potential sponsor, make sure you have cleared this with your tutor first. You must be able to show the potential sponsor that the event will be professionally organised and run, and that the organisation will get useful publicity out of the deal. Remember that organisations receive many requests for sponsorship throughout the year and your application needs to really interest them.

Grants

There are a number of different sources of potential grants, but you need to be sure that you qualify for them. Your tutor will be aware of a number of them and may be able to put you in touch with the right person. You could consider the following sources of grants:

▼ **your own centre**
▼ **your local council**
▼ **your local tourist board**
▼ **an educational grant provider**
▼ **a youth grant provider**

Grant providers need to know about the purposes of the proposed event and the information you have gathered in consideration of the parameters of the event will provide a useful background for this. If there is a grant available, it will probably not cover all the costs of the event, but will be of great use to you.

9.3.3 Estimate expected income from the event

Having looked at all the parameters of the event and considered the potential sources of income, you must now turn your attention to an estimate of the total income. At this stage you can only make some suggestions and estimates. Be on the pessimistic side, as you will not want to appear to be able to make a huge profit from it and then look stupid later on if the event does not work out as well as you expected.

This estimate will form the basis of the last part of the assignment which asks you to create a basic cash flow for the event. Your tutor will be able to recommend the preferred way of showing your estimated income.

9.3.4 Identify items of necessary expenditure for the event

ITEMS OF EXPENDITURE

This performance criterion looks at the most common items of expenditure for a leisure and tourism event, but, depending on the type of event planned, there may be others we have not considered.

Staff

Even if you are running the event on your own, you will have to consider the costs of the staff at the venue. You will probably be expected to make a contribution towards their wages. In a full-size event, the venue will charge the event organisers a fee for the use of the facilities, which include the staff that are on duty at that time. If you have decided to put on an event that needs the expertise of a specialist, trainer or coach, you should find out the cost of employing this person and make sure you have included it in your list of expenses.

Equipment

Any equipment used for the event will have to be costed out for the hire period. The providers of the equipment will be able to tell you whether they charge an hourly or daily rate for the hire. This again will have to be agreed in advance and included in your list of expenses. You may be lucky enough to be at a centre that has the equipment and will not charge you for the hire. You should find out how much it would cost to hire so that you can note this anyway.

Venue

Even small stands and displays can cost money if you use a venue. The venue owners charge a fee based on the amount of space you require and the length of time you use it. The larger the venue, the higher the hire charge. The owners may include everything in this charge, such as equipment use and the costs of the staff that are on duty. It is worth remembering that you should only rent the space you need, as you will have to pay for all the space whether you use it or not.

Publicity

As we have seen in earlier units, publicity is extremely important in making sure that the event is successful. If the visitors or customers are unaware that the event is taking place, you cannot expect them to appear on the day. Simple posters and fliers are ideal for small-scale events; you will have to think about the best places to put the posters and distribute the leaflets.

Materials

You will need a variety of consumable materials for the event. The exact list of items will depend on the nature of the event you are planning, but may include the following:

▼ **cloak-room tickets to act as entrance tickets**
▼ **information sheets and leaflets for customers to take away and read**
▼ **paper cups and plates for refreshments**
▼ **plastic rubbish sacks to collect the litter and discarded paper lying around after the event**

Insurance

It is likely that the venue's insurance will cover the event. However, it is a good idea to find out whether you are covered and, if not, how much it would cost to use the venue's insurance company. The venue will be able to help you with this and may insist that you organise insurance before allowing the event to take place. This expense may have to be covered well before the event date.

Other

This, obviously, covers all the items of expenditure that have not been considered so far. You may have to think about some of the following costs:

▼ **transport for customers/visitors to and from the event**
▼ **getting equipment and other items to the venue**
▼ **getting the event organisers to and from the venue**
▼ **replacing items due to wear and tear**

9.3.5 *Estimate expected expenditure for the event*

Having looked at all the parameters of the event and thought about the potential expenditure, you must now turn your attention to an estimate of the total cost. At this stage you can only make some suggestions and estimates. Again, be on the pessimistic side, as you will need to make sure that you have covered all the potential costs and have not missed out anything obvious.

This estimate will form the basis of the last part of the assignment which asks you to create a basic cash flow for the event. Your tutor will be able to recommend the preferred way of showing your estimated costs.

9.3.6 *Prepare a basic cash flow budget for the event*

BASIC CASH FLOW BUDGET

As you learnt in the previous two elements, leisure and tourism facilities must keep records of how much they spend and how much they receive so that they can calculate the profit they are making. This is important because the Inland Revenue Department needs to know this profit figure to work out how much tax the facility has to pay. It is also important to keep up-to-date and accurate financial records because of legal requirements. No matter how large or small, all facilities have to keep records. Private companies have to keep their accounts records on file for three years and a public company for six.

It is not, however, just outside organisations who need to know how the facility is doing. The managers and owners of the facility will also want to keep a careful check on the financial position of the business. We mentioned earlier the cash flow of a business. This is the amount of money that is available to pay the bills. It is in the best interests of any facility to collect any money owed to it quickly so that it can have this money to spend on other things. A wise facility would also take advantage of buying any goods needed for the running of the business on credit terms. This gives it time to pay for the goods and so keeps the money in the business for longer. This is known as **maximising cash flow**. If a facility is making a good profit, it may decide to invest the money it has left over so that it can earn interest, thus making more money.

When a facility receives a payment, it has to be recorded. These transactions can be recorded in many ways, but the three methods which we are concerned about here include:

▼ **in a cash book**
▼ **by a spreadsheet (which is a computer software package)**
▼ **on a payments received sheet**

As its name implies, a payments received sheet is only used to record any payments made to the facility. On the other hand, a cash book and a spreadsheet can be used to record both incoming and outgoing payments. The information contained in all three of these records of transactions is recorded by the accounts or finance department so that the annual accounts for the facility can be drawn up.

Cash book

A cash book is a manual method of recording financial transactions and it is used to list the cash and cheque transactions. It will record both the money coming into the facility and the money being paid out.

DEBIT (DR)	*CREDIT (CR)*
Money coming in	*Money going out*

DR					CASH BOOK			CR
DATE	DETAILS	CASH £	BANK £	DATE	DETAILS		CASH £	BANK £

Fig. 9.3.1
A blank cash book.

FIGURE IT OUT

PC 9.3.6
COM 1.1

00:10

*I*n pairs, try to work out why each of the headings given in Figure 9.3.1 (a blank cash book) are required. What information will come under the heading 'details'? Why are there two headings in each half called 'cash' and 'bank'? Discuss your thoughts with the rest of your group.

When a facility is completing the cash book with information about incoming and outgoing payments, it would begin on the first of the month by 'bringing down the balance' from the previous month. As you will see in Figure 9.3.2, this balance is transferred from the end of the previous month and is the amount of money the facility has in cash and in the bank. This is known as **the balance brought down**. The various transactions are recorded in date order. Any cash payments are entered on the CR side of the cash book in the 'cash' column. Any cheque payments are entered in the 'bank' column.

At the end of the month, the cash book must be balanced. This is done first by adding the two columns on the DR side of the cash book. It is assumed that the DR side will be larger than the CR side because we are hoping that the facility is a successful one and that it has received more money than it has paid out. The totals from the two columns on the DR side are then copied onto the two columns on the CR side.

Fig. 9.3.2 A part-completed cash book.

Fig. 9.3.3 A completed, but not yet balanced cash book.

In order to **balance** the cash book, the amounts entered into the CR side must be subtracted from the totals on the DR side. The difference between the two is inserted before the totals on the CR side.

The letters c/d appear after the balance to show the amount which will be **carried down** to the next month. This carried down figure is the **brought down** one that the facility will open its June cash book with.

DR		CASH BOOK						CR
DATE	DETAILS	CASH £	BANK £	DATE	DETAILS	CASH £	BANK £	
1 May	Balance b/d	550	4,650	3 May	Telephone bill		210	
4 May	Jones and Sons Ltd		1,560	6 May	Brian Phillips	225		
7 May	Carringtons Ltd		1,500	10 May	Wages		1,100	
12 May	Paul Riddlington	100		13 May	Garage bill		410	
14 May	Pettits of Dunwich		700	14 May	Petrol	20		
19 May	Jones and Sons Ltd		440	19 May	Wages		1,100	
23 May	Peter Smithson	150		27 May	Petrol	25		
29 May	Carringtons Ltd		1,000	30 May	Wages		1,100	
				31 May	Balance c/d	530	5,920	
		800	9,850			800	9,850	

Fig. 9.3.4 A balanced cash book.

FIGURE IT OUT

PC 9.3.6
COM 1.1, 1.2, 1.4

`00:30`

From the list of payments received and made by a facility given below, work out on which side of the cash book each would go. Also, identify whether it would be entered in the 'cash' or 'bank' column:

- *cheque for £430 received from Carringtons Ltd*
- *cheque for £390 paid to British Gas*
- *cash payment of £66.50 received from Paula Kane*
- *cash payment of £35 received from Bruce Wise*
- *cheque for £1,100 received from Capital Components*
- *cash payment of £29.50 made to the local garage*
- *cheque for £115 made to the local garage*

Estimated income

As we have already seen, a facility will receive money for the goods or services that it sells to customers. The facility may also receive money from:

▼ *interest on money in the bank –* although this is likely to be a small amount when compared to the money received through the sale of goods or services

▼ *any commission it may earn –* again this is likely to be a smaller amount than sales. Commission is a bonus payment which is earned if particular set targets are met by the facility

The facility is likely to receive its money from customers in a variety of ways. The customer may pay by cash, cheque, debit card or credit card, but this is all income to the facility. Whatever method of payment the customer uses, all transactions have to be recorded.

Estimated expenditure

In order to produce the products and services that the facility sells, it will be necessary for the facility to make a series of purchases. The purchases made could include the following:

▼ finished goods, which the facility buys in order to resell them to its customers. Examples of finished goods are:

–   CDs
–   clothes
–   ready-prepared food
–   furniture

▼ part-finished goods which the facility will finish processing in order to make the final product it sells. Examples of part-finished goods are:

–   potatoes to make oven chips or crisps
–   material to make clothes
–   the different components which make up a car to make the finished car

▼ raw materials which occur naturally and are 'extracted'. An example of a raw material is coal.

It does not matter what the facility buys, it still has to be paid for. Once the goods have been purchased by the facility, they become **stock**. This means that they are held by the facility until they are needed in the production process. Another example of stock are goods which the facility has finished making and which are being held await-ing a customer.

As well as having to find the money to pay for stock, the facility also has to pay for the follow-ing, which are known as **expenses**:

▼ **the rent or rates on the buildings or land where the facility is situated**
▼ **fuel, heating and lighting bills**
▼ **telephone and fax bills**
▼ **the wages of the employees**

Statement on the need for an advance of income

You will have identified certain items of expendi-ture that have to be dealt with before the event takes place. In this final part of the assignment you need to give an itemised total of the advance expenditure in order to make a request for this money. Remember that the finance provider will need to be certain that this money needs to be paid out ahead of the event for items that cannot be paid for out of the profits of the event. Although the event profits will pay for these items in the long run, the provider will have to cover the costs in the first instance.

Glossary of leisure and tourism terms

Academic qualifications This usually means GCSEs and A levels. Also see vocational qualifications.

Administration This is the part of an organisation that tends to support the rest of the departments by providing services such as photocopying and other office duties and tasks.

Appeal This is what might attract a visitor or customer to an attraction or facility.

Application form This is a document you may be asked to fill in if you apply for a job. There will be various sections of the form, all aimed at giving the employer the chance to find out about your qualifications, skills and other qualities.

Appointment This is the final part of the recruitment process. The successful candidate will be 'appointed' (offered the job) after the interviews have taken place.

Booking This involves making a series of arrangements for a visit or journey for an individual or a group of people. You would have to arrange the travel and confirm the arrangements with the traveller or visitor, as well as the organisations involved.

Cash book A cash book is used to note down all the transactions (cash or cheque) that have come into the business (incomings) and been paid out by the business (outgoings).

Cash flow This is all the incomings and outgoings of money in a particular business. The cash flow shows that the business is either taking more money than it is spending or spending more than it is making.

Chain of distribution This is made up of all of the different organisations in the UK travel industry. The tour operator purchases the products and services from the providers (principals), packages those products and services, then sells the package to the customers through the travel agencies.

Competition In business terms, competition is businesses trying to make sure that the public buy from them rather than any other organisation. They do this by advertising and promoting their products and services, as well as trying to offer the best deal to the customers.

Consumer This is another word used in business for customer or visitor.

Core skills These are the basic skills of communication and numeracy that are needed for most types of job.

Credit card This is a way of paying for products and services. When customers use one of these, they sign to prove that they are the true card holder and the credit card company pays the shop or supplier. The customers must then pay the credit card company back, but are charged interest for as long as they have a balance on the card.

Credit note This is given by the business to a customer that they owe money. Rather than refunding the money for faulty or returned products and services, the customer can use this as 'cash' against an invoice in the future.

Curriculum vitae (CV) This is a summary of your personal details (such as name, address and telephone number) and your achievements (qualifications) which is used to show an employer if you apply for a job.

Customer records These are information held by the organisation about the customer. This would include: personal details, customer complaints, customer enquiries, customer requests and sales.

Customer satisfaction This is achieved when the service given to the customer meets their needs.

Customer service This means delivering effective help to the customer in order to cater for their needs.

Electronic transfer of funds This is a new method of moving money from one account to another. It is carried out using computer terminals and allows immediate transfer. The money transferred can be used by the account holder straightaway.

European Union (EU) These are the countries, including the UK, that have signed the Maastricht Treaty.

Event   This is an activity that requires planning, resources and evaluation; it could include the provision of a product or a service.

Facility   This is a general term used to describe the equipment, buildings or features which provide the opportunity for leisure and tourism.

Health and safety   Health and safety laws require a business to carry out checks to ensure there are no dangers to the employees or customers as a result of the products made or services provided.

Health and safety equipment   These are items of equipment that can be found in the workplace. Examples are personal protective equipment like gloves, fire extinguishers, safety warning signs and first aid equipment.

Health and safety hazards   These are hazards, such as an untidy and cluttered work area, that could cause a health and safety problem.

Health and safety risks   These include smoking near inflammable liquids and unprotected machine wires and cords. If such risks are not looked out for, an accident could occur.

Interview   This is one of the most important parts of the recruitment process. After application forms or CVs have been received by the employer, the candidates are short-listed and the best are called in for interview. After the interview, one of the candidates will be offered the job.

Invoice   This is a document, sent out to the customer, which details the products and services bought and their cost. The customer is expected to pay the total shown on the invoice.

Itemised account   This is a statement which shows the individual transactions carried out between a business and a customer. It is useful because it breaks down every order and gives the date of purchase.

Job responsibilities   These are the main duties of the employee. For example, the job responsibilities of a wages clerk are to make sure that the wages and salaries are paid correctly and on time.

Job tasks   These are the individual duties and responsibilities of an employee. They are usually broken down into separate tasks so that they are clear.

Leisure   This is the time that individuals have left after completing all the things they have to do. It would normally involve an experience that the individual finds satisfying.

Leisure and recreation   This is a general term that would include: arts and entertainment, sports and physical activities, outdoor activities, heritage, play, catering and accommodation.

Letter of application   This is a simple letter which can be sent with an application form or CV when you apply for a job. In a letter of application, you would state which job you are applying for and your reasons for applying. You may also include a summary of your main qualifications, skills and experience.

Local authority   This is another term used to describe a local council, borough council, district council or county council. They are large employers and offer a wide range of services to the public and local businesses.

Locality   This is a flexible term which describes the immediate area in which you live.

Marketing   This is the department in an organisation that deals with the advertising and promotion of products and services. It will carry out research to find out about the organisation's customers and the best way of getting information about the products and service to them.

Media   These are the various forms in which information can be passed on to the customer, including the press, printed materials (leaflets, etc.), radio and TV.

Notices   These can be maps, timetables, opening times or publicity for special events that are on view to the public.

Paying-in slip   This document is used to prove that you have paid money into an account. The cashier will sign and stamp the paying-in slip and hand you back the counterfoil.

Payment received sheet   This is a document which records incoming money. A business would make sure that all incoming payments are put onto this document.

Petty cash voucher   This document is filled in by an employee who has spent some of the organisation's money on basic items such as coffee, fax paper or stamps. A receipt should always be stapled to the petty cash voucher.

Physical resources   These include facilities and equipment used by the various leisure and recreation centres.

Premises   This is another word for the buildings used by a business.

Principals   These are the basic products and services created and supplied by airlines, railways, car hire companies and shipping companies. Their products and services are sold to the customer via tour operators and travel agencies.

Private sector organisations   These are normally profit-making organisations. They include hotels, tourist attractions and health and fitness clubs.

Product/service   These are provided to the customer by a variety of different leisure and tourism facilities.

Public sector organisations   These are organisations that are usually funded by central or local government. They include tourist boards, local authorities, arts centres and tourist information centres.

Receipt   This is handwritten or printed proof that you have bought something for a particular amount on a particular day.

Record of achievement   This is a folder or binder that includes your certificates, personal details and career plans. Most students will have one of these by the time they leave school or will be encouraged to complete one.

Refunds   These are usually given if the customer returns something to the business because it is faulty or unsuitable. Refunds are normally given by the suppliers, but there are some cases when they are not required to do so.

Sales   This is the part of an organisation that handles selling to the customers. The sales department

works very closely with the marketing department so that the reps can be ready to sell products and services after the marketing department has advertised them.

Schedule   This shows the details and things you have to think about when organising a visit. It will include where the visit is to take place, who will be visited, arrival time, departure time and other information.

Spreadsheet   This is a computerised way of dealing with lots of numbers and figures. The spreadsheet will automatically total across and down so that you do not have to add the figures together yourself.

Statement of account   This document is sent out to customers (sometimes monthly) so that they can see all the transactions they have carried out with the supplier. The orders and payments are detailed, with the outstanding balance at the bottom of the document.

Student log   This is an outline of your activities and contribution during an assignment or work experience. You should keep a detailed account of what you do, where it is done, what materials you used and what equipment was needed.

Team plan   In many group activities, you will be required to organise the way in which you intend to carry out the work before you start the activity itself. It is wise to include all the steps that you need to follow. Your centre will have a particular form that you will need to fill in.

Till record   When a cash register, or till, prints a receipt, it also prints a copy onto a till roll. This is the business's record of the transactions carried out by the cashier.

Tourism   This is the movement of people to travel destinations and their activities at these places. It includes package holidays, day trips and excursions.

Tourism services   These consist of services offered by national and regional tourist boards, tourist information centres, tourist attractions, guiding services, currency exchange, accommodation, catering and transport.

Travel and tourism industry   This consists of travel and tourism services provided by travel agencies and tour operators.

Travel itinerary   This lists the travel arrangements that will have to be organised to meet the traveller's needs. It should contain the route selected, dates, calculated travel times and all the necessary stops.

Travel services   These are services provided by travel agencies, tour operators, airlines, railways, car hire companies and shipping companies.

Unique selling point (USP)   This is the feature of a product or service that makes it different from all other products on the market. If a pencil has a rubber on the end of it, then this is a USP compared to other pencils that do not have a rubber.

Vacancy   This is when a business has a job available.

Value added tax (VAT)   This is a government tax that is added to the normal price of most products and services. The current rate of VAT is 17.5 per cent.

Visitor attractions   These are recreational, cultural, entertainment or children's facilities that aim to attract visitors.

Vocational qualifications   These are non-academic achievements based on your ability to use skills and experience.

Voluntary sector organisations   These are organisations that are managed and operated largely by volunteers. They are often non-profit-making organisations or charities. These would include local sports clubs and playgroups.

Index